Building a Business Development Culture and Strategy

A Management Guide for Law Firm Leadership

AF867275

EDITED BY DEBORAH B. FARONE

Commissioning editor
Alex Davies

Managing director
Sian O'Neill

Building a Business Development Culture and Strategy: A Management Guide for Law Firm Leadership
is published by

Globe Law and Business Ltd
3 Mylor Close
Horsell
Woking
Surrey GU21 4DD
United Kingdom
Tel: +44 20 3745 4770
www.globelawandbusiness.com

Building a Business Development Culture and Strategy: A Management Guide for Law Firm Leadership

ISBN 978-1-83723-191-1
EPUB ISBN 978-1-83723-192-8
Adobe PDF ISBN 978-1-83723-193-5

© 2026 Globe Law and Business Ltd except where otherwise indicated.

The right of the contributors to be identified as authors of this work has been asserted by them in accordance with sections 77 and 78 of the Copyright, Designs and Patents Act 1988.

All rights reserved. No part of this publication may be reproduced in any material form (including photocopying, storing in any medium by electronic means or transmitting) without the written permission of the copyright owner, except in accordance with the provisions of the Copyright, Designs and Patents Act 1988 or under terms of a licence issued by the Copyright Licensing Agency Ltd (www.cla.co.uk). Applications for the copyright owner's written permission to reproduce any part of this publication should be addressed to the publisher.

GPSR Compliance: EU Authorised Representative: Easy Access System Europe - Mustamäe tee 50, 10621 Tallinn, Estonia, gpsr.requests@easproject.com

DISCLAIMER
This publication is intended as a general guide only. The information and opinions which it contains are not intended to be a comprehensive study, or to provide legal advice, and should not be treated as a substitute for legal advice concerning particular situations. Legal advice should always be sought before taking any action based on the information provided. The publisher bears no responsibility for any errors or omissions contained herein.

Contents

Part 4: Operations and Change Management

Executive summary

Globe Law and Business

What does it take to develop and sustain a culture that values marketing, business development, and client care as shared responsibilities across the firm?

Now more than ever, firms are recognizing that isolated efforts, such as one-off trainings, CRM implementations, or inspirational retreats, won't transform behaviors. What's needed is a holistic approach driven from the top.

Through practical frameworks, candid interviews with firm chairs and CMOs, and real-world examples, this book shows how to empower professionals at every level to contribute to the firm's brand and growth. Not only does it demystify how a strong marketing culture is built – from leadership vision and governance to talent development, systems, and incentives – it helps readers understand how to do this in the context of complex, partnership-based environments.

Introduced by the book's editor, Deborah B. Farone, the book is split into four parts. Part one looks at core marketing and business development. In chapter one, Deborah looks at how to build a firmwide marketing strategy, aligning marketing goals with the firm's vision and its clients' needs. She firstly looks at why a firmwide strategy is needed, what can go wrong without one, and then looks at how to start – from client development priorities to how the company wants to position itself. She then explores how to get buy-in for such a strategy, and ensure long-term alignment. Before concluding with ten steps to build an integrated marketing strategy, Deborah maintains that such strategy is "a practical necessity for any firm that is serious about growth ... and about creating an environment where talented lawyers at every stage of their careers can develop and thrive."

In a crowded legal marketplace where many firms claim similar strengths – client service, responsiveness, and deep expertise – true differentiation is difficult to articulate and even harder to sustain. Chapter two by Brandie Knox explores how law firm leaders can define a clear brand position grounded in strategy rather than marketing language. Drawing on more than two decades of experience advising law firms on brand and digital strategy, Brandie outlines a practical framework for developing meaningful brand positioning. The chapter begins with the discovery process – examining how firms are currently perceived by internal stakeholders, clients, and the external marketplace. Through structured interviews, competitive analysis, and internal alignment exercises, leadership teams can identify the gap between current perceptions and the firm's desired market position. The chapter provides practical tools and frameworks – including interview approaches, brand personality mapping techniques, and messaging pillars – that firms can use to clarify their value proposition.

Part two then gets into the tactics of business development strategy.

Chapter three realigns client relationships from episodic to strategic. JeanMarie Campbell provides law firm leaders and BD professionals with actionable frameworks that deepen trust with key clients, moving from a relationship "owner" mindset to a "client as our partner" mindset. Building a firm-wide key client account program that is scalable and practical is a business imperative, as clients are not simply sources of revenue, they are the firm's most important long-term strategic asset. Client relationship management skills are not soft, but instead strategic, skills that lawyers need to hone and practice. Firms that institutionalize client relationship management outperform peers in client retention, cross-selling/servicing, and reputation. The firms that win will be those that treat clients not as matters, but as long-term partnerships, intentionally, measured, and evolving.

Chapter four then reframes cross-selling as cross-investing – a disciplined, strategic approach to collaboration that breaks down silos and drives sustainable revenue across practices and offices.

Most firms struggle with cross-selling because the work is misunderstood. It's not about pushing services internally – it's about building shared value, aligning incentives, and creating a culture where partners invest in each other's success. Drawing on Julie Henson's experience advising managing partners and integrating lateral teams, the chapter explores why cross-selling fails – lack of trust, unclear structures, and compensation models that reward individualism – and how leading firms overcome these challenges. The chapter highlights how cross-investing strengthens the entire ecosystem, incorporating shared accountability, shared intelligence, and shared opportunity. When firms shift from transactional referrals to intentional collaboration, they unlock deeper client relationships, more effective lateral integration, and meaningful revenue expansion. Ultimately, this chapter argues that cross-investing isn't a program. It's a growth mindset – one that modern firms must adopt if they want to compete, adapt, and scale in today's legal market.

In chapter five, Heidi Gardner and Ivan Matviak show how to turn collaboration analytics into the insights that drive growth and create accountability. When collaboration remains a mere cultural aspiration rather than a measurable discipline, it becomes optional, overshadowed by individual goals. The chapter examines how to derive actionable insights at five levels where leaders can make a difference – firm, sector, practice, client, and partner. The authors show how to move from knowing that collaboration matters to actively managing it – identifying growth opportunities, spotting client and partner flight risks, and targeting cross-practice investments that drive ROI. Many firms are also placing big bets on lateral hires and mergers, yet too many fail to achieve their objectives. Collaboration analytics give leaders early, data-driven visibility into how these investments are integrating, while there is still time to intervene. Overall, the result is a practical framework for turning collaboration analytics into decisions that strengthen performance across the entire organization.

Building a law firm culture that prizes original thought leadership has never been more important. As AI takes over more routine work and can answer basic questions, law firms need to demonstrate insights and build trust, positioning them for strategic, high-level work.

The good news is that AI can help them do it by freeing up more time and providing new tools to generate content. But it's not as simple as it sounds. Law firms must find a way to get lawyers to view their work differently. Instead of merely serving as legal technicians, they need to become business advisors who can consider risks and opportunities for their clients in a broader context. They also need to recognize "BD" activities, such as thought leadership, as essential to client service – not merely "non-billable time". In chapter six, Jamie Diaferia and Andrew Longstreth talk to law firm CMOs who have developed cultures that reward thought leadership, whilst also considering what law firms need to know about building trust with clients in the new media landscape.

In chapter seven, Trish Lilley explores how lawyers can embed business development into their professional identity. At the core of that challenge is "purpose". Individuals pursue careers as lawyers for myriad reasons – developing a book of business doesn't top the list. Trish looks at ways in which lawyers can make BD fit into their own lawyering style, so that it feels natural rather than forced, and is something they do willingly rather than under duress. If we reframe business development effectively – as a core professional responsibility – we can more easily move beyond the pushback, the resistance, and the fear and apprehension that some lawyers experience when asked to "sell". This chapter offers helpful tips and tricks for firms seeking to embed client development holistically into lawyers' professional identities.

Part three of the book looks at developing human resources.

The legal profession has changed dramatically in recent decades. There are more laws and regulations, new practice areas, exceedingly complex transactions and disputes, and increased specialization – complicated by the fact that more legal issues are multi-disciplinary. Technology has sped up the pace of work, communications, and the ability to generate work product while automating some practice areas, making room for other professionals not practicing law to deliver certain services. The advent of artificial intelligence and its role in generating documents, analysis and strategy has further muddled how and what to learn.

Law is considered a 'practice' – a continual work in progress where ongoing learning is fundamental to keep current and develop the skills critical to law practice. However, the substantive law studied in law school is not sufficient to produce competent lawyers. Dynamic, complex modern law practice requires learning to act, work, and feel like a lawyer to become a professional with a strong professional identity. The process by which lawyers actually become effective practicing lawyers, however, remains something of a mystery.

The underlying assumption is that somehow, by osmosis or magic or grit, these qualities and abilities will manifest after law school. Magical thinking is not a viable strategy, so how does this transformation occur? The informal and incidental learning that takes place in the course of law practice fuel the process of moving from knowing the law to acting like a lawyer to being one. Chapter eight, by Diane Rosen and Natalie Loeb, looks at how mentoring, sponsorship and coaching can all help the lawyer gain the skillset and knowledge they need to be effective practitioners.

In professional services firms, business development is often framed through individual performance, incentives, or formal training. Chapter nine, by Allan Schoenberg and Renate Wagner, advances a broader and more durable perspective – sustained business development is rooted in firm culture, and culture is shaped, reinforced, and maintained through internal communications that are tied firmly to business goals. Readers will come away with the understanding that communications is not a downstream function or simply a distribution mechanism, but a leadership discipline that helps define how people understand their roles, collaborate across geographies, practices, and functions, and take shared responsibility for client relationships and outcomes. The chapter examines how strong internal communications strategy and execution directly influence morale, knowledge-sharing, firm cohesion, and ultimately client successes. The authors position internal communications as a strategic lever for building a firmwide business development culture that transforms culture from an abstract concept into a competitive advantage.

Chapter ten explores the often-overlooked link between business development culture, psychological safety, and wellbeing in law firms. While firms invest heavily in BD strategy (training programs, compensation structures, CRM systems), many struggle to achieve sustained behavior change. The missing ingredient is rarely motivation or capability – it is safety. Drawing on neuroscience and real-world law firm dynamics, Renee Branson explains how threat-based environments (scarcity mindsets, zero-sum credit systems, chronic cognitive overload) suppress the very relational and collaborative behaviors that effective business development requires.

Renee's chapter reframes common BD challenges – hoarding relationships, reluctance to cross-sell, avoidance of risk – as adaptive responses to unsafe systems rather than individual shortcomings. She offers leaders a practical lens for diagnosing when BD problems are actually culture and wellbeing problems, and why addressing psychological safety is not a "soft" intervention but a performance imperative. Her chapter concludes with actionable frameworks and leadership practices for designing BD cultures that support trust, shared ownership, sustainable growth and long-term wellbeing.

Part four then turns to operations and change management.

Chapter 11 positions AI not as a technical challenge but as a strategic opportunity for law firm leaders to fundamentally reimagine how they compete, differentiate, and grow. Rather than focusing on basic automation or efficiency gains, Jennifer Leonard explores how creative professionals can use AI as a co-intelligence to sharpen market positioning, deepen client relationships, and scale their impact during the transformative opening years of the AI era. The firms that will thrive aren't necessarily those with the largest technology budgets, but those whose leaders foster a culture of experimentation and understand AI as a strategic thought partner for business development rather than merely an efficiency tool. The most creative professionals – those willing to experiment, learn, and iterate – will gain significant competitive advantage during this pivotal moment in the profession's evolution.

Budgeting and ROI measurement sits at the heart of building a sustainable business development culture. It's how you know whether or not your change management efforts have been successful, as well as how and when to refine your approach over time. Chapter 12 by Monica Rodriguez Kuniyoshi positions budgeting and measurement not as isolated exercises, but as strategic tools for steering law firm investments toward measurable value despite the realities of limited data, lean teams, and uneven attorney engagement. The approaches and insights that Monica shares will be useful to any law firm undergoing the important work of building a business development culture – whether they are trying to change behavior among a small group of partners, shift the mindset of entire practices, or measure a large-scale program across hundreds of attorneys.

Lateral partner success doesn't start on day one – it starts before the first handshake. Chapter 13 by Jessica Grayson reframes lateral integration as a growth strategy that requires marketing and BD at the table throughout the entire process – identifying the right candidates, vetting their books of business, creating a great candidate experience, planning their launch, and building momentum that lasts. Drawing on real-world experience, this chapter gives law firm leaders practical frameworks for bringing their marketing and BD teams in earlier and more strategically. Jessica looks at how to use your firm's brand to attract top talent, conduct meaningful due diligence on portability, create an experience that wins candidates over, design business development plans before day one, execute market launches that actually work, and build integration systems that deliver real ROI. The bottom line is that lateral success is designed, not accidental. When you involve marketing and BD professionals as strategic partners (not just service providers) you reduce risk, set clearer expectations, help partners ramp up faster and get more consistent returns on your lateral investments.

Part five then explores the client-centric focus of a successful business development strategy.

Chapter 14 turns the focus to gathering insights to inform strategy and strengthen loyalty. Nat Slavin argues that most law firm business development challenges are not effort problems. They are intelligence problems. The data needed to drive better business development decisions almost always already exists somewhere inside the firm, but it is disaggregated and trapped in silos. Once it is integrated, it reveals five things firms cannot see otherwise – what clients actually want, how they think about cross-selling, why they would move work, the criteria that drive selection, and the areas where their needs are unmet. Each of these is a business development opportunity hiding in plain sight. Leadership's job is to integrate the intelligence, surface the patterns, and translate them into a business development strategy that reflects what clients have been telling the firm all along.

Chapter 15 explores succession planning and knowledge transfer as critical components of sustaining business development and ensuring continuity when firm leaders retire or transition out of practice. Ida Abbott examines why effective succession is vital to a firm's long-term health, client retention, performance and reputation, and how poorly managed transitions can jeopardize client relationships, goodwill, and institutional knowledge. The chapter considers the often-competing perspectives of the firm, clients, potential successors, and retiring partners, including client expectations for continuity and choice, the development and retention of future leaders, and the personal, financial, and cultural challenges that can create resistance to succession planning. Ida also addresses the particular risks succession poses to business development, such as loss of key relationships, stalled growth, and uncertainty around ownership of clients. Finally, the chapter outlines a practical framework for normalizing and managing retirement, clarifying expectations and processes, and establishing oversight and accountability.

Every law firm strategic plan declares that growing the business is a top priority and every stakeholder – particularly partners – must play a role in furthering this mission. However, in most law firms, a relatively small number of partners generate the majority of the firm's clients and matters. These partners are often among the highest paid partners. Firm managers are constantly exhorting all other partners to do more to grow their practices and the firm. Many firms employ marketing and business development professionals whose primary purpose is to promote the firm and support the lawyers' business development efforts. While many partners participate in training workshops, contribute thought leadership, and attend networking events, only a modest few make material progress each year in growing their practices. What can be done with those partners unable or unwilling to do more?

It might come as a surprise that our perceptions may be skewed and the familiar pattern repeated in so many law firms is not so much a battle to convert apathetic partners into hard-charging rainmakers, but a battle to overcome outdated partner compensation plans that impose significant and systemic barriers to generating more widespread business development success. In chapter 16, Tim Corcoran first highlights and reinforces the elements of law firm partner compensation plans that support business development efforts, and then unwinds the compensation plan elements that, in obvious and not so obvious ways, hinder partner business development efforts and even impose financial penalties on partners who are both capable and committed to growing their practices. He addresses topics such as origination, credit sharing, client succession, leverage, pricing, and long-standing KPIs that, despite good intentions, create a minefield of unintended consequences.

Given the unique nature of law firm cultures, what works well in one law firm may fall flat in another. Tim aids readers in identifying the partner compensation plan elements that warrant a deeper look in their own firms.

A strong digital presence and online reputation are key to successful business development for lawyers at the individual, practice, and firm levels. Developing a proper strategy and enforcing it throughout your firm's culture are key to accelerating future growth. This final chapter by Jaron Rubenstein covers key topics firm leadership must consider, including how to leverage AI-driven tools and services to maximize effectiveness, before concluding with a self-assessment tool for firm leaders to assess the maturity of their firm's digital presence and a methodology to prioritize an implementation roadmap based on that assessment.

About the editor

Deborah B. Farone has had the unique opportunity to play a seminal role in developing the best practices in professional services marketing by working with the most respected and demanding lawyers and management consultants in the world.

Her advisory practice focuses on working with law firms, legal technology companies, and individual lawyers in the US, Europe, Asia, and Latin America on business development strategy, and business development and marketing department creation. She is also highly regarded for her business development training sessions for all levels of lawyers, as well as practice groups. She has led strategic planning, and is an in-demand speaker at law firm retreats and workshops around the world.

Deborah is the author of two bestselling legal marketing books: *Best Practices in Law Firm Business Development and Marketing* (PLI, 2019) – a work based on more than 60 interviews with successful law firm leaders and marketers, general counsel, and innovators in the profession – and *Breaking Ground: How Successful Women Lawyers Build Thriving Practices* (PLI, 2026).

Heidi K. Gardner, PhD, Distinguished Fellow at Harvard Law School's Center on the Legal Profession, has called Deborah "the leading expert in law firm marketing. Not only has she studied this complex topic from the peak of the legal profession, her research into what works and what doesn't is priceless for anyone interested in growing their business."

Over the past two decades, Deborah has carved out a niche by distinguishing herself as the chief marketing officer of two of the world's most prestigious law firms – Cravath Swaine & Moore LLP and Debevoise & Plimpton LLP. Prior to diving into the legal marketing profession, she honed her business development and communications skills by working at the global management consulting firm Willis Towers Watson. In her early days, she worked both in the new business department and as an account executive at Ketchum Communications.

Deborah has also been involved in the corporate and academic arena. She recently spoke at Travelers legal department and has also spoken at McKinsey

& Company. On the academic side, she has lectured at Columbia Law School, the University of Pennsylvania's Carey Law School, Cornell Law School, and Fordham Law School. She has served as an adjunct assistant professor on the faculty of New York University.

Deborah is an officer of the International Bar Association's Law Firm Management Committee, past president of the Legal Marketing Association's New York Chapter, and past chair of the Association of the Bar of the City of New York's marketing communications committee. She was a charter member of the Luxury Marketing Council and serves as an advisor to the Chairman of the Board of the New York Public Library.

Deborah was recently inducted as a Fellow in the College of Law Practice Management. She has also been honored with the Legal Marketing Association's Legacy Award, in recognition of making "a distinguishable mark on the chapter and the profession", and is one of a few members named to the LMA's Hall of Fame. In addition, she was an honoree at the YWCA's Women Leader Luncheon and serves as a member of the organization's Academy of Women Leaders. For many years, Deborah served on the Board of Directors of The Girl Scouts Council of Greater New York.

Deborah has a B.S. in Marketing and Mass Communications from Boston University's College of Communications, graduating magna cum laude. Upon graduation, she was the recipient of the College's Alumni Award for Student Excellence and a member of Psi Chi, the International Honor Society in Psychology. While as an undergraduate, she served as a teaching assistant for courses in marketing and in psychology.

About the contributors

Ida Abbott is a retirement strategist who helps lawyers design happy and purposeful retirements and helps law firms design respectful and effective succession and retirement processes. She is an internationally recognized expert on legal talent and career development, especially mentoring, leadership, and – her current focus – retirement. Before becoming a consultant to law firms, Ida practiced law for 20 years. In recognition of her lifetime contributions to the legal profession, she was elected a fellow of both the American Bar Foundation and the College of Law Practice Management. She is an advisor, coach, speaker, and author of several seminal books, including *Retirement by Design*, named one of the best retirement books of 2020 by *The Wall Street Journal*.

Renee Branson is a resilience strategist, author, and international speaker who works with law firms and professional services organizations to strengthen performance through wellbeing, psychological safety, and trauma-informed leadership. She is the founder of RB Consulting, where she advises firm leaders on how resilience and organizational culture impact decision making, collaboration, and long-term business success. With a master's degree in counseling psychology, Renee spent nearly two decades working with survivors of trauma and crisis before bringing her expertise into the legal profession. Her work bridges neuroscience, behavioral science, and leadership strategy to help organizations reduce burnout, strengthen trust, and improve team performance. Renee speaks globally on the economics of wellbeing and the neuroscience of high performance, and collaborates with law firms in the United States, the United Kingdom, and Australia.

As chief marketing and business development officer at Jenner & Block, **JeanMarie Campbell** leads client growth initiatives that focus on driving revenue and elevating the client experience. Her work includes developing strategic marketing and branding campaigns to enhance market visibility while fostering a culture of innovation and teamwork. As a former practicing attorney for over nine years and with over 25 years of experience in client development, key account management and marketing roles, she brings a proven ability to contribute to strategy execution and strengthen client relationships. By leveraging her expertise in leadership, marketing strategy, account management and client development, JeanMarie aims to align initiatives with a law firm's broader objectives and deliver impactful client solutions. She enjoys writing and speaking on topics including leadership, client relationships, business development/marketing, and coaching for high performance. JeanMarie works with various law schools on their adjunct curriculum around marketing and business development. She is a certified executive coach and has a passion for coaching lawyers on business development, leadership, and career development.

Tim Corcoran guides law firm and law department leaders through the profitable disruption of outdated business models. Tim is a former CEO, a Fellow and past trustee of the College of Law Practice Management, past president and Hall of Fame member of the Legal Marketing Association, an American Lawyer Research Fellow, a past Teaching Fellow in the Master in Legal Business program at the Australian College of Law, a frequent keynote presenter and workshop facilitator at lawyer retreats and legal conferences, and a writer whose articles and commentary are published regularly in leading legal trade publications. Tim resides in the US and travels regularly to his global client base.

Jamie Diaferia, founder of Infinite, counsels leading professional services firms on their media, litigation, and crisis communications strategies. For 25 years, he has worked behind the scenes on many of the most significant stories in the news. In 2024 and 2025, *PRNews* recognized Jamie in its "People of the Year" award in the "Crisis Managers" category, which honors "standout communicators who have led overall communications efforts during a crisis, have proven their ability to protect an organization's reputation, and stay on message during a crisis". *PRNews* also included him among the "50 Game-Changers of PR" in 2017 and *Business Insider* recognized him on its 2020 list of the "19 top public relations experts CEOs scramble to hire in a crisis". Jamie has been named one of *Lawdragon*'s "100 Leading Legal Consultants and Strategists" every year since 2016 and has been ranked by *Chambers* in its Communications supplement since 2018. Before founding Infinite, Jamie was a journalist and lawyer.

Dr Heidi K. Gardner is a Distinguished Fellow at Harvard Law School and former professor at Harvard Business School, and a globally recognized authority on organizational performance. She is CEO of the research and advisory firm Gardner & Co, and has been named by Thinkers50 as one of the world's most influential leadership experts. Heidi is the bestselling author of *Smart Collaboration and Smarter Collaboration*, and has published more than 100 books, articles, and case studies. Her research has earned the top honors in her field, including awards from the Academy of Management, and has been selected more than ten times for Harvard Business Review's "Best of" collections. A Fulbright Fellow and former McKinsey consultant, Heidi has lived and worked on four continents. She holds a BA in Japanese from the University of Pennsylvania, a master's degree from the London School of Economics, and a second master's degree and PhD from London Business School.

Jessica Grayson is chief growth officer at Stradley Ronon, where she leads the firm's lateral partner and group acquisitions and integration, business development, and marketing initiatives. Under her leadership, the firm has achieved record lateral growth, expanding its capabilities, market reach, and geographic footprint. A member of the firm's management committee, Jessica works closely with firm leadership to drive financial growth, enhance market presence, and ensure seamless integration for incoming talent. Prior to joining Stradley Ronon, Jessica led lateral partner acquisitions and integration at an Am Law 10 firm and held C-suite marketing and business development roles at two New York City-based firms. She currently chairs the Law Firm Advisory Committee for the National Association of Legal Search Consultants (NALSC) and previously served on the Executive Committee of the Legal Marketing Association (LMA) Northeast Region Board.

Julie Henson is a growth strategist and chief growth officer at Decipher Investigative Intelligence, where she advises law firm leaders on revenue growth, talent strategy, market expansion, and competitive positioning. With more than 20 years of experience in the legal industry, she works closely with managing partners, executive committees, and c-suite leaders to help firms grow with greater precision and long-term alignment. Previously serving as chief client officer for an Am Law 100 firm, Julie led firmwide initiatives focused on client development, cross-investment, leadership engagement, and strategic expansion. She is known for helping firms identify high impact growth opportunities through data, market intelligence, and relationship strategy while strengthening collaboration across practices and offices. Julie regularly counsels firms on lateral growth, client investment strategies, leadership alignment, and the evolving business dynamics shaping the future of the legal industry.

Brandie Knox is founder and principal of Knox Design Strategy, a brand and digital strategy firm advising law firms. She helps firms clarify their positioning and create meaningful digital experiences for clients, prospective clients, and internal teams. Her work spans both external and internal law firm initiatives – from brand strategy and websites to knowledge management systems that help attorneys and staff access information and collaborate more effectively. With more than two decades of experience, Brandie previously managed the brand and design team at Shearman & Sterling (now A&O Shearman) before launching Knox Design Strategy in 2009.

Brandie is also the founder of Moxx, a digital case notebook designed to help litigation teams organize evidence, build case narratives, and collaborate more effectively throughout the lifecycle of a case. She brings a strategic perspective to brand positioning, helping law firms turn differentiation into something clients, prospective clients, and internal teams can see, understand, and trust.

Jen Leonard is the founder of Creative Lawyers, a company that works with legal leaders to drive creative solutions that respond to an era of significant change. Before launching her company, Jen was the first chief innovation officer and executive director of the Future of the Profession Initiative at Penn Carey Law School. At Penn Carey Law, Jen has taught Modern Law Firm Business Strategy, Design Thinking for Lawyers, and Generative AI in Law Practice. She has also taught design thinking to senior executives in Wharton's Executive MBA program. She hosts several podcasts, including *Fast-Tracked: Emergent Issues in the Legal Profession* (Practising Law Institute) and *AI and the Future of Law* (co-hosted with Bridget McCormack, president and CEO of the American Arbitration Association). She was named to the ABA's Women in Legal Tech list of honorees in 2024 and serves on the Board of Pro Bono Institute. Jen practiced law for ten years after graduating from Penn Carey Law.

Trish Lilley is an established leader in the legal industry with more than 25 years' experience shaping growth strategies for both US and global firms from 250 to 850+ attorneys and nearly $1B in annual revenue. She has led large-scale functional and cultural transformations across client development, marketing, employee relations, and communications. As chief marketing and business development officer at four Am Law firms, Trish is recognized for architecting modern, data-driven business development functions that align client needs, market intelligence, and firm capabilities to drive measurable results and position these functions as strategic engines for revenue and relationship expansion. Her work emphasizes practical innovation – integrating technology, analytics, and cross-functional collaboration to identify opportunities, strengthen client engagement, and accelerate growth. A frequent contributor on legal industry trends, Trish is widely regarded as a forward-thinking, insightful voice on how firms can modernize operations and growth strategies. She speaks often at industry conferences and law schools and has been published and quoted in various outlets, including *The American Lawyer* and *The New York Times*. Her work has been recognized for impact and innovation by the Managing Partner Forum, *The New York Law Journal*, the Web Marketing Association, and others.

Natalie Loeb is founder and CEO of Loeb Leadership, a leading coaching and development firm with 100+ consultants across the US and Europe. A visionary entrepreneur and seasoned female business leader, she has built a family owned company from the ground up and brings nearly 40 years of expertise in talent development, executive coaching, and organizational transformation. Previously on the human resources team at Skadden, Arps in New York, Natalie designed leadership academies and coached senior leaders – experiences that inspired her to found Loeb Leadership in 1997 to cultivate self aware, resilient, and inclusive leaders. She partners with senior teams to reshape culture, design workplace inclusion initiatives, streamline roles and processes, and deliver scalable leadership programs. Natalie holds an M.S. in Industrial/Organizational Psychology, executive coach training from Baruch College, and certifications in 15+ assessment tools. A prolific writer and sought after speaker, she is PLI faculty, authors the Coach's Counsel column, and co authored *Beyond the Courtroom*.

Andrew Longstreth is head writer at Infinite, an award-winning international communications firm. A former journalist with Reuters and *The American*

Lawyer, he has written about legal affairs and the legal industry for more than two decades.

Ivan Matviak is the co-founder and CEO of Smarter Collaboration International, where he leads the development of research backed technology that strengthens organizational collaboration and performance. He is the co author of the bestselling *Smarter Collaboration*, and a frequent contributor to *Harvard Business Review*, translating rigorous research into practical tools for leaders. Ivan previously served as president and chairman of Princeton Financial Systems, and as an executive vice president at Clearwater Analytics and State Street Bank, where he led global data, analytics, and fintech businesses. He has also advised Boston Consulting Group and Warburg Pincus on strategy, technology, and organizational effectiveness. Earlier in his career, Ivan held roles across Europe, Africa, and the United States at the Bank of Scotland, and Bain & Company. He holds degrees from the University of Pennsylvania, the Wharton School, and the Lauder Institute.

Monica Rodriguez Kuniyoshi, former chief marketing officer at Gunderson Dettmer, is the principal of MRK Strategies LLC, advising law firms on adoption, behavior change, and growth. With more than 25 years of experience, she is known for building and leading high-performing marketing and business development teams, supporting significant firm growth, and driving initiatives that strengthen client engagement and market position.

Drawing on a background in organizational development, Monica focuses on aligning attorney behavior with firm strategy to help leaders translate investment in marketing, technology, and talent into sustained adoption, stronger collaboration, and measurable business outcomes. She is also an advocate for the responsible use of AI and data-driven innovation to enhance client service, deepen relationships, and unlock new opportunities for growth.

Diane Rosen is an experienced coach, organizational consultant, training professional, lawyer, and mediator. She is the founder and president of dr2 Consultants LLC, which helps organizations, teams, and individuals achieve their goals, enhance existing resources, improve and optimize performance, manage transitions, support leadership development, and experience the extraordinary. Diane began her career at Weil Gotshal & Manges and Skadden Arps Slate Meagher & Flom, and maintains a private mediation practice in

New York. She was formerly counsel to Herrick Feinstein LLP and Ortoli Rosenstadt LLP where she handled real estate and corporate transactions. Diane has served on many non-profit boards and was the founding vice president of Girls Learn International, a non-profit organization that works to combat the global crisis in girls' education.

Jaron Rubenstein is a digital marketing technology innovator, software engineer, technology strategist, and proven business leader who brings deep operational, marketing, and data security expertise to professional services organizations. Jaron excels at aligning technical vision with business goals, building on decades of experience delivering sophisticated marketing technology solutions to leading law firms. Jaron is the founder and former CEO of RubyLaw, a legal marketing technology SaaS platform that powers websites, manages experience data, generates marketing documents for proposals and presentations, and ensures the integrity of digital content for law firms of all sizes. He established RubyLaw as the most modern marketing technology innovator, set the strategic vision, led the product and technology strategy, and grew RubyLaw to a significant share of the Am Law 200 market. In his current roles as a consulting CTO and chief AI officer, Jaron is designing and building the next generation of AI-enhanced digital marketing and business agents.

Allan Schoenberg is chief communications officer at Vinson & Elkins, where he leads the firm's brand strategy, media relations, internal communications, rankings, and digital media. He oversees an integrated, multi-channel communications platform designed to strengthen the firm's reputation through strategic storytelling, thought leadership, and market positioning. Before joining Vinson & Elkins, Allan held senior communications leadership roles at Nasdaq, CME Group, Bloomberg LP, and Accenture, building deep expertise in business-to-business communications and complex, highly regulated industries. He specializes in aligning communications strategy with business objectives, managing high-stakes issues, and leveraging data-driven insights to drive engagement and growth. Under his leadership, the communications function has become a strategic partner in advancing the firm's culture, visibility, and competitive advantage.

Nat Slavin is the CEO of ClientSignal, the AI-driven client intelligence platform for law firms, and founder and managing partner of Client Insight

Ventures, its consulting arm. For more than three decades Nat has been at the center of important conversations between law firms and their clients. As founder of one of the legal industry's leading client feedback practices, Nat has conducted thousands of confidential conversations with corporate counsel, general counsel, and C-suite executives, uncovering what clients really think about their law firms, what drives loyalty, what reveals competitive intelligence, and what puts relationships at risk. He has led the creation of client experience and service programs at firms across the Am Law 200 and regularly collaborates with firm leaders on client team strategy. Across both ventures, Nat brings the voice of the client directly to law firm partners, client teams, and firm leadership to inform and advise on business development and client growth strategies. Nat is an elected fellow in the College of Law Practice Management and a Legal Marketing Association Hall of Fame inductee.

Renate (Ren) Wagner is the director of internal communications at Vinson & Elkins, where she helps lead firmwide communications and engagement initiatives that support connection, culture, and strategic alignment across the organization. Since joining the firm in 2003, Ren has held roles spanning marketing, talent, inclusion, and employee engagement. In her current role, she oversees internal communications platforms and content, including a daily firmwide newsletter and the firm's intranet, and supports communications related to talent, recruiting, learning and development, benefits, and firm initiatives. She collaborates closely with leadership and cross-functional teams across communications, branding, business development, HR, and talent functions. Prior to joining Vinson & Elkins, Ren worked in communications for the American Airlines pilots' association and operated her own full-service design studio serving clients across multiple consumer and B2B industries.

Introduction

When I was first approached about putting together this book, I knew one thing right away – I did not want it to be another collection of generic advice about marketing, rainmaking, or business development formulas. There are already plenty of articles and conference panels offering easy answers to hard questions. Most law firm leaders know the basics. They know that relationships matter. They know that collaboration matters. They know that culture matters.

What they often struggle with is the harder part – how to actually build an environment where those things happen consistently, not just on a good day or in a strong quarter.

As I thought about what this book could be, I kept coming back to a practical question. If the chair of a law firm called me and said, "We want to strengthen our business development culture. Who are the smartest people you know to help us think this through?", who would I recommend? This book is my answer to that question.

Every contributor was chosen not simply because they are knowledgeable, but because they have lived these issues inside sophisticated, demanding professional environments. These are people I would trust to sit across the table from firm leadership and help them tackle some of the most important challenges facing law firms today, from client relationships and branding to AI, succession planning, psychological safety, thought leadership, digital reputation, internal communications, and cross-practice collaboration.

What emerged from their chapters was something even richer and more interconnected than I had originally expected.

At first glance, the topics may look unrelated. Branding. Culture. AI. Budgeting. Succession planning. Thought leadership. But as the chapters came together, several themes surfaced again and again.

The first is that business development is no longer a side activity. It cannot sit exclusively inside a marketing department or rest on the shoulders of a handful of rainmakers. Business development increasingly reflects the culture, leadership, systems, and behaviors of the entire institution. It is an essential factor of how law firm lawyers must think, on a daily basis.

The second is that collaboration has become a strategic necessity, not just a nice aspiration. Clients expect firms to work seamlessly across practices, offices, and disciplines. They assume lawyers inside a firm know one another, trust one another, and can bring the right resources forward efficiently. When firms fall short of that, clients notice, even if lawyers do not.

The third is trust. Again and again, contributors returned to the idea that trust is the foundation on which sustainable business development is built. Trust among partners. Trust between lawyers and clients. Trust between leadership and the broader organization. Several contributors approach this from different angles, including culture, psychological safety, communications, client teams, and succession planning, but the underlying principle is remarkably consistent. Firms grow more effectively when people feel safe sharing relationships, ideas, opportunities, and credit.

Authenticity is another theme that runs through nearly every chapter. One of the greatest misconceptions in professional services is that successful business development requires lawyers to become someone they are not. In reality, the most effective business developers tend to be those who find approaches aligned with their personalities, strengths, and values. Sustainable business development is not performative. It is relational. It depends on curiosity, generosity, responsiveness, consistency, and credibility far more than charisma.

Technology and AI also appear throughout these chapters, not simply as operational tools, but as forces reshaping the competitive landscape. As routine information becomes increasingly commoditized, differentiation shifts toward judgment, insight, interpretation, creativity, and human connection. In many ways, the rise of AI makes the human dimensions of professional relationships more important, not less.

Finally, nearly every contributor touches on leadership. Business development cultures do not emerge by accident. They are modeled, reinforced, incentivized, communicated, and protected by leadership. Lawyers pay close attention to what leadership rewards, tolerates, ignores, and celebrates. If collaboration, innovation, thought leadership, mentoring, and client service are truly priorities, lawyers need to see those values reflected consistently in firm systems and behaviors.

Throughout my career, both inside law firms and later as a consultant and author, I have seen firms invest enormous sums in marketing initiatives, technology, retreats, and strategic plans. Some succeeded brilliantly. Others struggled, despite significant resources and real talent. Often, the difference was not intelligence or ambition. It was alignment. The firms that thrived understood that business development is not a collection of activities. It is an ecosystem.

My hope is that this book offers practical ideas, frameworks, and inspiration for leaders who want to build stronger firms and stronger client relationships in a profession that continues to evolve rapidly. More than anything, I hope it encourages leaders to think about business development not as selling, but as one of the central expressions of culture, trust, service, and leadership inside a modern law firm.

Deborah B. Farone
June 2026

Chapter 1:
Building a firmwide marketing strategy – a roadmap for law firms ready to grow

By Deborah B. Farone

Many of the law firms that have people reading this book have a marketing department. Yet not each of those law firms has a marketing strategy.

That distinction matters more than most firm leaders realize. A department is a function. A strategy is your plan of action that comes before you consider tactics. It may be something like, "Grow our mid-market private equity practice in the northeast", or "Cross-sell our M&A work to our clients using us in litigation". It may be even more specific, such as "Dig deep to grow the relationships with these five clients". Strategy connects what you do every day – the tactics of PR, marketing, and business development – to the outcomes you are working toward. Without a strategy, even the most talented marketing professionals find themselves scrambling to execute tactics in a vacuum, responding to whoever makes the most noise rather than building toward something meaningful.

I spent two decades as chief marketing officer at two of the world's most respected law firms – Cravath, Swaine & Moore and Debevoise & Plimpton – and I have spent years since then advising firms and coaching individual lawyers around the world. For my first book, *Best Practices in Law Firm Business Development and Marketing*,[1] I interviewed more than 60 law firm chairs, rainmakers, general counsel, and innovators in the profession. For my latest book, *Breaking Ground: How Successful Women Lawyers Build Thriving Practices*,[2] I spoke to women rainmakers on four continents who have built some of the most powerful legal practices in the world.

In all of that work, one truth has surfaced again and again – the firms that consistently grow, attract great clients, and develop strong next-generation lawyers are the ones that are intentional. They have a strategy, they believe in it, and they execute on it.

What follows is a practical guide to building a firmwide marketing strategy that works. Not a theoretical framework, but a real-world roadmap for firm leaders, practice group heads, and marketing professionals who are ready to close the gap between intention and results.

Why you need a firmwide marketing strategy

The first question most lawyers ask is, why does a firmwide strategy matter? After all, many firms operate for years without one, relying instead on individual lawyer initiative and the accumulated relationships of their most senior partners.

The answer is that the legal market has changed, and the old model is no longer sufficient. Competition has changed, sophistication from the general counsel's office has changed, and the alternative to using traditional law firms has changed.

In my years working and consulting, I have seen a dramatic shift in how sophisticated clients select and retain outside counsel. General counsels at major companies now manage legal spend with the same discipline they apply to any other procurement decision. The days of relationships guaranteeing work are not entirely gone, but they are no longer enough on their own. According to the research behind *Breaking Ground*, the best business generators in the profession are not simply those with the deepest legacy relationships. They are the ones who are most intentional about how they build and sustain their practices.

That intentionality has to be modeled and supported at the firm level. Individual lawyers cannot be expected to build strong practices in isolation. As I have heard from CMOs at top firms, firms need to be transparent in establishing expectations and create mechanisms for rewarding attorneys who succeed. Without that structure, business development becomes ad hoc and unpredictable.

There is also a talent dimension. The best lawyers, especially younger ones, want to build practices, not just fill hours. When I conducted the interviews for *Breaking Ground*, one of the most striking findings was how often women lawyers said they rarely had role models for rainmaking or meaningful exposure to client development early in their careers. Many were included in pitch materials and even pitch meetings, but were never given a speaking role. That is both a loss for the individual and a missed opportunity for the firm.

A clear firmwide marketing strategy creates a framework in which all lawyers, regardless of seniority or background, understand where the firm is going and what role they play in getting there. That matters enormously for building the next generation of business generators.

The firms that take this seriously are the ones that will lead in the decade ahead.

What can go wrong without one

The absence of a firmwide strategy does not mean that nothing happens. It means that a lot happens without coordination, clear purpose, or measurable impact. The patterns I see most often when firms are operating without a strategy are remarkably consistent. I often call these tactics random acts of marketing. They can be divergent and work counter to one another and when not coordinated they can cause embarrassing outcomes. Think of two lawyers independently showing up at the same financial service client to pitch business, within the same week. Yes, in real life, these things happen.

Marketing can quickly become reactive, not only to every business opportunity – whether right or wrong for the firm – but in how the marketing professionals operate. Without a strategy, marketing teams spend most of their time responding to requests rather than driving initiatives. A partner wants a new bio. A practice group needs a pitch deck by tomorrow. An award opportunity arises and someone needs to decide whether to pursue it. All of this is legitimate work, but it is not strategic. The marketing and business development teams may be busy, but the firm is not necessarily moving forward.

Resources are spread too thin. When there is no strategy to guide prioritization, firms tend to say yes to everything. They sponsor every conference, apply to every directory and ranking submission, and spend money on initiatives with no clear connection to firm goals. The result is energy and money spread across dozens of activities, none of which receive the sustained investment needed to produce real results. Without intentional steps, firms risk playing on an uneven playing field where leadership and growth opportunities remain siloed and inaccessible to those who have not yet been tapped.

Some firms rely entirely on the rainmaking instincts of a handful of senior partners. When those partners retire or leave, the client relationships they carried often go with them. There is no institutional infrastructure to capture and build on what they built. This is one of the most significant business risks a firm can face, and it is preventable.

The firm's identity becomes muddled. Lawyers and law firms are often viewed by clients as parity products. On the surface, many firms look remarkably similar. The challenge I used to give my marketing students at NYU, drawn from my own professor's assignment years ago, was to think about how you market a parity product, where the features are barely distinguishable from the competition's. The answer is always the same – differentiation requires clarity, consistency, and a deep understanding of what your client actually values. A firm without a clear strategy rarely has that clarity.

Talented lawyers do not develop. Business development is a skill, not a gift. It is a talent that needs to be strengthened by using it over and over again. Without a firmwide commitment to building these capabilities, many lawyers never develop them. And the lawyers who miss out most often are not the ones with the least potential. They are the ones who were never given the right exposure or support.

How to start – match it to the firm's direction

A marketing strategy is only as good as the overall firm strategy it is designed to support. This is where many firms go wrong at the outset. They ask their marketing department to develop a strategy without first anchoring it to the firm's larger goals and direction.

The starting point is clarity about where the firm is going. What are the firm's strategic priorities for the next three to five years? Which practice areas and industries represent the greatest growth opportunity? What geographic markets matter most? What kind of clients does the firm most want to serve? What do the best client relationships look like, and how does the firm want to be known?

These are questions that need to be answered at the firm leadership level before the marketing strategy can be built. If firm leadership has not done this work, the marketing strategy process can actually serve as a useful catalyst for it. In many of the firm retreats I have moderated, the process of developing a marketing strategy surfaces important strategic conversations that have been deferred for years.

Once you have clarity on firm direction, the marketing strategy should address several key dimensions.

Positioning and differentiation

Lawyers who build thriving practices are known for something specific. The same principle applies at the firm level. What is the firm's story? What makes it the right choice for the clients it most wants to serve? The best firm-level positioning works the same way. It is rooted in genuine strengths and expressed with specificity, not in the vague claims of excellence that appear on every law firm website.

Client development priorities

Not all clients are created equal. A smart marketing strategy identifies where the firm has its strongest relationships and where the best opportunities exist to deepen and expand them. It also identifies target clients where growth is most strategic and creates a plan for how the firm will pursue those relationships over time. The transition from transactional service to trusted advisor happens at the firm level, as well as the individual level. It requires sustained investment and attention.

Thought leadership and visibility

One of the most consistent findings across both of my books is that the lawyers who build the most powerful practices are known for something. They are visible. They are contributing to the conversation in their fields. True thought leadership requires taking a point of view. It demands intellectual courage. At the firm level, a marketing strategy should identify where the firm has genuine expertise that clients care about, which lawyers will be the voices for the firm in those areas, and how the firm will support and amplify their efforts consistently.

Business development infrastructure

What systems and processes does the firm need to support effective business development? CRM systems like Salesforce, Foundation, Next, and Dealcloud have been game changers for many firms by giving marketing and business development teams a comprehensive view of client interactions and relationship history. One of the most powerful things a firm can do is help its lawyers understand and position their outreach within the context of the broader firm relationship with a client. Today's technology can make that possible at scale.

Talent and development

How will the firm build business development capability across its lawyer population? Business development is not an inborn talent. It is a teachable skill. The firms that understand this and make continuous investment in building that skill from the associate level through partner create a pipeline of business generators rather than relying on the same few people forever. In today's world where half of lateral partners leave after five years at a firm, it's too risky to lose rainmakers. Certain partners may be fantastic lawyers but have never had the coaching or exposure they need to build a book of business. Firms that provide that support change the trajectory of careers and the trajectory of the firm.

How to get buy-in

Even the best marketing strategy will fail if it does not have genuine buy-in from firm leadership and key partners. This is one of the most important and most underestimated challenges in the process.

Buy-in is not the same as approval

Approval means people say yes in a meeting. Buy-in means people actually believe in the strategy and are willing to act on it, even when it requires effort, change, or sacrifice of the status quo. Getting there takes a deliberate approach.

Involve people in the process

The surest path to buy-in is participation. When lawyers and leaders are genuinely part of developing the strategy, they have ownership of it. One of the most powerful things I observed in my years as a CMO, and have continued to see in my consulting work, is how different the energy is in a room when people feel they've contributed to a plan versus when they feel it was handed to them. Practice group chairs, rainmakers, managing partners, and marketing leadership should all be genuinely part of the conversation. Their perspectives should shape the strategy, not just receive it.

Connect the strategy to what people care about

Partners care about clients, compensation, and their own professional success. If the marketing strategy is presented as an abstract firm initiative, it will generate polite interest at best. Connect it to outcomes that matter to individual lawyers. Show people how a stronger firmwide strategy makes their own practices more successful. The connection between firm investment in marketing infrastructure and individual lawyer success at building a book of business is direct. Make it explicit.

Make the business case

Law firm partners respond to evidence. The lawyers who build the most powerful practices are intentional. They know what they stand for, they invest consistently in their relationships and their visibility, and they do not wait for opportunities to come to them. Firms that support that intentionality outperform those that leave it to chance. If you can demonstrate that case with data and concrete examples, you have a compelling argument. The more specific the evidence, the more credible the initiative.

Find and cultivate your champions

In every firm, there are lawyers who genuinely believe in business development and who have the credibility to influence their peers. Identify them. Bring them into the process. Give them a platform to share what they are doing and why it works. A respected partner advocating for a more strategic approach to marketing is far more persuasive than any presentation from the marketing department alone. Many firm leaders understand this and are champions of the firm's business development and marketing programs, while many are not. Which firms do you think perform better and have greater participation from their lawyers? Those who have the backing of firm leadership, or those that do not? At Morgan Lewis, Jami McKeon understood this well. ML Women, her signature business development program, gained traction in part because it was grounded in the firm's core mission and led by someone with enormous credibility and conviction.

Address resistance directly

There will be skeptics. Some partners will view a firmwide marketing strategy as unnecessary overhead or as a threat to their autonomy. We know who those people are and there seem to be a few naysayers at every firm. Do not ignore this resistance. Engage with it. Understand where it comes from. If partners believe the strategy will add bureaucracy without adding value, that concern is worth taking seriously. Show people how the strategy will remove friction, not add it.

Leadership must model the behavior they want

If firm leaders talk about the importance of business development but do not engage in it themselves, or do not allocate meaningful resources to it, the message is clear. Commitment and action at the top are the most powerful signal the firm can send. The firms where marketing strategy takes hold are almost always the ones where managing partners and firm chairs are active participants in executing it.

Keeping everyone on target and aligned

Launching a strategy is one thing. Sustaining it is another. Many firms do the hard work of developing a thoughtful marketing strategy, only to watch it fade over the following months as daily pressures crowd it out. It's much like the strategic plans that firms spend a fortune to produce, with layers of outside consultants. Preventing this requires ongoing structure, communication, and accountability.

Translate strategy into clear accountabilities. Every element of the marketing strategy should be assigned to someone who owns its execution and is accountable for results. This means defining what success looks like, setting timelines, and establishing how progress will be measured and reported. One of the most common failure modes I see is a strategy that is everyone's responsibility and therefore no one's. Specificity about who does what by when is not bureaucracy. It is the difference between a plan and a wish. Each element, whether public relations, client interviews, or branding should have SMART goals – goals that are:

S – Specific: The goal clearly defines what you want to accomplish, who is involved, and why. "Increase the number of client alerts" is vague. "Publish two client alerts per quarter in the M&A practice group" is specific.
M – Measurable: There's a concrete way to track progress and know when you've succeeded. Numbers, percentages, and deadlines make goals measurable. For example, "Each partner in the practice agrees to meet with three new-to-them in-house counsel each quarter".
A – Achievable: The goal is realistic given your resources, time, and capacity. Ambitious is good, unattainable sets the team up for frustration.
R – Relevant: The goal connects to broader priorities. For a law firm, a marketing goal should tie back to the firm's overall business strategy.
T – Time-bound: There's a defined deadline or timeframe. Without one, goals drift indefinitely.

Build in regular reviews
A quarterly review of marketing and business development activity, measured against the strategic plan, keeps the strategy alive and creates natural opportunities to address what is and is not working. These reviews should not be pro forma. They should be substantive conversations about progress, obstacles, and adjustments needed. Bring the data but also make room for the qualitative conversation about what is really happening in the market and with your clients. I often suggest that my clients pre-schedule these meetings so that they have them booked on partners' calendars in advance.

Use the strategy as a decision filter
One of the most practical tests of whether a strategy is real is whether it guides resource allocation and prioritization. When a new opportunity arises, asking whether it aligns with the strategy is a discipline that prevents drift

and keeps the firm focused. Not every good idea fits the strategy, and that is fine. The strategy should provide a filter, so that decisions about where to invest time and money are made intentionally rather than reactively. This will also allow your marketing and business development people to say no to certain projects that don't fit with this year's strategy.

Invest in continuous development

Any lawyer training, including business development training, should not be viewed as a one-time event. It should be woven into a lawyer's time at the firm from associate to partner and beyond. The worst thing is when someone becomes partner and says, "I really don't know anyone outside the firm. I've just been sitting in my office for eight years." That outcome is entirely preventable, but only if the firm builds development into its culture from the start.

Early exposure matters

Consistent reinforcement matters. Many law firms are starting to do this right, with skills programs for various levels of seniority and allocated funds for private coaching. Not only does this help the firm increase revenue, but it also supports the associate by saying, "We care about you and we are making an investment in you".

Celebrate progress

Business development is hard work, and it often takes time to produce visible results. Recognizing the efforts of lawyers who are investing in their practices, even before the results are fully visible, reinforces the culture you are trying to build. It signals that the firm values this work and is paying attention. Recognizing lawyers who are doing that invisible foundational work is how you sustain a culture of business development over time. Be sure to mention these developments and provide kudos to those partners that are taking the right steps, whether that means they are cross-selling, helping to train and mentor other lawyers, or bringing in business.

Communicate consistently

The strategy should not live only in a slide deck that gets presented at a partner retreat and then filed away. It should be referenced in meetings, reflected in practice group plans, and woven into the conversations that firm leaders have with their lawyers. Repetition and consistency are what turn a strategy into a shared culture. As I observed in my years at Cravath and Debevoise, and have continued to see in my advisory work, the firms where marketing is truly embedded in the culture are the ones where it gets talked about regularly at every level, not just by the marketing department.

Keep it current

Markets change. Client needs evolve. New competitors emerge. A marketing strategy is not a document that gets written once and revisited every five years. It should be a living framework, updated as circumstances change. An annual strategic review, separate from quarterly check-ins, ensures that the strategy stays relevant and that the firm is always looking forward.

The bottom line

A firmwide marketing strategy is not a luxury. It is a practical necessity for any firm that is serious about growth, about building something that lasts, and about creating an environment where talented lawyers at every stage of their careers can develop and thrive.

The lawyers who build the most powerful practices are intentional. As Donna Wilson, CEO and managing partner of Manatt, Phelps & Phillips, told me for *Breaking Ground*, the path to building a practice comes down to two words – hustle and consistency. Those are not qualities you can outsource. But they are qualities a firm can support, encourage, and reward. That is what a firmwide marketing strategy makes possible.

The same principle applies at the institutional level. Strategy is intention made operational. It is the difference between hoping good things happen and building the conditions that make them likely.

The firms that will lead in the decade ahead are the ones that start building that foundation now.

Ten steps to building a firmwide business development and marketing strategy

When building a firmwide business development and marketing strategy, the sequence matters as much as the substance. These ten steps provide a practical framework for getting started and sustaining momentum.

1 Align with firm leadership first

Before building a marketing strategy, ensure firm leaders have clarity on the firm's overall direction – which practices and industries to prioritize, which clients to pursue, and how the firm wants to be known. Marketing strategy must follow business strategy, not precede it.

2 Conduct an honest assessment of where you stand

Audit what is currently working and what is not. Review your client base, your competitive positioning, your brand visibility, and your existing marketing infrastructure. Identify the gaps between where you are and where you want to be. You cannot chart a course without knowing your starting point.

3 Define your differentiation

Articulate, with specificity, what makes your firm the right choice for the clients you most want to serve. Avoid vague claims of excellence that every firm makes. Ground your positioning in genuine strengths. As the research behind *Breaking Ground*[3] confirms, lawyers and firms that are known for something specific win more work.

4 Identify your priority clients and targets

Not all clients represent equal opportunity. Map your most important existing relationships and determine where you have the best prospects for growth. Then identify the target clients where growth is most strategic and create a plan for how the firm will pursue those relationships over time.

5 Build a thought leadership plan

Determine where the firm has genuine expertise that matters to clients and identify which lawyers will serve as the firm's visible voices in those areas. Create an editorial calendar that is consistent and connected to your positioning. True thought leadership requires taking a point of view, not simply producing content for content's sake.

6 **Invest in the right infrastructure**
Put systems in place that enable effective business development at scale. A well-implemented CRM system, an experience management platform, and content tools give marketing and business development teams the visibility they need to support coordinated, strategic outreach. Technology does not replace relationships, but it makes them easier to manage and develop.

7 **Establish clear roles and accountabilities**
Assign ownership for every element of the strategy. Define what success looks like, set timelines, and establish how progress will be measured. A strategy without clear accountability is aspirational at best. Specificity about who does what by when is what separates a plan from a wish.

8 Set SMART goals
Translate strategy into goals that are Specific, Measurable, Achievable, Relevant, and Time-bound. A goal like 'improve thought leadership' is not actionable. 'Publish six bylined articles in top-tier publications this year, with each practice group responsible for two, tracked quarterly' is. SMART goals create accountability and make it possible to measure real progress.

9 **Commit to continuous development**
Make business development training an ongoing investment, not a one-time event. From associates learning relationship-building basics to newly promoted partners developing their books of business, training should be woven into every stage of a lawyer's career at the firm. As one of the leading lawyers featured in *Breaking Ground*[4] put it, business development is not an inborn talent. It is a teachable skill.

10 **Review, adjust, and keep the strategy alive**
Build in quarterly reviews to assess progress, address obstacles, and make course corrections. Conduct an annual strategic review to ensure the strategy stays relevant as the market evolves. Communicate the strategy consistently at every level of the firm. The goal is to turn a document into a shared culture, one in which everyone understands where the firm is headed and the role they play in getting there.

References

1 *Best Practices in Law Firm Business Development and Marketing*, Deborah B. Farone, Practising Law Institute, 2019

2 *Breaking Ground: How Successful Women Lawyers Build Thriving Practices*, Deborah B. Farone, Practising Law Institute, 2026

3 *Ibid.*

4 *Ibid.*

Chapter 2: Brand positioning and differentiation – a practical framework

By Brandie Knox, principal and lead strategist, Knox Design Strategy

Brand positioning is not about creating a logo or crafting a tagline. Instead, it is about establishing and owning a distinct, positive, and authentic place in the mind of your target audience, relative to your competitors. This unique position sets your firm apart, resonates with prospects, clients, and recruits, and is lived by attorneys and business support staff.

You have a brand, even if you're not aware of it.

"A brand is not what *you* say it is. It's what *they* say it is."[1] In other words, certain experience, attributes, and culture already come to mind when these audiences think of your firm.

You can, however, influence how your firm is positioned in the mind of your clients, prospects, and recruits by making intentional, strategic choices to shape that perception. Ultimately, it comes down to this: when your target audience thinks about your firm, what do you want them to remember – and why does it matter?

I've spent more than two decades working with law firms on brand strategy, and one of the most consistent challenges I see is this – firms struggle to clearly articulate what makes them different. A review of law firm websites and marketing materials often reveals the same language, e.g., client service, responsiveness, experience.

The problem is none of it is differentiating.

Law firms are understandably hesitant to take a strong position in the market. There is often a fear that, by leaning into a specific strength or focus, the firm may exclude other opportunities. Instead, firms rely on generic, cliché messages and design.

This creates ambiguity.

Our brains do not remember what is ambiguous. We remember what is different. Moreover, firms often describe themselves one way while the market experiences them another. Identifying the gap between internal belief and external reality is essential to shaping a brand strategy that is both credible and effective.

A thoughtful, well-planned process challenges these assumptions and internal opinions, and should bring together diverse input, including leadership, attorneys, business support staff, and clients. This approach ensures that a firm's brand is built on real insights and authentic experiences, rather than guesswork.

The process demands discipline – asking the right questions, synthesizing outcomes, and aligning stakeholders around a clear direction.

It requires a willingness to challenge long-held assumptions about the firm and how it presents itself. This work becomes the foundation for everything that follows – language used for marketing initiatives, visual brand identity, the website user experience (UX) and user interface (UI), and market and business development initiatives – ultimately shaping how the firm shows up in the market.

There have been entire books and articles written about this topic and I've read many of them. This chapter is not meant to replace these resources but is intended to offer practical, tested frameworks for approaching brand positioning, differentiation, and developing a brand strategy within law firms

The process – a practical framework

With a clear, shared understanding of what brand positioning is – and what it is not – the next question is how to approach it in a way that is structured, efficient, and grounded in real insight.

The process can be broken into four phases:

1. *Planning*. Define the firm's goals, scope, and stakeholders, while also establishing a clear structure for how decisions will be made.
2. *Discovery*. Gather input through individual research, collaborative workshops and one-on-one interviews.
3. *Synthesis*. Identify and document patterns, core themes and outliers.
4. *Strategy*. Determine how the positioning will be communicated both verbally and visually in all brand touchpoints.

Each phase builds on the one before it. Skipping steps or compressing the process often leads to misalignment, generic messaging, or a strategy that is not fully adopted internally.

The sections that follow present each phase in more detail, beginning with planning and the steps required to set the foundation.

1. Planning – setting the foundation

The initial step involves clarifying and documenting business goals and objectives, and setting clear expectations before the work begins. What are the underlying motivations behind the initiative? And why now? For example, is the firm seeking to:

- Reposition itself in the market because of a merger?
- Expand or strengthen its reputation in new practice areas, industries or geography?
- Address inconsistent or undesired perceptions in the market?

The answers to these business questions will shape the subsequent work.

Identifying stakeholders, roles, and responsibilities

It is important to recognize that this is not a marketing-only exercise. Effective brand positioning requires participation from firm leadership, input from attorneys and business support staff at all levels, and – often excluded – actual perspective from clients. Without this breadth of input, the strategy risks reflecting internal assumptions from a few, rather than comprehensive, internal and external perspectives.

A frequently overlooked part of planning is determining who needs to be involved and how decisions will be made. In law firms, layered leadership structures and multiple practice groups can quickly complicate this work. Without clarity upfront, the process risks slowing down, losing focus, or defaulting to diluted outcomes. At the start of the project, clearly define and document:

- *Who is accountable for leading the process* – including managing the work, facilitating discussions, synthesizing the feedback, developing the strategy, and reporting back to the key decision-makers.
- *Who will provide input and in what capacity* – stakeholders who participate in workshops or interviews to inform the strategy but are not responsible for final decisions.
- *Who has final decision-making authority* – the individuals responsible for resolving differing viewpoints and approving the direction.
- *Who needs visibility, but not active involvement* – individuals who should be informed throughout the process but not in a way that influences outcomes.

Brand positioning is a strategic exercise, not a consensus-driven one.

Management will need to align on the direction and path forward – but not on every detail.

Securing buy-in

In law firms, buy-in is often the most challenging part of the process, not only because attorneys are often resistant to change, but because there are many stakeholders, opinions, and competing priorities.

How the process is positioned internally has a significant impact on buy-in. If the process (or resulting work) is framed as a marketing exercise or without appropriate context, it is more likely to elicit subjective personal opinions rather than constructive feedback based on research and desired outcomes. The strategy should be presented, evaluated, and decisions made based on how well they support the firm's business goals and objectives.

Buy-in does not require unanimous agreement on every detail. It requires alignment around the direction. That distinction matters, and without it, the process can become an exercise in trying to satisfy every individual perspective, which often leads back to generic positioning the firm is trying to avoid.

One of the most common misconceptions is that buy-in happens at the end, once the positioning and resulting messaging or brand identity has been developed. Instead, trust must be earned, and buy-in must be integrated into the process from the start, through conversations and questions – and active listening.

Common pitfalls

There are a few patterns that come up consistently:

- *Too many decision-makers.* When roles are undefined and everyone has equal say, feedback becomes misaligned or diluted, and it becomes difficult to move forward with clarity.
- *Late-stage objections.* Stakeholders who were not involved early may raise concerns near the end, often requiring the work to be revisited.
- *Feedback based on personal preference, not strategy.* Comments such as, "I don't like this" or "This doesn't feel right" happens when the process or resulting work is not tied back to the strategy.

2. Discovery

With a clear plan in place and stakeholder roles set, the discovery phase begins, consisting of design thinking workshops and one-on-one interviews. The purpose of this phase is to gather comprehensive information about the firm. Prior to this step, facilitators have requested and reviewed material that helps inform and guide the discussion, but nothing should be assumed. Before beginning the collaborative exercises, it's important to cover some general groundwork about the firm:

- *Success metrics:* one to three outcomes per participant to guide and measure progress throughout and beyond the project.
- *Mission:* the firm's purpose and key objectives.
- *Vision:* the firm's long-term aspirations and future goals.
- *Values:* the core principles that guide the firm's behavior and decision making.
- *Marketing:* current efforts, including what's working and what's not working.
- *Messaging:* key messages that need to be better communicated.

Use workshops instead of meetings

Design thinking workshops provide a structured environment for gathering input, aligning stakeholders, and uncovering insights that are difficult to capture through individual conversations alone. Workshops bring people into the same conversation at the same time. In a law firm setting, where perspectives can vary significantly across leadership, practice groups, and roles, this is critical. Workshops are one of the most effective tools in this phase for several reasons:

- *They are active and not passive.* Workshops require participation from everyone. Meetings, by contrast, are often centered around a moderator, often with one or two attendees dominating the conversation.
- *They mitigate false consensus.* During the structured exercises, participants brainstorm individually – without the influence of others – then come together to share and discuss. This ensures all voices are heard – not just the loudest ones.
- *They are collaborative.* Insights and outliers are discussed collectively. Participants have an opportunity to react and make trade-offs, leading to clearer alignment and faster decision making.

What to cover – tools and exercises

While there are many approaches that might fit a firm's unique needs, the key is to transition from open-ended conversations to focused, structured exercises. The following activities are designed to help workshop participants generate meaningful, actionable insights.

SWOT analysis

Most everyone, at some point, has participated in a SWOT analysis. This is a highly effective exercise for surfacing both internal and external Strengths, Weaknesses, Opportunities, and Threats, enabling group discussion and deeper insight. Ask each attendee to provide three firm strengths and weaknesses. Repeat the process for opportunities and threats. Outputs should be clustered, grouping similar ideas to identify patterns, while also highlighting any outliers that do not neatly fit into those categories. Openly discuss each category as a group.

Target audience personas

Personas are fictional representations of the firm's target audience and include characteristics, goals, and pain points of each. Identify three to four clients and prospects the firm currently serves or aims to target (including a recruit persona). Based on your initial research, it is best to pre-determine collective questions you need answered for the personas. Have workshop participants pair up to complete these, as it provides more well-rounded results. At the end, have them present each persona back to the group for open discussion.

Competitive landscape

Discuss how the firm views itself relative to its top three to five competitors. Evaluate at a firmwide level and, if necessary, a practice level. Discuss how the firm is different from these competitors. Conversations should focus on positioning, services, and visual design. What makes your firm different? Why does a prospect hire your firm over the competition? If a prospect is evaluating your firm alongside three competing firms, what makes your firm memorable? Review the firms' websites, and ask the following question – if all logos were removed, could you distinguish one firm from another?

Brand personality spectrum

This is an easy way to gauge individual stakeholders' aspirational brand attributes. Distribute a single print-out to each participant. The handout should include four to six pairs of contrasting attributes – such as traditional versus modern; personal versus corporate. Invite each participant to mark their position along each continuum. Like the SWOT analysis, outputs should be reviewed collectively to identify patterns, alignment, and divergence. This will assist in defining attributes and tone of voice.

The workshops are not about reaching any immediate conclusions. They are about gathering input, identifying themes, and creating a shared understanding of the current state, and a desired future state.

Common pitfalls

A few things to watch for:

- *Staying at a high level:* Conversations that never move beyond generalities.
- *Dominant voices:* One or two individuals shaping the discussion disproportionately.
- *Jumping to solutions too quickly:* Trying to define positioning before enough input has been gathered.

Facilitating the conversation

The quality of insight gathered during discovery depends as much on how conversations are facilitated as on the tools used. Workshops and interviews should be based on prior research and must create space for candid input while remaining focused and productive. Effective facilitation means:

- Redirecting conversations that stay at too high a level or drift off course.
- Probing for specificity, examples, and underlying reasoning.
- Challenging assumptions when needed.
- Ensuring all voices are heard – not just the most senior or most vocal.

Just as important is allowing room for disagreement. Differences in perspective are not problems to solve in the moment – they are valuable inputs.

Interviews

Workshop outcomes will inform how to then approach the interviews. For example:

- What insights were gathered that need validation or additional exploration?
- Was there a lack of agreement on competitors? (This is often the case, as competitors tend to be highly focused on practice.)
- What cultural insights surfaced that require more research and understanding?

Internal interviews

Internal interviews are an opportunity to go deeper with firm attorneys and employees at all levels. One-on-one conversations create space for more specific and, often, more candid feedback. These interviews should include:

- Firm leadership;
- Practice group leaders;
- Attorneys at all levels; and
- Business support staff.

Remember – differing perspectives offer valuable insights.

Client interviews

Select client participants who represent the personas identified during the workshop and use these conversations to further develop and refine those profiles. These interviewees provide a perspective that the firm cannot generate internally. This is from where some of the most valuable insights emerge, yet client interviews are often skipped. Without this input, positioning is based on assumption and opinion rather than direct evidence. Clients can confirm strengths, highlight blind spots, and bring clarity to what differentiates the firm in practice. They can speak to why they chose the firm, what they value, how they compare it to other firms, what other firms they considered as part of the hiring process – and whether expectations are met, or not. The interview script should be shaped by insights gathered from the workshop and internal interviews.

Meaningful results depend on attentive listening and thoughtful follow-up questions. Be ready to probe deeper as recurring themes and patterns – or outliers – surface. Some common outcomes to listen for include:

- Consistency or inconsistency in how the firm is described.
- Primary brand touchpoints, e.g., how clients engage with the firm along the client journey.
- Experiences with individual attorneys, client teams, and/or business support staff.
- Differentiators, including those revealed during the competitive discussion.
- Language clients use to describe the firm versus language the firm uses to describe itself.

That last point is particularly important. This alignment or potential gap between what your internal stakeholders say about the firm and what the firm's clients say about the firm is a critical aspect of positioning.

Common pitfalls

- Asking leading questions or steering the conversation toward a desired answer.
- Filtering feedback too quickly – dismissing input that does not align with internal assumptions.
- Drawing conclusions from too small a sample, i.e., not speaking with enough clients.
- Skipping external input altogether and relying solely on internal perspectives.

Interviews do not replace workshops, and workshops do not replace interviews. Each format contributes to the project, and together, they create a more complete and balanced view of the firm.

Competitive audit

The competitive audit involves a thorough examination of the previously identified competing firms. Beginning the audit early can help inform all aspects of the process, and should be revisited regularly to ensure alignment, as no doubt, this will be an ever-evolving list requiring refinement as the process progresses from workshops to client interviews. The audit, at a minimum, should include a review of the following.

Positioning and communication

- Firm positioning
- Key messages
- Differentiators
- Taglines
- Tone of voice
- Personality
- Organization of practices, services, and industries
- Thought leadership
- Social media presence

Visual brand identity and user experience

- Brandmark/logo

- Color
- Typography
- Imagery
- Graphics
- Shape
- Information architecture
- User Experience / User Interface (UX/UI) design

Having completed the discovery phase and gathered information through workshops, interviews, and the competitive audit, the next critical step in the process is making sense of what you heard.

3. Synthesis – making sense of what you heard

By this point in the process, a significant amount of insight has been gathered. Workshops have surfaced internal perspectives, and interviews have added depth, validation, and in some cases contradiction.

This phase is about identifying patterns and themes across all inputs and evaluating them against competitors to determine opportunities for differentiation. It is about positioning the firm in the mind of its target audience so that when there is a specific need, your firm is the one that comes to mind before any others. In other words, it is about owning a place in the mind of clients, prospects, and recruits that no other firm can own.

It might be that the firm delivers services for a particular industry or client type. It may be how the firm staffs cases that is particularly meaningful to its target audience. It could be a cross-practice service model in which clients hire the firm for specific experience, and business needs are met through a distinct approach that infiltrates all other practices. Perhaps your firm's approach provides a holistic view of all parties involved – not just those you represent – allowing the firm to complete transactions faster. These are a few examples, and it is impossible to predict, because what emerges will be unique to your firm.

Many outputs will be accurate descriptions of the firm. Fewer will distinguish it in the market. Strong client service, experience, responsiveness – these may all be true, but they are also expected. They do not differentiate. It's when the same themes consistently emerge that they begin to signal what truly matters, not because they are unanimous, but because they are persistent.

"If you try to stand for everything, you end up standing for nothing."[2]

Developing a positioning statement

With the target audience defined, the competitive audit complete, and the firm's core differentiators and value proposition identified, it's time to write the positioning statement. A simple framework is as follows:

> *"For [target market], our brand is the only one among all [competitive set] that [unique value claim or primary point of difference] because [reasons to believe]."*[3]

All future marketing and business development decisions should be evaluated against the approved positioning statement.

Firmwide vs practice- and attorney-level positioning

Depending on the firm's structure and size, positioning can become complex. Competitors, client expectations, and differentiators vary significantly at the practice level – and even at the individual attorney level, which is where relationships are built and trust is earned. A litigation practice may be competing against an entirely different set of firms than a corporate or regulatory group, and within those practices, individual attorneys may be known for distinct areas of specialization and have developed reputations and formed long-term relationships.

Firmwide positioning provides an important foundation, yet it may be necessary to drill down further to differentiate individual practices.

To truly differentiate at the practice level, the process outlined in this chapter may be adapted and repeated with core practice groups. This does not mean starting from scratch but rather applying the same principles to define how each practice (and even the attorneys within it) show up in the market – who they are targeting, who they are competing against, and what they want to be known for.

It is critical, however, that this work align with the firm's overarching positioning. Practice- and attorney-level differentiation should add specificity and depth – not inconsistency and confusion.

4. Strategy

If brand positioning is about establishing and owning a distinct, positive, and authentic place in the mind of your target audience relative to your competitors, then brand strategy is the process of defining *how* to implement and communicate brand positioning. It is not an endpoint but a guide for everything that follows – from how individuals behave and speak, to how the brand shows up in the market through content development, visual brand identity, and all marketing and business development efforts. A well-defined and documented brand strategy creates alignment and clarity and ensures the brand communicates consistently and authentically – verbally and visually – through every brand touchpoint.

At this stage, a readout with key stakeholders is necessary for review, discussion, and sign-off. The presentation should be succinct and to the point. Key takeaways can be presented in the form of an executive summary or key slides – however, all the raw data and work that resulted in the strategy should also be delivered for key stakeholder review. The readout should cover key components, including but not limited to:

- Mission;
- Vision;
- Values;
- Target audience personas;
- Brand promise;
- Competitive analysis;
- Key differentiators;
- Positioning statement;
- Key messages and messaging pillars; and
- Tone of voice.

Once the strategy has been signed off, copywriting and creative ideation can begin.

Creative recommendations

While the brand strategy addresses the *how* with respect to long-term positioning, the creative recommendations focus on the visual language of the firm's brand. Leveraging the approved brand strategy, the creative team ideates and explores different directions for how the often-intangible strategy can be translated to the overall look and feel – one that will be distinctive from competitors, and memorable. For example:

- What combinations of color, typography, and imagery stand out from competitors while adhering to the desired brand personality?
- How will the website's information architecture support the firm's business goals and objectives?
- How will key messages drive particular audiences to desired services or thought-leadership content?

At least two – but no more than three – different approaches to the creative should be articulated clearly and succinctly, in writing, for review and discussion, and eventual approval. More than three, and the leadership team is bogged down in the decision-making process. Furthermore, the creative team are the experts, so while they may have worked through many conceptual approaches, their job is to refine and prioritize the solutions that are most appropriate and aligned with the strategy. Visual concepts should not be presented at this stage. Each written concept should only explore the following in relationship to the strategy:

- Color.
- Typography.
- Imagery.
- Graphics/shape.

Once the proposed creative directions have been approved, the creative team initiates visual exploration across a select group of key representative touchpoints. These initial applications serve as the foundation for further development and are presented for approval, establishing standards that will guide all subsequent creative work and ultimately extend across a wide range of materials. The primary objective is to build consensus around a unified visual language before expanding to additional touchpoints and platforms.

Common pitfalls

- Offering too many options, which delays the decision-making process and leads to combined, diluted solutions.
- Giving feedback based on personal preference instead of strategic alignment.
- Dismissing good ideas too early because of risk aversion.

Conclusion

A firm's position is not a tagline or a design choice – it is the distinct, credible place the firm earns in the minds of clients, prospects, and recruits, and it must be reinforced internally by attorneys and business support staff. Getting there requires a disciplined process. Planning clarifies the business goals, scope, stakeholders, and decision making. Discovery, through research, workshops, interviews, and audits, surfaces both alignment and disagreement, replacing assumption with evidence.

Synthesis is where the work becomes strategy – patterns are identified, tested against the competitive landscape, and translated into a point of view the market can actually remember. Many observations will be true; fewer will be differentiating. The objective is to define what the firm should be known for – and why it matters. A documented brand strategy then defines how that positioning is expressed both verbally and visually across every touchpoint – behavior, voice, content, visual identity, the website experience, and marketing and business development efforts.

This is not the endpoint – it is the starting point. Execution and activation are what make the positioning real, and without them even the best strategy remains theoretical.

References

1 Neumeier, Marty. *The Brand Gap*. Indianapolis, IN: New Riders, 2003.

2 Author unknown, commonly cited in marketing and business development contexts.

3 Allen, Sallie. "Crafting the Perfect Brand Positioning Statement," *Harvard Business Review*, 29 October 2024. https://online.hbs.edu/blog/post/brand-positioning-statement

Works consulted

Wheeler, Alina. *Designing Brand Identity: An Essential Guide for the Entire Branding Team*, Fifth Edition. Hoboken, NJ: John Wiley & Sons, 2018.

Neumeier, Marty. *The Brand Gap*. Indianapolis, IN: New Riders, 2003.

Chapter 3:
Client relationships as strategic capital – how to build an enduring key client program

By JeanMarie Campbell, chief marketing and business development officer, Jenner & Block

The purpose of this chapter is to provide practical insight when creating a key client program. A successful key client program should provide law firm leaders and business development professionals with:

- A process to increase communication and collaboration among lawyers who are servicing particular clients;
- A framework for communicating with clients that deepens trust and promotes information sharing; and
- Most importantly, a program that moves lawyers away from a "my client" owner mindset to a collaborative "our client" mindset. Building a key client program that is scalable and practical is a business imperative, as clients are not simply sources of revenue, but instead are the firm's most important long-term asset. The first mindset shift is to realign the notion of what a client relationship looks and feels like – from episodic to strategic.

The new reality of client relationships in law firms

Clients have become more organized and focused on their legal budget, demanding more value

The introduction of procurement and legal operations professionals into client buying behavior has changed the focus clients previously had on selecting legal counsel based on their network and relationships. Procurement and operations professionals have been charged with safeguarding and rationalizing the organization's outside counsel legal spend. This process has become less dependent on the lawyer–client relationship and more focused on law firms providing value and decreased costs. Having a key client program can help solidify relationships with clients and their business professionals who are often gatekeepers of the outside counsel budget. A key client program has frameworks and metrics in place that provide data to the client on how the client is utilizing the law firm's services, including costs, discounts, number and types of matters, value-add services, and overall cost savings.

For example, a global law firm that I worked at made sure that the law firm business professional – known as a client relationship manager (or client relationship director or executive) – connected with the client procurement/operations professional on a regular basis. It was part of the defined roles included in the key client program. That law firm client manager created such a strong relationship with the client operations professional that most billing issues were addressed and solved through their relationship and when there were quality concerns that the client that had not yet surfaced to the law firm partners, the client manager was apprised and the partners proactively addressed these items before things escalated. This is just one example of how a key client program can add value to the law firm–client relationship.

Clients are less tolerant of inconsistency in service delivery, quality, and cost

When a key client program is in place, there are internal processes that promote quality control in service delivery methods. In a mature key client program, there can be a service level agreement, commonly known as an SLA. SLAs are documented agreements defining the expected level of service provided to the client. For example, an SLA may include a directive on how a client prefers to receive their bills, when and who will provide a status update, who at the client you should contact for a certain inquiry, and so on.

Whether you have an SLA or not, making a concerted effort to provide consistent service levels is critical to maintaining a strong relationship with a client. When lawyers are part of a key client program and participate on a client team that meets regularly to discuss the work being provided, they can spot issues and inconsistencies and flag client concerns before they blow up. Being acutely aware of the client's needs and getting ahead of client issues is a benefit of having a key client program.

At a large law firm that I worked at with a mature key client program, we put in place an SLA, mostly because the client was very particular about who the law firm contacted about particular issues. They wanted billing issues to only go through their biller assigned to our law firm. They wanted a monthly update on fees and the budget in a certain format. They asked for a quarterly update on our value-add services that we provided in a dashboard similar to their billing template. All of these particulars derived from a conversation that we set up at the onset of the matter. Even asking these questions about how the client likes to receive communication and updates sends a message to the client that they are important, what they want matters, and that they are part of a program for the law firm's most important clients.

Clients are less loyal to law firms

Given the budget constraints they are under, if necessary, clients will move work to another law firm if they feel that they are not getting the service, value, or quality they deserve. Having a key client program sends a message to the client that they:

- Are one of the most important clients at the law firm;
- Are part of a program that values that client relationship; and
- Receive special treatment from the law firm, in the form of educational programming, social events, and thought leadership.

For example, at one international law firm, a program was developed to help general counsel nurture and grow their pipeline for their next generation leadership. General counsel advised that they found it hard to find the time to provide education, skill building, and opportunities for their deputy general counsel to move to the next level. This law firm created a year-long program for the deputy general counsel and other senior leaders to help the GCs with this pipeline succession issue. The law firm invested considerable time, sweat equity, and expense in building this program – all for those clients who were part of the key client program. The result was a tangible, visible, value-add provided to those important clients, yielding stronger relationships with both the general counsel and the deputy general counsel, who would one day be a GC. The data also showed increased revenue from those clients over a period of time, rewarding this goodwill and relationship-building efforts.

A practical framework to bring consistency to key client management – the RELATE model

The RELATE model in key client management is not a universal acronym, but instead a framework that those who focus on key account management use as a guide.

R: Relationship mapping is an important component when initiating a key client program. Some look to R for "research", but I believe that a combination of both research and relationship mapping provide a guidepost for identifying decision makers, ambassadors, influencers, and blockers at the client, both on the personal and enterprise level. Knowing who the players are sets the stage for productive client engagement. Most business development professionals are well-versed in driving a relationship mapping exercise and adept at keeping this information up to date.

E: Enterprise understanding and empathy provide a lens to better manage a client's pain points and issues. As a starting point, a law firm needs to educate itself on its client's strategy, risks, and risk tolerance, as well as Board priorities. Investigating a client's outside counsel budget is part of this process, as well as identifying spend drivers and procurement protocols/ timing. The marketing and business development team can research this information and prepare a briefing packet for the client team to discuss at their inaugural meeting.

L: Leadership alignment sets the tone that this key client program is a high priority for the law firm and deserves attention and resources. Procuring visible leadership support ensures that leadership is invested in this program and can help navigate issues. Creating defined roles for lead partners, supporting partners, associates, and business professionals streamlines the process and provides clear information on expectations and action. If leadership is asked to support such a program, knowing what is expected of them is critical as well. Getting leadership on board early to get their input on the program, the processes, the client roster, and which partners will be driving the effort is an important success factor in creating and sustaining a key client program.

A: Action planning is about developing strategic, data-driven plans that drive growth, retention, and collaboration. Such plans outline the goals, tactics, and execution methods to achieve these goals. An important factor to keep in mind when developing client action plans is the value of including cross-collaboration targeting among practices and geographies. An important element of a key client program is the ability to include a diverse set of lawyers available to the client to offer capabilities outside the usual legal offerings. Considering both diversity of practice and geography is important.

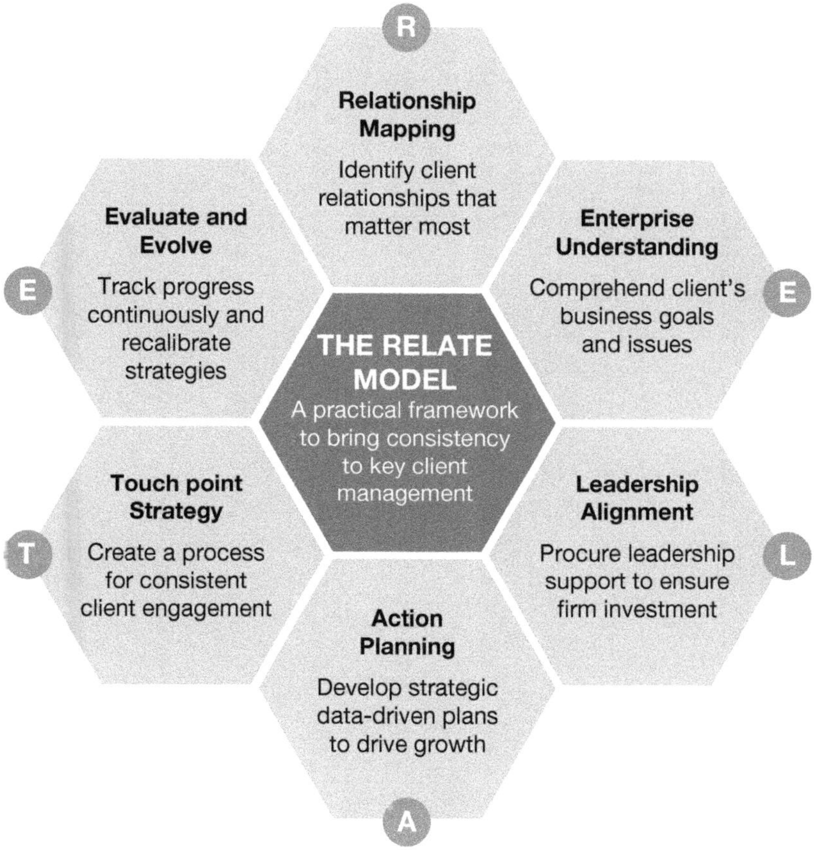

Figure 1: The RELATE model.

T: Touch point strategy creates a process for the lawyers on the client team to engage with the client on a regular basis. Creating a process for an intentional cadence outside of active matters is where the magic happens. Consistent communication builds authentic, sustainable connections with the client, as well as trust. Building trust helps to develop personalized solutions for client issues, including value-add offerings and thought leadership. Getting to know the client outside of work and in between matters helps to solidify a trusted relationship that can help withstand stresses that come from outside factors.

E: Evaluate and Evolve are defining factors to help measure success and make necessary changes to the program where and when needed. Regular check-ins with the client, providing opportunities for client listening sessions and measuring success all help to drive and recalibrate strategy. Instituting regular internal law firm meetings to discuss the status of matters, opportunities for growth, and ways to provide value-add services to the client, helps to keep the lawyers and business professionals focused on action and ownership. Incorporating regular intervals during the year to stop and review the client relationship with a critical eye can help spot issues, forecast trends, and provide a proactive client service-oriented experience that sets one law firm apart from others.

Figure 1 showcases each element of the RELATE model, demonstrating how each reinforces the others, creating a continuous cycle of relationship strengthening.

How strong are your client relationships?

Self-assessment tools are helpful to shed light on this question as you start the process to determine which clients should participate in a key client program. Below is a list of areas to consider to help initiate this assessment. Relationship partners should score themselves on a 1-5 scale, with 5 as Strong and 1 as Weak.

Client relationship maturity (quantitative)

Client knowledge depth: How well do you know the client, the person you engage with on a regular basis, on a personal level? Score 1-5.

Client relationship breadth: How well do you understand the client's business and their industry? Score 1-5.

Cross collaboration acumen: How often do you invite others from the firm to a meeting or to engage in a conversation with the client to share other ways you can bring value to the client? Score 1-5.

Proactive engagement: Do you take initiative and contact the client in between matters to share information/thought leadership or make introductions to others and/or invite them to events? Score 1-5.

Proactive service delivery: When you are engaged in a matter, how good are you and the team at proactive outreach on the matter at hand, providing information on upcoming deadlines, billing, and updates on the legal work underway? Score 1-5.

Proactive client feedback requests: How would you rate yourself and the team on asking the client for feedback on a regular basis? Score 1-5.

Process for measurement: How good are you at assessing and measuring the service you and the team are delivering to the client? Do you have a process in place to ensure that you are regularly measuring what the client thinks of the service provided? Score 1-5.

Rating scale: Add up your score and review:

- 20-35: There is a strategic partnership.
- 13-19: There is a strong relationship but it could be vulnerable.
- Below 13: The relationship is at risk.

Client relationship strength (qualitative – sample questions)

- Do you know the top three business imperatives for the client for the next year?
- Are you included in key strategic discussions with the client?
- Do you have access to the decision makers at the client?
- If the key relationship partner at the firm left tomorrow, do you think that the client would follow them to a different law firm?

These questions provide a qualitative look at the relationship strength and, paired with the quantitative analysis, can assist in analyzing whether a certain client should be placed in a key client program.

Data and process provide consistency and scale to a key client program

The following are examples of success factors when designing a key client program:

- Have clear selection criteria when identifying clients for the program, including:
  - Three-year revenue horizon;
  - Specific growth potential;
  - How the client's business needs align with firm capabilities; and
  - Depth of the client relationship
- Conduct a client mapping exercise:
  - Demonstrating where there are strengths and opportunities; and
  - Showcasing a visual to help partners see where gaps lie and opportunities abound.

- Create one-page client plans, to include:
    - Key objectives and a timeline;
    - Client priorities and how the firm aligns;
    - Opportunities to grow the client by practice area;
    - Opportunities to grow the client by geography;
    - Client relationship partners and their role in the relationship; and
    - Other important players at the firm who can contribute to the client relationship.
- Client listening protocols:
    - Devise a process for regular client outreach;
    - Create a cadence that includes annual check-in meetings at the onset of a client's fiscal year;
    - Ask the client for feedback after every substantial matter – offer to meet in person at their office or remotely if they prefer;
    - Check in with the client casually on a regular basis to ensure the little things are going well; and
    - Offer a chairman or firm leader visit to thank the client for choosing the firm.
- Utilize client feedback to drive strategy:
    - When receiving feedback from a client, always institute changes based on this information;
    - Share the effect that the client feedback had on how the firm services the client and thank them for the feedback; and
    - Celebrate internally when client feedback creates a change in process and has a positive impact on the client relationship.

Example: A law firm used information from a client listening meeting to revamp its billing process. AT the very end of the client listening meeting, a question was asked about what other law firms do that are great and could be incorporated into the current law firm process. It was apparent that the client was immensely disappointed with the current inefficient billing process. This question prompted an entire revamp of the law firm billing process, which delighted the client. Without that one last question during the meeting, the law firm may not have identified this area of improvement. The lesson is: ask the question and be willing to do the work to effect changes.

Case studies

These examples spotlight two issues that occur when addressing implementation of a key client program.

Transforming a single practice client to a firm client

Problem: One dominant partner appears to "own" the client relationship.
Solution: Put in place a cross-selling incentive program to reward expansion of practice offerings and introductions of other partners to the client relationship.
Result: Expanded client contacts, deeper connection with the client across various practices and geographies, resulting in a reduced flight risk and higher probability of increased revenue.

Launch of a new key client account program

Problem: Resistance from partners.
Solution: Spotlight leadership buy-in of the program offering clear governance, a process for all to participate, and periodic measurement to keep the program in check. Provide public recognition of those adopting the behaviors needed for the program to thrive and incentives to those who embrace the program.
Result: Deeper focus on clients and their needs, retention of clients who may been a flight risk, potential revenue increase.

Implementation is about making things stick

Below are a few common pitfalls that can derail a key client program, along with examples of what contributes to the success of a key client program. Be on the lookout for both as you design your program.

Common pitfalls:

- Over-engineering the program – keep it simple and practical and people will participate.
- Designating the marketing and business development team as merely administrative support, instead of inviting them to the table to actively participate and help drive strategy.
- Not holding partners accountable for the roles and responsibilities they agreed to.

Success factors:

- Visible leadership support of the program.
- Clear communication around process, client selection criteria and roles/responsibilities.
- Scalable processes that may be revised based on client feedback.
- Public recognition of the partners and clients that are engaging and thriving in the program.

In conclusion, client relationship management skills are not soft skills, but instead are strategic skills that lawyers need to hone and practice. Firms that institutionalize client relationship management outperform peers in client retention, cross-selling/servicing and reputation. The law firms that win will be those that treat clients not as matters, but as long-term partnerships that tie into firm strategy.

Chapter 4: Cross-selling to cross-investing – breaking silos to build enterprise value and win

By Julie Henson, chief growth officer, Decipher Investigative Intelligence

Why cross-selling fails in most law firms (and why that's the wrong diagnosis)

Cross-selling fails in most law firms for a reason few leaders are willing to say out loud – lawyers did not choose this profession to sell. They went to law school to win. To solve complex problems. To reduce risk. To advocate. To change outcomes. And yes, to be highly compensated for doing so.

But not to sell services internally.

Yet firm leadership continues to treat cross-selling as if it is simply a matter of effort. If partners would just try harder. Be more collaborative. Mention other practices. Make more introductions.

When it does not happen, the conclusion is predictable: "They just won't do it."

That diagnosis is wrong.

To understand why cross-selling feels unnatural, you have to understand how lawyers are wired. Research by Dr Larry Richard[1] – who has studied lawyer personality traits for more than three decades – shows that lawyers score significantly higher than the general population in skepticism, autonomy, and urgency, and lower in sociability and resilience. Decades of empirical personality testing confirm that the very traits that make lawyers exceptional advocates can also create friction in collaborative commercial behavior.[2]

These traits are not flaws – they are adaptive advantages in legal work. Skepticism drives risk spotting. Autonomy fuels independence of judgment. But those same traits can make internal selling feel unnatural. Lawyers are trained to challenge assumptions, not to promote services. They are rewarded for protecting clients from risk – not for expanding institutional relationships.

In other words, the legal mindset is optimized for analysis and control – not persuasion and internal promotion.

When leadership launches a "cross-selling initiative", resistance is almost guaranteed. Not because lawyers are selfish. Not because they lack ambition. But because the request feels misaligned with how they see themselves.

I learned this early in my career. The moment I would mention cross-selling while coaching attorneys on growth, I could see it happen – the subtle shift, the eye roll, the disengagement. The phrase itself triggered resistance. To many partners, cross-selling felt political, transactional, even desperate. And if something feels forced inside a partnership culture built on autonomy, it will fail.

The persistent frustration leaders feel around cross-selling is not proof that partners are broken. It is evidence that the system is misaligned. If cross-selling feels forced, it is the structure that deserves scrutiny – not the lawyers.

Most firms treat the lack of cross-selling as a behavioral issue. They focus on training programs, marketing scripts, or reminders to "think firm first". But they rarely confront the harder questions:

- Are we compensating individual production while preaching collaboration?
- Are we measuring utilization and originations while expecting enterprise thinking?
- Have we built enough internal trust for partners to confidently introduce their most valuable clients to one another?
- Are we supporting collaboration – or simply mandating it?

Partners behave rationally within the system you design. If collaboration is economically risky, politically ambiguous, or structurally unsupported, it will not happen. Not because lawyers lack character. But because they are responding logically to incentives.

My perspective on this shifted dramatically when I began conducting client interviews. Clients could immediately tell which firms were integrated and which were fragmented. They experienced it in the coordination of teams, in how well lawyers understood the broader business, in whether advice felt connected or siloed.

Clients assume firms collaborate. They expect it.

When they sense fragmentation, they do not always complain. They quietly consolidate work elsewhere.

When I brought client feedback directly to partners – when the message came from the client instead of from me – resistance softened. That is when the conversation changed.

It was also when I retired the phrase "cross-selling".

Language matters. Cross-selling suggests pushing services. It centers credit. It triggers internal politics.

I began using a different term – cross-investing. The shift was immediate.

Cross-investing reframes the behavior. It is not about selling someone else's services. It is about investing in the firm's collective client relationships. It is about long-term enterprise value over short-term credit. It signals shared ownership instead of transactional referral.

It asks a better question – not, "Who gets the origination?" but, "How do we deepen value inside clients we already serve?"

When approached this way, collaboration stops feeling like a mandate and starts feeling like strategy.

Done well, cross-investing drives measurable revenue growth from existing clients. It strengthens retention. It accelerates lateral integration. It reduces concentration risk. It builds institutional trust inside the client relationship.

But it does not happen by accident. It requires trust. It requires leadership. It requires structure. It requires support. Above all, it requires patience.

Cross-investing is not a marketing program. It is not a quarterly campaign. It is a growth discipline embedded in how the firm operates. It must be modeled by respected partners who already do it well. Their stories must be told. Their behavior must be visible. And the firm must build systems that make collaboration safe and rewarded.

In this chapter, we will examine why cross-selling fails when treated as a behavioral problem and how firms can reframe it as a structural growth strategy. We will explore how trust and incentives shape partner behavior, why laterals expose collaboration gaps faster than any internal initiative, and what leadership must do to create durable, enterprise-wide growth.

The goal is not to turn lawyers into salespeople. The goal is to design a firm where collaboration is the rational, supported, and trusted path forward. When that happens, revenue follows. Not because lawyers changed who they are but because leadership changed the system.

From transactions to trust – the cultural foundation of cross-investing

Trust is the true currency of collaboration. Not messaging, not mandates, not compensation tweaks. Trust.

After working alongside lawyers for more than 20 years, I have learned one consistent truth. If a partner does not understand another practice group – or does not genuinely know and respect the lawyer behind it – they will not put their client in that lawyer's hands. Period.

That client relationship is not just revenue. It represents years of credibility, performance, and personal investment. It is identity. It is security. It is reputation.

Lawyers are trained to protect what carries risk.

When leadership asks, "Why won't they cross-sell?" the more honest question is, "Have we built enough internal trust for them to feel safe doing so?"

Heidi Gardner's research on professional service firms reinforces this reality. In *Smart Collaboration*,[3] Gardner demonstrates that collaboration is not driven by goodwill; it is driven by relational capital – the accumulated trust, familiarity, and confidence professionals have in one another's competence. Without that relational capital, autonomy feels safer than integration.

Lawyers default to protecting what they control. That is not resistance. It is rational behavior in a system that has not sufficiently invested in internal trust.

Partners hesitate to introduce clients across practices for logical reasons:

- They are unsure of the other lawyer's technical excellence.
- They do not understand how that practice operates under pressure.
- They fear inconsistent client experience.
- They worry about reputational exposure if something goes wrong.
- They fear losing control of the relationship they built.

This is not selfishness. It is professional risk management. Research in organizational behavior consistently shows that trust reduces perceived risk and increases cooperative behavior. When trust is low, individuals default to self-protective decision making. In partnership models – where autonomy is structurally reinforced – that instinct becomes even stronger.

The mistake firms make is confusing collegiality with trust. You can enjoy someone socially and still not trust them with your most important client. Operational trust is different. Operational trust means I believe you will enhance my client relationship, not jeopardize it. I believe you will communicate proactively. I believe you will protect the institutional relationship, not compete for it.

Without that level of confidence, cross-investing will always feel like a gamble.

Gardner's empirical findings go further – firms that successfully collaborate across practices see stronger client loyalty and higher margins because clients perceive integrated teams as lower risk.[4] In other words, the market rewards collaboration – even when internal structures do not.

This mirrors what I began seeing years ago when conducting structured client interviews. Clients could immediately identify which firms operated as institutions and which operated as collections of individual practices. They experienced it in responsiveness, coordination, and depth of understanding. They rarely framed it as "cross-selling". They described it as seamlessness.

Clients assume you collaborate. They expect it. When they sense fragmentation, they may not complain. They simply consolidate work elsewhere.

That external perspective reframes the issue. Collaboration is not an internal political exercise. It is a client expectation.

But expectation alone does not build trust.

Firm structures often reinforce siloed identity. Practice group leaders are evaluated on growing their own revenue, headcount, and influence. They are not typically rewarded for investing in other practices. Governance structures emphasize domain strength, not enterprise integration.

The signal is clear: grow your territory. If you want cross-investing, you must intentionally counter that signal.

Trust grows from visibility, repeated positive experience, and shared wins. It requires structured opportunities for lawyers to understand one another's work – not just at the surface level, but in how they think, operate, and serve clients.

Research on social capital further supports this dynamic.[5] High-performing professional organizations intentionally cultivate dense internal networks because familiarity increases cooperation and reduces coordination costs. When lawyers lack internal network density – when they do not meaningfully interact across practices – collaboration remains inefficient and psychologically costly.

Partners will never refer work to someone they do not like, let alone trust. That is human nature.

The question is not whether that instinct exists. The question is whether the firm is investing internally the same way it expects lawyers to invest externally.

We train lawyers relentlessly on how to build client trust. Be responsive. Deliver consistently.

Communicate clearly. Demonstrate expertise over time.

Yet we rarely apply those same disciplines internally. If cross-investing is going to become mandatory behavior, then internal trust-building must become mandatory leadership work.

That means:

- Creating structured cross-practice visibility.
- Sharing client feedback that reinforces integrated value.
- Elevating and celebrating enterprise behavior publicly.
- Establishing consistent standards for client experience across practices.
- Protecting collaborative efforts from short-term political backlash.

Trust is slow. It compounds through evidence. It requires patience. But once relational capital exists, collaboration accelerates naturally. The friction decreases. The fear decreases. The perceived risk decreases.

And when trust is institutionalized – not just interpersonal – cross-investing becomes rational.

Without trust, no compensation system will fix the problem. Without trust, mandates will fail.

Without trust, cross-selling will always feel forced. Cross-investing begins here. Everything else is structural reinforcement.

The economics of individualism – how compensation and metrics undermine collaboration

Even when trust exists, structure can still sabotage collaboration. The most powerful structural signal in any law firm is compensation – and traditional compensation systems overwhelmingly reward autonomy over enterprise value.

We can talk about culture all day. We can preach "firm first". We can celebrate collaboration in partner meetings. But at the end of the year, partners look at one thing – how the system allocates credit and compensation. That is the truth serum.

Most legacy compensation models are built around originations, collections, and individual production. Those metrics reinforce independence. They reward control. They reward keeping the client relationship tightly held.

And then firms act surprised when partners hesitate to cross-invest. Partners behave rationally within the economic system you design. Origination hoarding is not moral failure. It is rational incentive optimization.

The hidden cost of that optimization, however, is enormous. When partners hoard originations:

- Client relationships remain shallow and dependent on one individual.
- Succession becomes fragile.
- Institutional depth erodes.
- Rising partners disengage when they see no path to shared opportunity.
- Laterals struggle to integrate into closed systems.
- The firm confuses short-term revenue protection with long-term stability.

One of the most common responses I hear from leaders is, "But we encourage credit sharing".

Encouraging credit sharing is step one. It is not the solution. Some partners believe that once they "share credit", they have done their part. They pat themselves on the back. The box is checked.

But sharing credit is not the same as investing in enterprise growth. Credit sharing without structural reinforcement often becomes symbolic. It does not necessarily change behavior, deepen relationships, or alter long-term economic incentives. In many cases, the sharing is partial, negotiated, or politically calculated.

I have had clients ask directly, "Who is actually getting credit for this work?" Think about that.

Clients – external clients – asking how internal compensation is allocated because they want certain lawyers recognized for the value they deliver. In more than one instance, credit only got meaningfully shared because the client advocated for it. If the client had not insisted, it would not have happened.

That is a structural failure on multiple levels. First, it signals to the next generation of partners that contribution alone is not enough. Advocacy is required. Politics matter. Second, it reveals that the system does not automatically reward collaborative behavior. Third, it demonstrates that leadership is often unaware of how frequently this dynamic plays out.

Economic fear is real inside partnerships. Leaders underestimate it. Just because a partner has built a significant book of business does not mean they feel secure. In fact, often the opposite is true. The larger the book, the more intertwined it becomes with identity and lifestyle. That relationship is not just revenue – it is status, influence, control, and personal worth.

This is one reason partners struggle to retire. Letting go of clients feels like letting go of relevance. Compensation systems that tie identity tightly to originations reinforce that fear.

If cross-investing requires partners to loosen control, they must believe the system will protect them when they do. Without that belief, autonomy will always win.

Rewriting compensation systems requires courage. It requires confronting political realities. It requires transparency. But it does not require a complete overhaul. This is where many firms hesitate. They assume that meaningful change demands total reconstruction. It does not. Smaller, intentional shifts can send powerful signals.

For example:

- Recognizing enterprise contribution explicitly in compensation criteria.
- Rewarding successful cross-practice client expansion.
- Elevating succession planning as a measurable performance metric.
- Publicly highlighting collaborative revenue wins.
- Tying leadership roles to demonstrable enterprise behavior.

These are not radical moves. But they alter perception. When rising partners see that collaboration leads to advancement, not marginalization, behavior changes.

Retention is directly tied to this dynamic. If high-performing rising partners believe their growth is capped because originations are locked up above them, they will find another platform. And they will not leave alone. They will take their relationships – and their momentum – with them.

Cross-investing is not only about revenue expansion. It is about talent retention. You cannot tell emerging leaders that they are the future of the firm while simultaneously denying them meaningful participation in enterprise relationships.

Economic alignment builds trust. Trust enables collaboration. Collaboration drives revenue.

The sequence matters. Compensation does not need to be equal. It needs to be aligned with enterprise value creation. The firms that recognize this early will retain their rising stars and institutionalize client relationships. The firms that do not will continue to experience quiet departures and fragile succession. Cross-investing requires trust – but trust without structural alignment will always collapse under economic pressure. If collaboration is economically risky, it will remain rare. If it is economically rational, it will become cultural.

Cross-investing defined – a growth strategy, not a courtesy

If cross-selling is a tactic, cross-investing is a growth strategy. That distinction matters.

Cross-selling suggests a moment. A referral. A handoff. A transaction. Cross-investing is different. It is a deliberate decision to deepen institutional value inside the clients you already serve. It shifts the focus from individual credit to enterprise expansion. The question is no longer, "Who can I introduce?" It becomes, "Where are we underpenetrated, and how do we unlock that together?"

Cross-investing is about increasing client lifetime value, not spreading work around internally. It is about expanding the surface area of the firm inside a client relationship so that the client sees the institution – not just the relationship partner.

When firms get this right, several things happen:

- Revenue growth becomes more predictable because it comes from existing relationships.
- Client retention strengthens because the relationship is institutionalized.
- Succession becomes less fragile because knowledge and trust are distributed.
- Lateral integration accelerates because new partners plug into shared growth plans instead of isolated silos.

This is not theory. It is math. It costs exponentially more to acquire a new client than to expand an existing one. Yet many firms focus more energy on lateral acquisition and market expansion than on fully leveraging the clients already inside the portfolio.

Cross-investing flips that equation. It requires firms to map client relationships intentionally:

- Where are we strong?
- Where are we absent?
- Where are competitors gaining ground?
- Which practices should be aligned around industry opportunities?

It also requires clarity around ownership. Cross-investing does not eliminate relationship partners. It elevates them into enterprise stewards. Their role shifts from gatekeeper to growth architect.

That is a leadership evolution. The firms that treat cross-investing as a formal growth discipline – supported by data, reinforced by compensation, modeled by leadership – create durable revenue expansion. The firms that treat it as an informal expectation continue to rely on personality and luck. Cross-investing is not about being generous with work. It is about institutionalizing value inside relationships. In a market where clients expect integrated expertise, strategy (not courtesy) wins.

Lateral integration as the ultimate stress test for collaboration

If you want to know whether a firm truly practices cross-investing, watch what happens after a lateral walks in the door. Laterals expose collaboration gaps faster than any internal initiative. On the front end, energy is high. The deal gets negotiated. Compensation is structured. The press release goes out. Leadership celebrates the win.

Then the lawyer arrives and reality sets in. The lateral is immediately consumed by logistics. Conflicts. Client transitions. Billing systems. Technology. Assistants. Internal processes.

At the same time, they are under pressure to migrate clients quickly. Anxiety is high. Expectations are high. Survival becomes the priority.

Very few firms build structured cross-investing into this window. By the time the lateral is ready to focus on internal relationships, the initial excitement has faded. Leadership attention has shifted. The lawyer retreats into what feels safest, serving their existing clients.

That is when the silo hardens. What could have become enterprise integration becomes isolated production. This is not a personality problem. It is a structural one.

Firms are often so focused on getting the deal done that they underinvest in what happens after the signature. They assume collaboration will follow naturally. It does not.

Common integration failures are predictable. There is no pre-hire mapping of cross-practice opportunity. There is no defined growth plan aligned with industry or client teams. There is no accountability for internal relationship development. There is no structured visibility into how the book strengthens the enterprise.

The result is revenue without integration. Production without institutional depth.

Cross-investing changes the equation.

Integration should begin before the offer letter is signed. Firms should validate not just portability, but enterprise opportunity. Where does this lawyer create adjacency? Which practices should align immediately? Where is the whitespace inside their client base?

This is where shared intelligence matters.

Data-driven validation of books of business, analyzing client overlap, industry exposure, revenue durability, and cross-practice potential transforms lateral hiring from acquisition to investment. When you map opportunity before day one, integration becomes intentional. Without that discipline, even strong laterals default to autonomy. Not because they resist collaboration, but because autonomy feels safer.

Cross-investing is the difference between adding revenue and building enterprise value. If your firm cannot cross-invest in laterals, it cannot scale. Scaling requires institutionalizing relationships. It requires distributing trust. It requires aligning talent around shared growth strategy. Without integration discipline, growth remains fragile and personality dependent.

Lateral integration is not a recruiting function. It is a collaboration audit of your firm's structure.

The firms that treat it that way build deeper platforms, retain talent more effectively, and convert individual books into enterprise strength.

Leadership's role – what managing partners must model (and enforce)

This is the moment where leadership proves it is serious or reveals that it is not. Cross-investing cannot be delegated to a committee. It cannot be assigned to marketing. It cannot be announced at a retreat and then left to culture to figure out.

This is where the managing partner must walk the walk, not just talk the talk. Every firm says it values collaboration. Very few structure their leadership behavior around it. Tone at the top is not symbolic. It is operational. Partners watch what leaders reward. They watch what leaders protect. They watch whose behavior is elevated and whose is tolerated. They watch how compensation decisions are explained. They watch which conflicts are addressed and which are ignored.

Culture follows that.

The hardest truth is this. The first changes required to support cross-investing will most directly affect the most senior partners. The partners who built large books. The partners who have operated autonomously for decades. The partners whose identity and compensation are tightly linked to individual originations.

That is where resistance will surface. And that is why this requires courage.

Managing partners cannot softly suggest enterprise behavior while privately preserving legacy structures. They cannot call for shared ownership while protecting political comfort. If collaboration is the strategy, leadership must model it visibly.

That means publicly supporting shared credit decisions. It means aligning compensation criteria with enterprise contribution. It means challenging gatekeeping behavior even when it is politically uncomfortable. It means rewarding succession planning, not just production.

It also means demanding the same from practice leaders. Practice group heads cannot be evaluated solely on growing their own revenue. They must be evaluated on how effectively they integrate with other practices and how intentionally they invest in firm-wide opportunity. If leadership behavior remains siloed, the partnership will follow.

This is not about forcing older partners into compliance. It is about setting a new expectation of what leadership looks like. Enterprise stewardship replaces territorial protection. The managing partner sets that standard first. If they cross-invest in relationships. If they share credit visibly. If they align themselves with enterprise wins rather than personal alliances. The signal is unmistakable.

Partners do not need perfection. They need clarity, and they need to see that leadership is willing to absorb short-term friction in exchange for long-term stability.

The firms that succeed in building cross-investing cultures are not the firms with the most eloquent strategy documents. They are the firms where leadership behavior is consistent, transparent, and disciplined. If managing partners want collaboration to be mandatory behavior, they must first make it mandatory leadership behavior and model it visibly. It starts with them.

Building the infrastructure for collaboration

Trust creates the foundation. Compensation creates alignment. Leadership sets the tone. But none of it sustains without infrastructure.

Collaboration cannot rely on personality. It cannot depend on who happens to know each other. It cannot be fueled by occasional wins that leadership celebrates and then moves on from. It requires ownership.

Firms that are serious about cross-investing must invest at the C level in a dedicated growth leader whose responsibility is enterprise alignment. Not marketing. Not operations. Not recruiting. Growth.

The managing partner cannot do this alone. The COO cannot do this alone.

Especially not in firms that are navigating mergers, acquisitions, and lateral expansion. The complexity is too great. There is no single executive who can "also" manage enterprise integration on top of everything else. If growth is truly a strategy, it must have a steward. That steward's role is not to sell. It is to see the entire platform clearly. To understand how practices intersect. To identify where alliances create scale. To hold leaders accountable for integration. To ensure that cross-investing is not episodic but disciplined.

Without that role, integration becomes fragmented. This is particularly visible in mergers and combinations. Firms spend months negotiating terms, aligning compensation systems, managing brand decisions, and integrating operational teams. There is energy around the deal itself. There is celebration when one or two collaborative matters close.

Then momentum fades. Each practice group focuses on integrating its own operations. Each office focuses on its own logistics. The broader growth thesis that justified the combination begins to dilute. The cross-investment opportunity that once looked expansive becomes tactical and small. The firm tells itself the deal is working because revenue is stable. But stability is not the same as enterprise growth.

The real opportunity in combinations is adjacency. It is industry overlap. It is cross-practice expansion inside shared clients. It is leveraging scale to unlock new markets.

Those opportunities do not materialize automatically. They require someone whose job is to see them, quantify them, and push them forward. That is the future of the legal profession.

As firms grow more complex, as mergers accelerate, as lateral movement increases, the coordination challenge becomes exponential. Expecting managing partners to hold the long-term growth strategy together while also managing governance, partner politics, and firm operations is unrealistic. Infrastructure means clarity. Clear growth priorities. Clear accountability. Clear measurement. Clear integration plans tied to profit, not activity.

When firms institutionalize this function, cross-investing becomes systemic rather than situational. Without it, collaboration rises and falls with personalities. The vision gets watered down. The initial excitement of combinations fades. And the mass opportunity sitting inside the platform remains unrealized.

Cross-investing is not self-executing. It requires structure. It requires discipline. It requires leadership capacity dedicated to enterprise growth. Anything less leaves scale to chance.

The firms that cross-invest will win

The legal market is not standing still. Revenue expectations continue to rise. Profits per partner are expected to grow year over year. At the same time, billable rates are flattening in many practices. Clients are pushing back. AI investment is accelerating. Margin pressure is real.

Firms are spending millions on technology, talent acquisition, and combinations to stay competitive. And yet one of the most powerful revenue levers remains underutilized – cross-investing. This is not theoretical growth. It is immediate opportunity inside relationships you already have. It does not require acquiring a new client. It does not require entering a new geography. It does not require a headline merger.

It requires discipline. It requires trust. It requires structural alignment. It requires leadership courage. Firms that fail to cross-invest will be outgrown by those that do – not because their lawyers are less capable or their brand is weaker, but because they are leaving enterprise value on the table while others are institutionalizing it.

When collaboration is embedded into strategy, revenue becomes more durable. Client relationships become less fragile. Succession becomes intentional rather than reactive. Laterals integrate faster. Rising partners see a future. When collaboration remains optional, growth remains personality dependent.

Cross-investing must be built into the firm's strategy. Not as a side initiative. Not as a quarterly campaign. As a core operating principle tied to compensation, leadership evaluation, lateral integration, and succession planning.

The firms that embrace this shift will create platforms that scale. The firms that resist will continue to rely on individual rainmakers to carry the enterprise. In a market defined by consolidation, technological disruption, and margin pressure, that is not sustainable.

Cross-investing is not easy. It challenges legacy behavior and it affects compensation dynamics. It requires senior partners to loosen control. It demands that leaders absorb political friction in the short-term. But it is one of the few growth levers that is entirely within your control.

The question is not whether it works. The research supports it. Clients expect it. The economics reinforce it.

The question is whether you have the courage to build it into your strategy.

The firms that build cross-investing into their strategy will not simply compete in the market. They will win it.

References

1 Richard, Larry. "Herding Cats: The Lawyer Personality Revealed." *Report to Legal Management*, Hildebrandt International, 2002.

2 Daicoff, Susan. *Lawyer, Know Thyself: A Psychological Analysis of Personality Strengths and Weaknesses*. American Psychological Association, 2004.

3 Gardner, Heidi K. *Smart Collaboration: How Professionals and Their Firms Succeed by Breaking Down Silos*. Harvard Business Review Press, 2017.

4 Gardner, Heidi K., and Ivan Matviak. "Collaborating for Growth: Using Teamwork to Drive Revenue and Profit." Harvard Business School Research findings.

5 Mayer, Roger C., James H. Davis, and F. David Schoorman. "An Integrative Model of Organizational Trust." *Academy of Management Review*, vol. 20, no. 3, 1995, pp. 709-734.

Chapter 5: Smarter collaboration analytics – turning data into performance

By Heidi K. Gardner, distinguished Fellow, Harvard Law School, and Ivan Matvick, CEO, Smarter Collaboration

Why collaboration analytics is the new frontier for law-firm growth

When *Smart Collaboration* hit the market, it jolted law firm leaders and partners into understanding that collaboration is the key to growth.[1] When partners work across practices, they gain deeper insight into client needs, build greater trust, and deliver more strategic, higher-value work. These clients, in turn, are more loyal and more profitable.

In the intervening decade, more than 80 percent of top firms globally have inserted some aspects of collaboration in their vision statements and strategic plans. And yet, most fail to deliver on it. Firms struggle to generate the consistent, everyday behaviors required for genuine cross-practice and cross-office client service.

Why? Our decade-plus of research at Harvard and beyond, involving more than 10,000 partners across professional service firms globally, has documented many of the key barriers that inhibit collaboration – trust, understanding where expertise lies within the firm, and the lack of collaboration skills.[2]

Often the most salient obstacle is the massive gap between the aspirational way of working and the reality of both the performance management system and the culture it breeds. Leaders declare collaboration a priority, but the system signals that individual performance is what really matters. Partners hear the rhetoric, but then they look at what is actually measured, celebrated, and rewarded. They conclude collaboration is optional.

Our most recent analysis has identified data as the root cause that inhibits leaders – managing partners, business development professionals, learning and development teams – from helping develop a collaborative culture. Few firms have the ability to strategically analyze the data required to understand where collaboration is happening and where the gaps exist at a firm, group, and individual level.

Without data, leaders cannot diagnose the current state, set targets, or create accountability. As a result, the aspiration for a collaborative culture becomes little more than rhetoric, and is overshadowed by individual goals. When collaboration is invisible, it inevitably becomes optional.

Yet a path forward exists. Most firms already possess, or can readily access, the necessary data – though often fragmented across systems. This chapter explores how that data can be harnessed to identify growth opportunities and manage risks throughout the firm.

This chapter is organized into five sections. Section one outlines how firms move from data to insights to action – and ultimately to measurable growth. Sections two through six examine collaboration analytics at each level of the firm – firmwide, sector, practice, client, and partner. Each level requires a distinct set of analyses that reveal the firm's collaboration patterns, surface growth opportunities, and highlight emerging risks. Section seven then shows how cross-functional collaboration – across marketing and BD, L&D/HR, and firm leadership – turns those insights into sustained action.

Moving from data → insights → action → growth

Firms typically stumble, not because they lack data, but because they lack a they lack a clear, end-to-end approach for translating data into insight, insight into action, and action into growth.

We hear from many law firm CFOs that "we have the data". That's true – the raw data underlying insightful network analytics comes from a firm's core platforms, such as billing and people systems. However, the business value comes from the insights and action stages, where most firms fall down. See Figure 1.

But having data is not the same as having insight, and having insight is not the same as taking action. Most firms are stuck in the first two stages.

The real value of the data comes from analyzing collaboration patterns:

- Who works with whom to develop clients, practices, and sectors, and which practices feed others.
- Which clients are underpenetrated.
- Where partners and teams are isolated, particularly lateral hires and newly promoted partners.
- Who are the unrecognized stars that are growing relationships, integrating laterals, sending work to new hires, and building bridges across merged business.

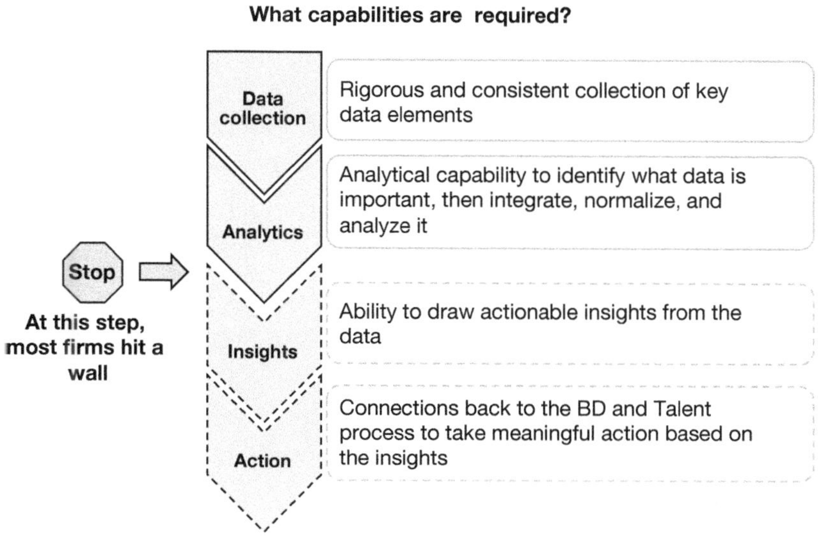

Figure 1: Translating data into insight.

In other words, firms lack an integrated end-to-end system to make this happen.

Leaders (managing partners, practice and sector leads, heads of business development and marketing, heads of learning and development) need to collaborate in business planning and skill development to translate these insights into BD activities, key client programs, partner development, sector strategies, and lateral integration. Firms must finally move from "what happened?" to "what should we do next?"

Analytics only matter if they change behavior. Without a strong cross-functional system, collaboration analytics become just another dashboard that gathers dust.

The next decade will belong to firms that understand and embed cross-silo collaboration into their client service, not those that chase solo star rainmakers. Winning firms will be the ones with the clearest picture of how collaboration actually happens, and the discipline to act on it.

Firm-level insights – understanding the collaboration signature

Collaboration drives growth – both for the firm and for individual partners. Across dozens of law firms, our analyses consistently show the same pattern – when cross-practice penetration increases, growth accelerates.[3] That is, when law firms increase the number of practices serving each client, revenue and profits rise disproportionately. The opposite is also true – when firms serve clients in more siloed ways, they suffer worse margins, resource allocation, and client turnover.[4]

The core point is that cross-practice client service does not merely add revenue. Rather, it changes the fundamental economics of the client relationship. When firms break out of silos, they shift from linear to exponential growth because trust, insight, and access compound over time.

To understand and manage these patterns, senior leaders – managing partners, business development heads, L&D leaders, compensation committee members – must begin by examining collaboration at the firm level. This reveals the firm's "collaboration signature" – its unique pattern of how work actually flows across practices, partners, and clients.

Client transformation example

A five-year example from a global law firm illustrates this dynamic clearly. In 2017, the firm's highest level of cross-practice penetration was five practices. Revenue increased linearly as more practices served a client – one plus one equaled two. Clients with one practice generated roughly $160k in revenue; those with two practices generated $320k. The firm also had a long tail of single-practice clients.

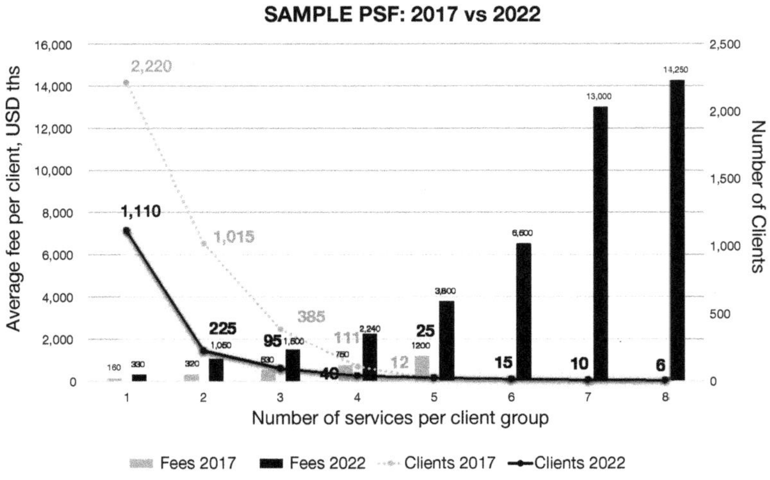

Figure 2: Cross-practice penetration example.

Five years later, the picture was radically different. The firm was serving clients with up to eight practices, and revenue grew exponentially – one plus one now equaled three. The client portfolio had shifted meaningfully to the right – more clients were receiving multi-practice service, and the tail of single-practice clients had shrunk. Notably, the firm did not aggressively "cut the tail". Instead, as partners focused on strategic, multi-practice collaboration, smaller non-strategic clients naturally drifted away.

This transformation occurred because the firm built a system for cross-practice engagement, not just a set of initiatives. Trust deepened, partners shared more information, and clients began viewing the firm as a strategic advisor rather than a group of disconnected specialists. As multi-practice relationships expanded, the firm saw more touchpoints, deeper knowledge of client needs, more cross-partner conversations about industries and opportunities, greater senior-level engagement, and a rise in complex, high-margin engagements. At the same time, risk decreased. Single-practice or single-partner clients are inherently fragile – shifting clients to the right creates a more stable, diversified, and resilient portfolio.

Figure 2 provides an essential starting point by showing the distribution of clients across levels of cross-practice penetration. The strategic goal is clear – deepen cross-practice engagement and shift clients steadily to the right. Leaders should carefully examine both ends of the chart.

Leaders must understand what drives the left-side pattern, showing clients served by only one or two practices. Often, it begins with leadership signals – what is recognized, highlighted, and praised? Firms frequently celebrate landing new client logos; they rarely spotlight teams that add the third practice to an existing client relationship, even though that move creates far greater strategic and financial value. Key questions include:

- Which partners and practices are spending disproportionate time on mono-line clients?
- What trends characterize this segment?
- What is the year-over-year churn rate?
- How many of these clients move to the right annually?

Turning to the right side – clients served by multiple practices – leaders should examine the dynamics of their most strategic relationships:

- Which partners and practices are driving multi-line growth?
- Which sectors, practices, or offices are underrepresented?
- Which parts of the firm generate the most multi-disciplinary opportunities?

This right side represents the firm's strategic engine. If the right side is thin, the firm is leaving substantial value unrealized.

Analytics are essential here. Leaders may believe they understand where collaboration flourishes or where silos persist, but data often reveals unexpected dependencies, gaps, or "super-connectors" whose networks disproportionately sustain the firm's growth. Identifying these patterns is critical to reducing risk, allocating resources, and designing interventions that improve the overall system.

With this insight, leaders can develop a clear set of metrics to track progress over time. Effective measures include:

- Ratio of single-practice clients vs premium clients.
- Number and practice-concentration of "at risk" single-partner clients.
- Share of clients moving to the right, with associated revenue uplift.
- Percentage of new matters that are multi-practice.

One firm we worked with, for example, achieved a 16 percent increase in revenue from premium clients (those served by at least three practices) in the first year by developing these insights, then setting goals and monitoring progress.

These metrics are not merely reporting tools – they are management tools. They should shape leadership discussions, strategic planning, and resource allocation.

Post-merger integration

While M&A is perhaps the highest-risk move a firm can make, leaders do a poor job of actively analyzing how the merger is progressing. For nearly every combination announced over the last three years, the "merger thesis" boils down to smarter collaboration – creating a broader platform with greater reach across geographies and/or services to deliver enhanced offerings to clients.

Despite this goal, firms spend nearly all their effort on integrating systems, but devote precious little focus to how collaboration is evolving post-merger.

Post-merger, network analysis helps leaders understand:

- Which sectors, practices, offices, and leaders are collaborating across the legacy firms.
- Which clients show early promise of cross-firm development.
- Which partners are initiating collaboration with peers from the "other" firm.
- Where isolated pockets exist that require intervention.

These insights provide both evidence of early success and clear signals of where behavioral change is needed.

When firms make collaboration visible and measurable, they give themselves the ability to manage it. Once it is managed, collaboration shifts from aspiration to a disciplined driver of growth, profitability, and reduced portfolio risk.

Sector-level insights – where the market demands collaboration

We have long argued that a robust, well-resourced sector strategy is one of the most powerful levers for growth. Yet many firms remain early in their maturity curve. Ask any client about their business, and they will answer in sector terms – "we're in energy"; "we're a global sports-apparel brand". What they will *not* say is "we're buyers of tax advice". Clients define themselves by industry, and they expect their advisors to share that lens.[5] As one GC put it, *"I want a partner who helps me see around corners".*

Meeting that expectation requires more than deep technical expertise. It demands genuine cross-practice integration. As Gardner and Harvey note, *"If all the partners serving an industry are from the same practice group, it's almost certain that you're not delivering the holistic insights that your clients need".* [6] Sectors, therefore, become the natural focal point for collaboration analytics – they reveal whether the firm is delivering the joined-up perspective clients assume is already happening.

To do this well, client teams must understand the environment in which clients operate, including market dynamics, competitive pressures, regulatory trends, and emerging risks. They must engage clients proactively with cross-practice insights. The goal is not mechanical cross-selling – it is demonstrating a deep understanding of the client's business and generating integrated solutions to advance it.

Within each sector, collaboration analytics illuminate how practices come together to serve and develop clients. The starting point is simple – which practice groups are generating work in the sector? Which partners are originating cross-practice matters and drawing in colleagues from other groups to deliver?

From there, we drill down to the partner level. The sector-filtered scatterplot shown in Figure 3 quickly exposes where the engines of growth truly lie. In one analysis of the corporate sector, three practices – Corporate, Corporate Real Estate, and Property Litigation – drove the majority of revenue.

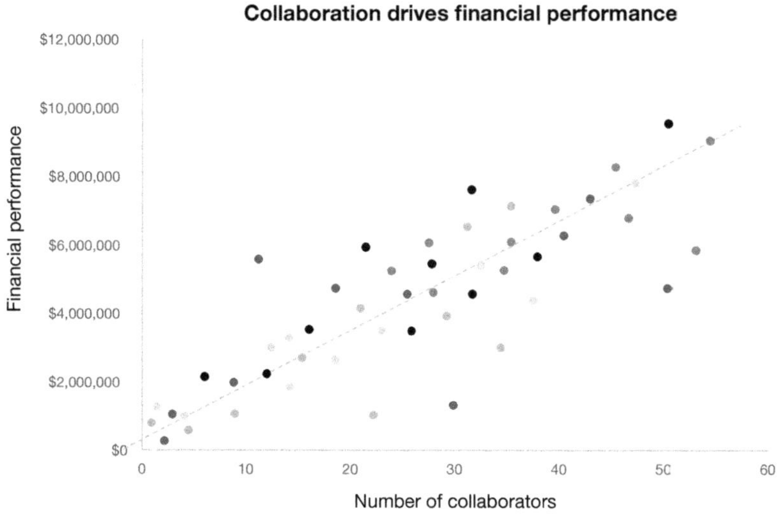

Figure 3: Engines of growth.

A tenure lens provided deeper insight – several newly elevated partners were outperforming many long-tenured peers, while a cluster of senior partners across practices lagged. Their collaboration networks revealed the structural reasons; more on that later in the chapter.

Sector leadership and accountability are equally critical. Effective sector strategies require leaders who can mobilize partners, set expectations, and hold people accountable for contributing to sector success, not simply affiliating with it. High-performing sector leaders spend their time externally – engaging clients, prospecting, and building domain expertise. Collaboration analytics reinforce this shift by tracking not just revenue but activity – which partners are generating cross-practice opportunities, investing in sector initiatives, and elevating the sector's market profile.

Sectors are where client reality and firm capability meet. Sector-level collaboration surfaces growth opportunities, highlights partner and client risks, and provides the evidence base that sector leaders need to set priorities, allocate resources, and drive accountability.

Practice-level insights – the hidden pipelines between practices

For many firms, especially those without a sector approach, the practice is the focal point for network analytics. A central question for firm and practice leaders is straightforward: *Which practices are working together, and where are the gaps?*

Practice leaders should develop strategic plans jointly with their counterpart peers to identify and pursue cross-practice client opportunities. Yet in many firms we advise, performance expectations are set almost exclusively around each practice's stand-alone growth. Targets rarely include explicit goals for cross-practice client development. The result is predictable – siloed practices, underdeveloped client relationships, and subtle competition among groups rather than a unified partnership expanding clients together. When leaders are evaluated solely on their own P&L, the structure itself suppresses collaboration.[7] Analytics help break that cycle.

Figure 4 is a basic data display that illustrates the trade flows between practices and quickly highlights where collaboration is flourishing and where it is lacking. Which practices are generating work for others? Which are receiving it? How does client work actually move through the firm?

Generation: Sending work to other practice groups

Execution: Receiving work from other practice groups

	Corporate	Litigation	Intellectual property
Corporate	$10m	$5m	$1m
Litigation	$50m	$10m	$1m
Intellectual property	$50m	$5m	$50m

Figure 4: Trade flows between practices.

The key is moving from this data to genuine insights – firm and practice leaders must define the strategic role of each practice and how it should interact with the rest of the firm's ecosystem.

- *"Magnets"* draw other practices into client matters.
- *"Importers"* execute work largely generated elsewhere.
- *"Islands"* neither import nor export – they deliver most of the work they originate.

See Figure 5.

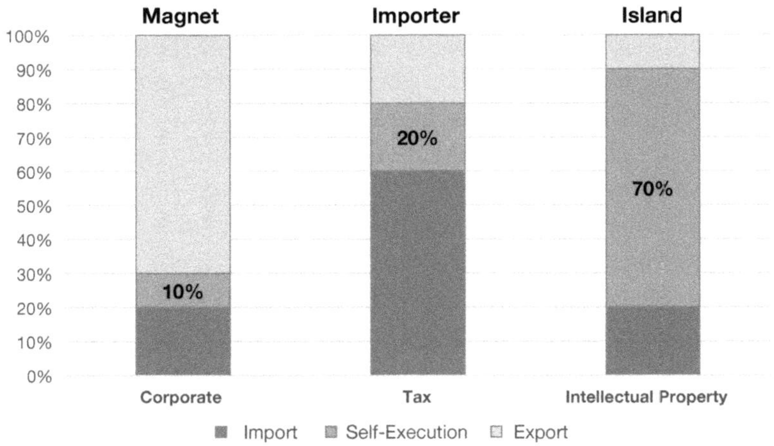

Figure 5: Magnets, importers, and islands.

Drilling deeper, we assess whether practice leaders themselves role-model the collaborative behavior expected across their groups. Key indicators include the number of partners, practices, and offices to which they export work, and the breadth of their collaborator base by practice, tenure, and office. Analytics also help surface areas of risk, such as practices that are disproportionately dependent on a small number of partners or clients.

Most firms should also analyze collaboration patterns across offices – particularly those expanding into new markets or integrating through mergers. We frequently see new offices founded to serve a specific client segment, such as a Houston office for the energy sector, becoming isolated "micro-practices" focused only on local expertise. Without visibility into collaboration patterns, leaders don't see the early warning signs that these groups are failing to integrate with the broader firm. When they underuse the full range of experts available, this undermines the expansion rationale, and client service suffers. Riskier still, this dynamic creates a strong risk that this isolated group will be the target of a lift-out. Although the underlying analysis mirrors the practice-level approach, the cultural implications can be even more significant.

Practice-level analytics reveal the "ecosystem" of the firm – which practices feed others, which operate as islands, and which act as true magnets for cross-practice work. Practice leaders must be role models – if they are not exporting work to others, their partners won't either.

Client-level insights – turning under-penetration into growth

Ultimately, all the firm's collaboration patterns across sectors and practices converge at the client. This is where business development and marketing teams and key account leaders spend most of their attention, and for good reason – understanding where the firm is at risk, where it is under-penetrated, and where the most immediate growth opportunities lie is fundamental to sustainable performance.

A core finding from our research is that moving clients "to the right" – increasing cross-practice engagement while reducing the long tail of small, single-practice relationships (see Figure 2) – simultaneously drives revenue and de-risks the portfolio. Clients served by a single practice, or worse, by a single partner, are disproportionately vulnerable.

Across thousands of clients and hundreds of firms, we consistently see a shocking percentage of clients tied to a single partner.[8] In one European firm we worked with, 46 percent of all clients were served by just one partner (Figure 6).

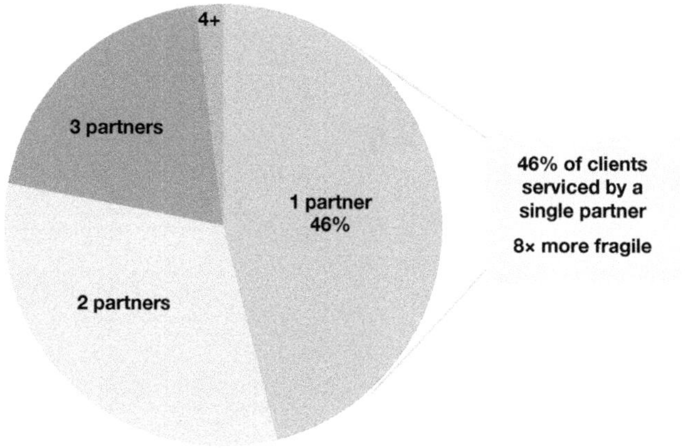

Figure 6 At risk clients – percentage of clients served by one partner.

That concentration created real, quantifiable risk:

- *Client-side change.* Single-partner relationships almost always anchor on a narrow set of contacts. A general counsel change or client reorganization exposes the firm.
- *Low strategic relevance.* Without multi-stakeholder, multi-practice engagement, one misstep can trigger a competitive review, or simply a switch to another firm.

- *Partner mobility*. Partners may get poached, retire, or leave for other personal reasons. If the client relationship isn't institutionalized, it is at risk the moment the partner departs.

Our research shows that a client served by a single partner is eight times more likely to leave the firm if that partner exits. This pure, quantifiable risk metric should be central to every management discussion, and yet most firms fail to even track it.

Drilling down – identifying patterns of opportunity and risk

Using the bar-and-line chart introduced earlier (Figure 2), we drill down to the most granular levels of individual relationships and matters to identify patterns of penetration, opportunity, and risk. We categorize clients by the number of partners serving them, flagging those that are single-threaded and therefore high-risk (see Figure 7).

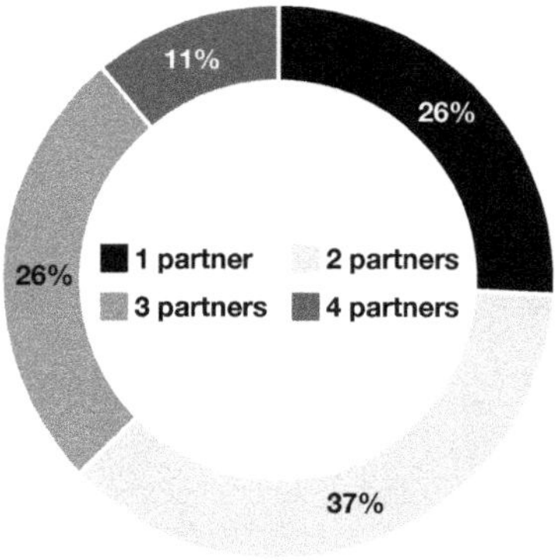

Client	Partners	Revenue	Client risk level
5078	2	$1,790,000	Medium
1856	5	$43,560,000	Low
4667	1	$8,800,000	High
8309	8	$49,990.000	Low
1415	2	$11,675,000	High

Figure 7: Percentage of clients served by number of partners.

These clients, and the partners supporting them, warrant deeper analysis to determine:

- Why is the relationship single-threaded?
- Does the client represent a strategic opportunity for the firm?
- If the client is large, does it represent a strategic risk if left unchanged?

From there, it is useful to zoom back out to examine cross-practice dynamics. For each client, analytics show which practices generate work, and which workstreams the client is sourcing elsewhere. Figure 8 highlights these asymmetries and helps leaders pinpoint immediate opportunities for expansion.

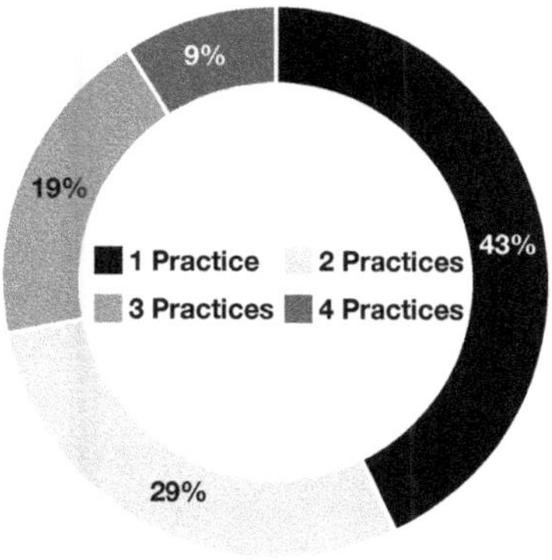

Client	Partners	Revenue	Client risk level
5544	1	$980,000	High
8973	1	$1,100,000	High
2231	1	$1,350,000	High
1234	1	$2,650.000	High
9876	1	$3,125,000	High

Figure 8: Percentage of clients served by number of practices.

Visualizing the work flows

Client-level network graphs provide a powerful view of how work flows between partners generating business and those executing it. In a single visual, we see:

- The direction and magnitude of workflows;
- Which partners drive the relationship; and
- Key demographics such as sector, practice, office, tenure, gender, and more.

Figure 9 offers this evidence in an intuitive form, enabling BD teams and practice heads to identify structural patterns and genuine insights about strengths and vulnerabilities that would otherwise remain invisible.

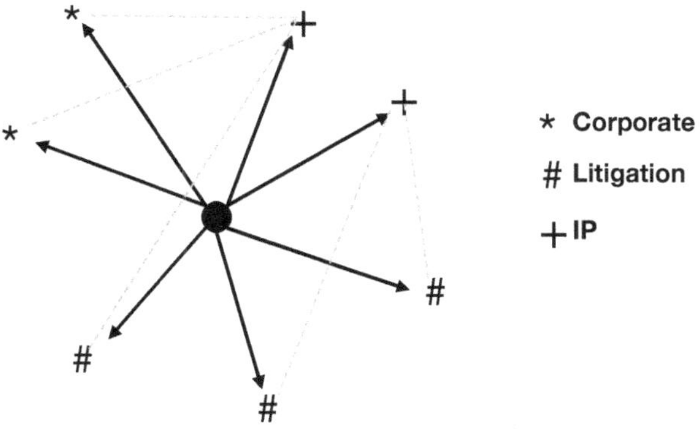

Figure 9: Client-level network graph.

Strategic questions for practice and BD leaders

This client-level analysis surfaces essential questions that should guide account management:

- Is the client strategic, and should they remain in the portfolio?
- Do we have the right account lead?
- Do we have the right key client team?
- Are there well-defined cross-practice pursuit strategies and account plans?

Under-penetration is not a failure – it is a roadmap for growth. Client-level analytics provide the clearest insights into opportunity, risk, and prioritization. They should be a standard component of every key account review and a central input to firm-wide strategic planning.

Partner-level collaboration – the business case, the benchmarks, and the early warning system

As Figure 2 shows, cross-practice collaboration delivers clear firm-level benefits – higher revenue, stronger margins, and stickier, more strategic client relationships. Yet partners often ask the reasonable question: "What's in it for me? I understand the benefit to the firm, but how does collaborating help build my business?" The answer becomes compelling when we analyze collaboration at the individual partner level.

The individual ROI of collaboration – the "twin partners" analysis

To assess the business case for an individual partner, we analyzed two nearly identical partners in a single firm – same practice, same year of promotion, similar hours, similar demographics. We nicknamed them "the twins". And yet their financial outcomes diverged dramatically.

Figure 10 shows their internal networks. Each node represents a partner whom they worked with for at least five hours over the course of a year; node colors represent practice groups.

- Twin 1 had a small network of six partners across four practices, with half of those relationships inside his own practice. His network resembled a hub-and-spoke model with limited cross-practice integration.
- Twin 2 had a far larger, more diverse network spanning more practices, with dense interconnections among the partners in his network.

The result was unequivocal – Twin 2 delivered financial outcomes four times stronger than Twin 1. We see this pattern everywhere we run network

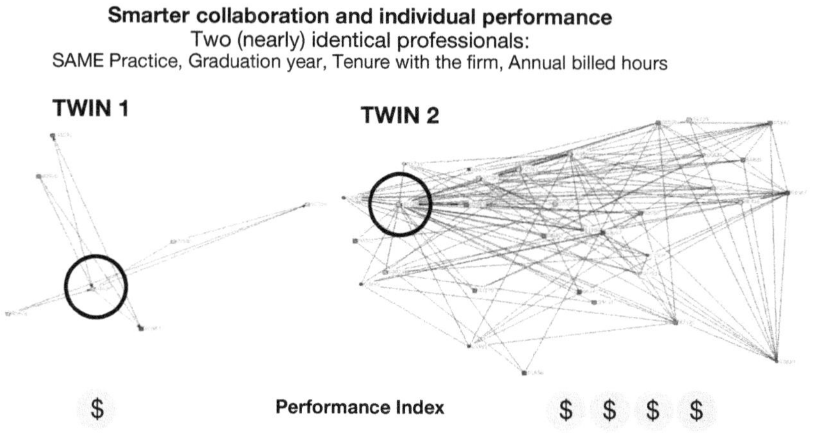

Figure 10: Translating data into insight.

analyses. The difference is not explained by tenure or demographics – it is directly correlated to collaboration patterns.

- A broader, deeper, more reciprocal network delivers tangible benefits:
- Better visibility into firm capabilities and institutional knowledge.
- Early insights into market and client developments.
- More opportunities to focus on expertise by exporting work to complementary experts.
- More inbound opportunities from colleagues.
- More resilient, multi-stakeholder client relationships.

The "twin partners" analysis makes the business case personal – and impossible to ignore.

The scatterplot – a wake-up call for partners

Partners vary widely in their views on collaboration, often shaped by firm culture. These range from "eat-what-you-kill" environments to strongly team-oriented cultures. For skeptics, the scatterplot is transformative.

In Figure 11, we filtered for a single practice and highlighted partners by tenure. Patterns appear immediately:

- A near-perfect 45-degree slope showing correlation between network development and financial outcomes.
- Higher-tenure partners [*] clustering toward the top right.
- Lower-tenure partners [▪]clustering bottom left.
- Wide dispersion within each tenure band – some junior partners dramatically outperforming peers due to stronger networks.

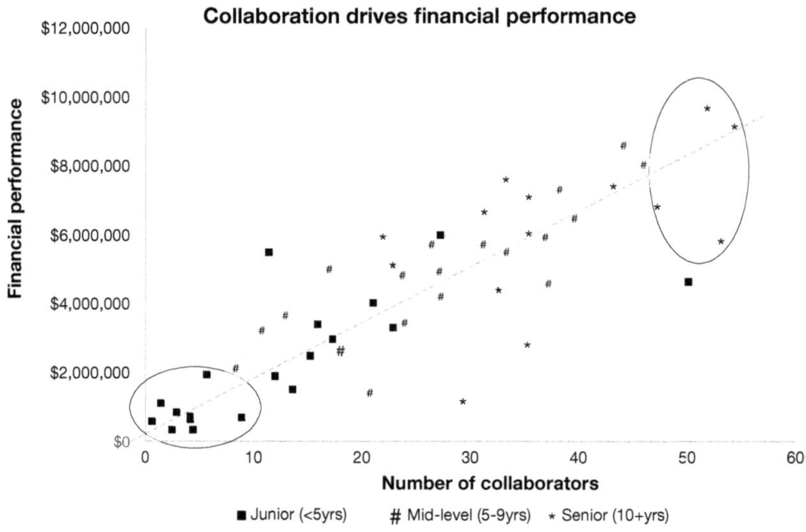

Figure 11: Highlighting partners by tenure.

Although we recommend keeping others' names hidden, showing someone their own dot is often catalytic. Partners instantly see the connection between their network and their outcomes – and begin exploring how to move up and to the right.

Partner-level diagnostics – how well is a partner actually collaborating?

For each partner, we drill into a set of core questions:

- How well-developed is their network – size, diversity, and distribution?
- How effectively are they generating cross-practice opportunities with clients?
- How does work flow – inbound, outbound, reciprocal?
- How do they perform on key collaboration metrics?
- Where do they need targeted coaching?

Let's look at an example of a corporate partner's network (Figure 12) and benchmarks (Figure 13). In this firm, Corporate is considered a "Magnet" practice – partners are expected to collaborate broadly and generate work for other practices.

The direction of the arrows shows the work flows, with solid lines showing relationships that meet the threshold for "core" and dotted lines showing those that are relatively small. The focus partner, Diego, exports work to four partners and imports from five. But none of his outbound ties are "core"; his deeper ties are all inbound. None are reciprocal (i.e., double-headed arrows).

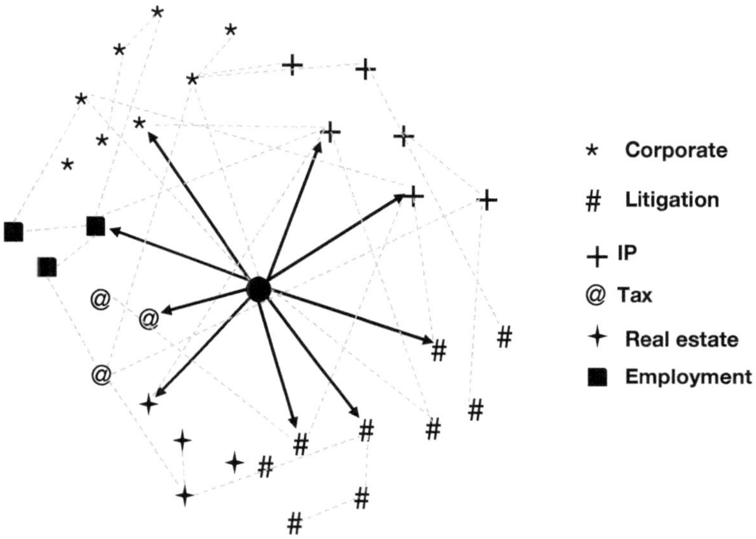

Figure 12: Corporate partner network.

His benchmarks (Figure 13) show underperformance relative to other partners in his practice, sector, and firm on most core metrics – number of collaborators, number of practices worked with, delegation rate (percentage of revenue generated that was exported to others). One bright spot: 98 percent of the matters he generated involved at least two practices, signaling strong performance on "complex generation".

Metric	Self	Practice Avg	Sector Avg	Firm Avg	Var to Practice	Var to Sector	Var to Firm
Total collaborators	9	20	18	14	-11	-9	-5
Generation $	3	10	8	7	-7	-5	-4
Complex generation %	$1.7m	$2.3m	$2.1m	$3.1m	-$0.6m	-$0.4m	-$2.4m
Network – practices	4	5	5	4	-1	-1	0
Network – offices	3	3	3	3	0	0	0
Delegation rate	21%	45%	35%	50%	-24%	-14%	-29%

Figure 13: Corporate partner benchmarks.

For BD leaders and L&D coaches, this opens targeted conversations:

- Where is the partner collaborating – and where could the network strategically expand?
- Where are this partner's multi-practice opportunities succeeding or stalling?
- How does the partner engage colleagues across levels?
- What is the balance between self execution and delegation?

Lateral integration – a critical use case

For lateral hires, behavior-based collaboration analytics are indispensable – see Figure 14. Our research shows that if a lateral is not well integrated within nine months, the risk of derailing is high.[9]

Firms often track a lateral hire's matter and revenue generation, but that is insufficient, misleading, and post-hoc. By the time leaders have documented a lateral's lack of progress, it is often too late to course-correct because that partner has already lost credibility with peers.

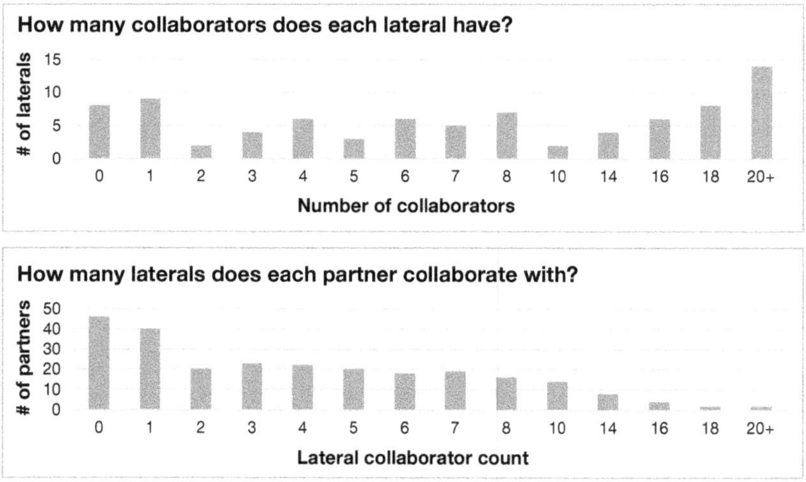

Figure 14: Behavior-based collaboration analytics.

Leaders must track:

- How many partners the lateral is importing work from.
- How many partners they are exporting to.
- Are relationships becoming reciprocal?
- How are relationships developing across clients, practices, and offices?
- Who is isolated?

These are the earliest signals of whether a lateral is embedding or operating as an island – regardless of how much business they initially bring. See Figure 15.

Isolated laterals **6 at Risk**

Partner	Office	Practice	Collaborators
Ellie James	New York	Anti-Trust	1
Hunter Morgan	Chicago	Exec Comp	1
Julian King	London	Exec Comp	1
Daniel Wilson	New York	Corp	2
James Lee	Tokyo	Corp	2
Hazel Chavez	Dallas	Tax	2

Top lateral integrators **Top 6**

Partner	Office	Practice	Collaborators
Jaydon Torres	Boston	Corp	1
Michael Hernandez	Boston	Real Estate	1
Lily Wood	London	Anti-Trust	1
Tom Carter	London	Corp	2
Ethan Gonzalez	Tokyo	Corp	2
Damian Moore	Boston	Tax	2

Figure 15: Comparing isolated laterals with integrated laterals.

Equally important is the inverse. Which existing partners are collaborating with laterals? In most firms, a small number of partners build strong networks with laterals, while many avoid them, often seeing them as competitors. This is destructive and must be actively managed.

Identifying the hidden gems

Network analytics also reveal the partners who quietly power collaborative performance – the firm's "hidden gems". Every firm has its high-profile stars and rainmakers, but beneath the surface are partners who consistently advance the firm's strategy through their collaborative behaviors, often without fanfare. These under-the-radar integrators are essential to sustaining a collaborative culture. Analytics ensure they are identified, supported, and celebrated.

Hidden gems who support laterals accelerate a lateral's integration and dramatically increase the odds of success. They make proactive introductions to key partners, bring the lateral into client work, and champion their business development efforts. They view the lateral as a strategic investment in the practice or sector – not a threat – and act accordingly.

Hidden gems who support newly elevated partners play an equally critical role. Ideally, these are the same tenured partners who engaged the individual as an associate. Too often, however, the opposite occurs – after elevation, support evaporates as former mentors begin to see the new partner as a competitor. Hidden gems understand that the first two to three years post-elevation are decisive for both the partner and the practice. They help the new partner build internal relationships, secure meaningful client work, and establish a credible BD rhythm.

The role of leaders, including managing partners, practice and sector heads, and L&D is threefold:

1. Identify the hidden gems whose behaviors exemplify the firm's collaborative expectations.
2. Champion them by making their contributions visible and celebrating their impact.
3. Replicate their behaviors by encouraging others to follow their example – and by spotlighting where support is missing but should exist.

Hidden gems are not just "nice to have". They are the connective tissue that makes collaboration real, scalable, and durable. Recognizing and empowering them is a high-leverage action a leadership team should take.

The early warning system – partner-level risk indicators

When a valued partner leaves a firm, the impacts are broad – on revenue, client relationships, and firm morale. And yet, firms are too often surprised when it happens. Collaboration analytics provide the most reliable early warning indicators of partner-level risk:

- Which partners are isolated (few collaborators, few intros received)?
- Which partners are stretched thin (many small relationships)?
- Which partners are islands (high self-execution, low collaboration)?
- Which partners are captive (high concentration of work with a small set of colleagues)?

- Which partners are self-dealing, and on which clients?
- Which partners are struggling, and what patterns explain the gap?

These indicators should be standard in every firm's leadership dashboard. They are the earliest and most reliable predictors of future performance and retention issues.

Turning collaboration analytics into behavioral change and performance

Even the most sophisticated collaboration analytics will fail to create impact if they remain trapped in a dashboard or owned by a single function. Firms that translate insight into sustained growth treat collaboration as a cross-silo discipline – one that requires coordinated action across marketing and business development, learning and development, HR, firm leadership, and the partnership itself. Analytics reveal *what is happening*; execution determines *what changes* as a result.

Put simply, analytics are the spark. Transformation depends on how deliberately the firm organizes around them.

Marketing and BD – turning insights into pursuits

Marketing and business development teams are often the first to feel the practical value of collaboration analytics because they sit closest to client development. Historically, BD teams have relied on anecdote, partner recollection, or incomplete CRM data to identify opportunities. Collaboration analytics transform that equation by providing an objective, firm-wide view of where strong cross-practice relationships already exist, where clients are under-penetrated, and where growth is most likely.

This shift enables BD to move from reactive support to proactive leadership. Rather than asking partners where they want to focus, BD teams can lead conversations with evidence – which clients offer the greatest multi-practice upside, which partners are best positioned to engage them, and which practices naturally reinforce one another. Pursuit strategies become more focused, more defensible, and more likely to succeed.

Sector initiatives benefit even more. Many sector programs struggle because they are built around partner self-identification rather than client-level reality. Collaboration analytics reveal which practices generate strategic work in a sector, which partners collaborate across sector-relevant matters, and where cross-practice pipelines already exist. BD teams can then design sector campaigns that reflect how the firm truly operates – not how it aspires to operate. The result is sharper thought leadership, stronger pitch teams, and sector strategies that feel grounded rather than rhetorical.

Perhaps most importantly, analytics equip partners with evidence-based client conversations. Partners often struggle to articulate the full breadth of the firm's capabilities to clients. Analytics make those capabilities visible – showing how the firm serves comparable clients, where integrated teams have delivered value, and how cross-practice engagement improves outcomes. These insights, often developed by the BD team and used by partners, strengthen pitches, deepen client dialogue, and increase partner confidence.

Finally, collaboration analytics allow BD teams to redesign client teams around reality rather than hierarchy or internal politics. Teams can be built around the partners who actually drive relationships, generate cross-practice work, and hold critical client trust – creating client teams that are more coherent, more collaborative, and more effective.

Learning and development / HR – building collaboration as a skill

One of the clearest conclusions from our research is that collaboration is not a personality trait. Smarter collaboration involves a set of behaviors that can be taught, coached, measured, and reinforced. Learning and Development and HR play a central role in embedding these behaviors into the firm's talent systems.

Collaboration analytics give these teams a level of precision they have never had before – and take the "heat" out of difficult conversations. Rather than relying on self-assessment or generic competency models, they can see exactly how partners build networks – who they work with, how reciprocal those relationships are, whether they delegate or self-execute, and how well they integrate laterals and new partners. This allows L&D to design individualized coaching plans that target personalized, specific behaviors rather than broad themes. Moreover, partners respond best to evidence – coaches armed with data-driven insights are far more likely to create breakthroughs when conversations start with "let's see what the numbers say" – a framing that feels less judgmental and more objective.

Leadership programs also become more credible. Many firms run partner academies or leadership cohorts, but few explicitly teach collaboration as a core leadership capability. Analytics equip firms to incorporate real, anonymized firm data into learning programs; to illustrate what effective and ineffective collaboration looks like; and to help partners understand their own collaboration "signature". This creates a shared language and clearer expectations across the partnership.

Perhaps the most transformative contribution L&D can make is the ability to track behavioral change over time. This is like the "holy grail" of L&D – demonstrating how well development programs and coaching are working, whether networks are expanding, delegation is increasing, reciprocal ties are forming, and cross-practice matter generation is improving. Partner development shifts from a series of isolated interventions to a longitudinal, evidence-based process.

HR can then integrate these insights into performance management. Compensation, promotion, and succession decisions all benefit from a clearer view of how partners contribute beyond their individual book of business. Analytics help surface high-potential future leaders, identify "hidden gems" who quietly drive cross-practice work, and flag partners who are isolated or at risk. When HR uses these insights, collaboration becomes something the firm not only encourages but also rewards.

Leadership – embedding collaboration into strategy and accountability

Leaders' role is not simply to endorse collaboration – they must operationalize it. Collaboration analytics give leaders the visibility they need to set strategy, allocate resources, and hold partners accountable.

The first requirement is strategic clarity. Analytics help leaders identify which clients should be prioritized for cross-practice growth, which practices need to collaborate more effectively, which sectors require multi-disciplinary solutions, and where the firm is overly dependent on a small number of partners. These insights equip leaders to set clear, fair, measurable collaboration goals – reducing single-partner clients, increasing multi-practice matter generation, improving delegation rates, or expanding cross-office collaboration in key sectors.

The second requirement is incentive alignment. Compensation is one of the strongest signals of what a firm truly values. Collaboration analytics allow leaders to reward partners who export work, recognize those who integrate laterals, spotlight strong network builders, and address persistent self-dealing or isolation. When incentives shift, behavior often follows.

Leaders must also ensure that practice, sector, and client leaders have access to accurate collaboration insights. Most leaders assume they understand how collaboration works in their groups, but their view is often shaped by anecdote. Analytics reveal how work really flows, who drives growth, where risks are emerging, and how collaboration patterns are evolving – enabling proactive rather than reactive leadership.

Transparency is another powerful lever. When collaboration analytics are shared appropriately across the partnership, they create peer awareness and shared standards. Partners can see what "good" looks like and how they stack up, leaders can reinforce desired behaviors, and collaboration becomes visible rather than optional. Transparency, when handled well, accelerates cultural change.

Ultimately, leaders' role is to create an environment where collaboration is the default, not the exception. That requires consistent messaging, aligned incentives, visible role modeling, investment in cross-practice initiatives, and recognition of collaborative successes. It also requires consequences for persistent siloed behavior. Collaboration analytics give leaders the tools to build this culture with precision and discipline.

Peer-to-peer feedback – building a culture of collaborative accountability

Even with strong systems and leadership support, collaboration will not endure unless partners hold one another accountable. Peer-to-peer feedback is the most powerful – and most underutilized – mechanism for sustaining collaborative behavior.

Partners are far more likely to change when the message comes not from a dashboard or a coach, but from a respected colleague whose success depends on shared effort. In most law firms, however, feedback between partners is informal, inconsistent, or avoided altogether.

Even partners who have a formal remit, such as practice group leaders, hesitate to challenge one another's behaviors, despite those behaviors undermine client service or team cohesion.

Collaboration analytics create a new opening – they give partners a shared language and shared evidence that make feedback feel less personal and more constructive. Instead of "I think you're not collaborating," the conversation becomes, "Here's what the data shows about how we're working together – and here's how we can improve it".

Well-designed, collaboration-focused 360-degree tools can support this process, but only when used for development, not evaluation. They help partners understand how colleagues experience working with them – where they build trust, where they create friction, and where small behavioral changes could unlock greater impact. When separated from performance ratings, 360s help partners see blind spots that no amount of self-reflection or financial reporting could reveal. In contrast, peer feedback used for year-end assessments rarely focuses on how to build specific behaviors, but rather on outcomes. Even worse, research shows that feedback providers in an assessment process are far less honest than in a developmental one.

But formal feedback alone is not enough. Culture changes most powerfully through ongoing, informal feedback – debriefs after pitches, post-matter reflections, and candid conversations about how to collaborate more effectively next time. This real-time dialogue normalizes feedback, reduces defensiveness, and embeds collaboration in daily work.

Over time, peer feedback becomes a form of social accountability that no formal system can replicate. Strong collaborators become role models. Isolated partners feel pressure to engage. Teams normalize discussions about reciprocity and delegation. Collaboration shifts from an initiative to a professional norm.

Institutionalizing collaboration for competitive advantage

Analytics alone do not change a firm. What changes a firm is the system built around those insights – BD teams that translate them into targeted pursuits; L&D and HR teams that embed them into development and evaluation; leaders who align strategy, incentives, and accountability; and partners who use feedback to help one another improve.

But the final – and often decisive – layer is the partnership itself. When partners use both formal tools, like development-focused 360s, and informal, real-time feedback to help one another grow, collaboration stops being a program and becomes a shared professional norm. And at that point, analytics are no longer just information – they are the catalyst for a culture that continuously sustains itself and compounds advantage over time.

Conclusion – collaboration analytics as a competitive advantage

Most firms describe collaboration as a cultural aspiration. A smaller number treat it as a strategic priority. Very few, however, manage it as a source of enduring institutional advantage – one that can be measured, actively managed, and systematically scaled. Collaboration analytics are the catalyst for that shift. They illuminate what has historically been invisible – how work flows, how partners behave (when nobody seems to be watching), and how clients experience the firm in practice.

But analytics alone don't change firms. They simply reveal the truth. What matters is how leaders respond to what the data reveals.

The first requirement is recognizing that collaboration analytics are not reporting tools – they are management tools. They allow leaders to move from intuition to evidence, from anecdotes to patterns, and from isolated success stories to firm-wide truths. They reveal where the firm is creating value, where it is exposed, and where growth opportunities have been hiding in plain sight. But insight without discipline is merely information. Firms capture real value only when analytics are embedded into leadership routines – annual planning, sector strategy, client reviews, partner development, and succession decisions.

The second requirement is shifting from individual effort to collective action. Collaboration has traditionally been framed as a personal choice or personal virtue. Analytics challenge that framing. They demonstrate that collaboration is heavily shaped by structure, expectations, and accountability. Business development teams use analytics to direct the firm's growth engine. HR and Learning and Development teams use them to help partners build the behaviors that drive cross-practice success. Leaders use them to clarify priorities and reinforce consequences.

Yet the most powerful force in the system remains the partnership itself. Partners change when peers expect them to change. They grow when colleagues give them direct, honest, constructive feedback. They collaborate when they see collaboration modeled, rewarded, and reciprocated. Development-oriented 360 tools, when used thoughtfully, help partners understand how they are experienced by others. Informal, real-time feedback reinforces those insights in the flow of work. Together, these mechanisms create a culture in which collaboration is continuous rather than episodic.

At its core, collaboration analytics help firms move from silos to shared success. They reveal which practices act as magnets, which operate as islands, which clients are under-penetrated, and which partners quietly drive cross-practice growth. This level of visibility allows leaders to intervene with precision rather than broad, undifferentiated initiatives.

To thrive in the coming decade, as competition and volatility continue to ramp up, winning will demand that firms treat collaboration not as a stated value but as a capability – one that can be measured, developed, and scaled. When analytics, leadership, cross-functional support, and peer accountability reinforce one another, collaboration becomes self-sustaining. The firm becomes something more than the sum of its practices – a unified institution capable of delivering the kind of integrated value clients cannot find anywhere else.

References

1 Heidi K. Gardner, *Smart Collaboration: How Professionals and Their Firms Succeed by Breaking Down Silos*. Boston: Harvard Business Review Press, 2017.

2 Heidi K. Gardner and Ivan A. Matviak, *Smarter Collaboration: A New Approach to Breaking Down Barriers and Transforming Work*. Boston: Harvard Business Review Press, 2022.

3 Heidi K. Gardner, "Why It Pays to Collaborate," *The American Lawyer*, March 2015.

4 Heidi K. Gardner, "By Failing to Collaborate, Law Firms Are Leaving Money on the Table." *The American Lawyer* (International Edition), 9 October 2018.

5 Heidi K. Gardner and David Harvey, "Cutting Through the Noise: How to Use Industry Expertise to Get Clients' Attention." Law.com, May 2020.

6 Heidi K. Gardner and David Harvey, "Why Your Firm Needs a Sector-Based Strategy – and How to Build One." *The American Lawyer*, November 2019.

7 Heidi K. Gardner and Ivan A. Matviak, "Performance Management Shouldn't Kill Collaboration." *Harvard Business Review*, September 2022.

8 Heidi K. Gardner, "When and Why Clients Want You to Collaborate." *The American Lawyer*, June 2016.

9 Gardner, Heidi K. and Gillespie, Anusia E., *Smart Collaboration for Lateral Hiring: Successful Strategies to Recruit and Integrate Laterals in Law Firms*, 2018. Globe Law and Business. www.globelawandbusiness.com/special-reports/smart-collaboration-for-lateral-hiring

Chapter 6:
Content differentiation in the age of information abundance

By Andrew Longstreth, head writer, and Jamie Diaferia, founder and CEO, Infinite

Differentiation. It's the existential challenge facing law firms today. How do you distinguish your firm in a market where legal excellence is assumed?

Not so long ago, firms could rely on work quality and responsiveness to build brand equity. But today, attributes such as legal talent, size, and geographic coverage are table stakes. They are expected, not exceptional.

More recently, firms have attempted to differentiate themselves through industry focus. Rather than listing dozens of practice areas on their websites, they highlight integrated capabilities across sectors such as healthcare, energy, and financial services. This shift reflects a simple truth – clients do not have legal problems; they have business problems. It also acknowledges that law firms are no longer merely in the legal business. They are in the advisory business.

Yet genuine opportunities to demonstrate deep, differentiated knowledge tailored to client needs remain rare.

Generative AI intensifies the challenge. Clients now have tools that can handle routine legal work and surface answers to common legal questions in seconds. When information is abundant, firms compete on interpretation, synthesis, and strategic insight.

One powerful path forward is original analysis with practical takeaways – what we will call thought leadership in this chapter. When done well, it demonstrates strategic depth, builds trust, and positions firms for higher-level, higher-value work.

But success today requires a new playbook.

Distinctiveness over volume

Content distribution mechanics are changing rapidly. Traditional search is under pressure. Clients seeking answers online no longer have to settle for a list of links – they can seek AI-generated summaries that cite only a handful of sources. The low-hanging fruit once captured through search engine optimization is disappearing.

The media industry's upheaval offers a warning for law firms. Publishers anticipate significant declines in search-driven traffic in the coming years, forcing a fundamental rethink of their models. In response, they are doubling down on what cannot be commoditized – original reporting, sharp analysis, community-building, and opinion-driven commentary. Generic evergreen content is losing ground.

The lesson for law firms is clear – in a world of expanding information, distinctive insight aimed at defined audiences wins; mass content loses.

But distinctiveness cannot be achieved through tactics alone. It requires a cultural shift – one that prioritizes originality and tolerates failure in its pursuit.

When professionals cannot clearly articulate original thinking, they default to clichés and recycled frameworks, which can erode market reputation. AI won't save them. Yes, it will make content creation easier. But precisely because it does, law firms have to become more ambitious. As firms gain access to the same tools and content becomes frictionless, advantage will come not from volume but from sharper thinking and clearer signals.

Generative AI will not eliminate legal insight, but it will commoditize basic explanation. When any lawyer – or client – can generate a passable summary of a new regulation in seconds, the value shifts to interpretation. What does it mean? What should we do about it?

To consistently produce fresh insights, firm leaders must help lawyers see their roles differently. Instead of functioning primarily as legal technicians, they must see themselves as business advisors – professionals capable of assessing risks and opportunities within a broader strategic context.

Creating a culture of thought leadership requires more than encouraging lawyers to publish. It requires four institutional conditions – leadership signal, strategic focus, editorial infrastructure, and meaningful recognition. When those elements align, thought leadership moves from sporadic activity to institutional capability.

Leadership sets the signal

A culture that prizes thought leadership does not emerge organically. It does not appear because a marketing team launches an initiative or because a few motivated partners enjoy writing. It takes root only with visible, sustained support from the top.

In many law firms, leadership buy-in requires a fundamentally different view of how value is created. For decades, business development has often been treated as a necessary but secondary activity – non-billable time that competes with the real work of serving clients.

In that framework, thought leadership is treated as discretionary. Something to do if time allows. Lawyers are acutely attuned to signals from firm leadership. If they do not hear consistent reinforcement about the importance of thought leadership, they will reasonably conclude that it ranks below billable hours and client urgencies.

The result is predictable – inconsistent effort, sporadic output, and disjointed initiatives that fail to build real distinction. It reflects a dynamic that organizational psychologists describe as the "shadow of the leader".

Leaders cast long shadows. Their visible priorities shape what others believe truly matters. When leaders consistently elevate intellectual contribution, curiosity, and external engagement, those priorities cascade through the organization.

The question, then, is practical: How do leaders extend that shadow in support of thought leadership?

One powerful method is to lead by example.

For five years, name partner John Quinn of Quinn Emanuel Urquhart & Sullivan has hosted the podcast *Law, Disrupted*.[1] Through conversations on topics ranging from AI to litigation finance to emerging markets, the podcast has kept forward-looking issues at the center of the firm's identity. With more than 250,000 downloads as of mid-2025, it has become more than a marketing channel – it is a signal. When the firm's most senior leader invests time in publicly exploring big ideas, it signals that intellectual engagement is central to the firm's brand.

Leaders don't have to get behind a microphone to show their commitment, however – they can also provide structural support. At Morgan Lewis, firm management, including chair Jamie McKeon, appointed senior partners to lead editorial output in areas critical to client industries. These leaders were empowered to do more than just review articles before publication. They were tasked with convening cross-practice discussions to synthesize the implications of regulatory shifts, market volatility, and emerging risks. The goal was not to produce more content. It was to foster clearer thinking that only a global law firm could.

The approach crystallized during the pandemic. Under leadership direction, Morgan Lewis organized a cross-disciplinary COVID task force to address unprecedented operational questions from clients. Because the issues were novel and interconnected, the response had to be as well. The task force became not merely reactive but a coordinated platform for generating timely, integrated insight. In these examples, leadership did more than approve thought leadership. They participated, structured around it, and legitimized it.

"Our leadership makes our jobs easy because we never have to sell our value," says Morgan Lewis' chief marketing officer, Mona Zeiberg. "There's always been an emphasis on demonstrating insights to clients through our content."

The legitimacy that leaders confer on activities like content changes behavior. When leaders consistently demonstrate that original thinking is valued – by investing their own time, allocating institutional resources, and elevating those who contribute – thought leadership ceases to be "extra". It becomes part of what it means to practice at the firm.

Culture follows the shadow.

Strategy sharpens the focus

Leadership engagement alone is insufficient. Thought leadership must be tightly aligned with a firm's strategy. Research consistently shows that professionals invest discretionary effort when their work is clearly connected to organizational purpose. In professional service firms – where publishing and speaking are rarely mandatory – clarity of objectives reduces ambiguity and increases motivation. Lawyers are particularly sensitive to three questions:

- Is this aligned with firm strategy?
- Will this help my practice?
- Is this valued by leadership?

If the firm's objectives are unclear, thought leadership can feel like personal branding detached from institutional priorities – or worse, marketing "busywork" that competes with billable time. A clear strategic framework reduces that cognitive friction. Lawyers do not have to guess whether the effort matters.

The connection between insight and business impact is explicit. Clarity also sharpens execution. When a firm defines its narrative themes, priority industries, and distinctive positioning, it moves beyond a "throw-it-at-the-wall-and-see-what-sticks" approach. Content becomes intentional rather than episodic.

Goodwin Procter provides a strong example. Guided by its "Goodwin

2033" strategy, the firm aims to position itself as an elite, industry-focused firm that fuses legal excellence with strategic business advisory across its core industries – technology, life sciences, investment funds, private equity, real estate, and healthcare. A flagship initiative supporting this strategy is Forces of Law,[2] a collection of editorially driven articles developed by a dedicated in-house team.

Rather than offering narrow legal analysis, the pieces examine shifting legal landscapes and deliver strategic business insight with a legal overlay. The initiative directly mirrors the firm's broader ambition – to serve as high-level advisors to CEOs facing consequential "bet-the-company" decisions.

"We want them to call us, not necessarily because we're the best legal advisors to them, but because we're the best overall advisors who really understand their industry," says Goodwin's chief growth officer, Konstantin Shishkin.

Goodwin treated the project not as a routine publication effort but as a campaign – complete with custom illustration and deliberate positioning. By leading with distinctive, idea-driven content, the firm reinforces its identity in the market and internally clarifies what kind of advisor it seeks to be. Alignment turns thought leadership from activity into advantage.

Infrastructure for sustainability

If signal and strategy are necessary to set content cultures in motion, infrastructure is what makes them sustainable. Building that infrastructure requires empowering people who define editorial excellence, create effective processes, and own the function.

Creating a culture of thought leadership does not mean expecting every lawyer to become a prolific public commentator. But it does mean recognizing that business development exists on a continuum – and that the editorial function is equally important.

As the longtime law firm marketing leader Murray Coffey notes, lawyers who generate intellectual capital – those who synthesize trends, articulate frameworks, and shape market conversations – must be treated as co-equal to the outgoing partners who generate business through personal networks. Both create value. One converts relationships into revenue. The other builds the intellectual platform that enables those relationships.

"Just because you can walk into a dinner party and walk out with business doesn't mean you're any more valuable than the person who's cranking out that piece of intellectual capital that is going to help distinguish the practice," says Coffey, senior strategic advisor to the chair, Americas, at Willkie Farr & Gallagher. "Successful firms require a balance of magicians who predict the future, client handlers, salespeople, and scholars who document intellectual capabilities. Without the scholars working in the background to put that intellectual capital out into the market, the traditional salespeople would have nothing to sell."

That cultural recognition must be supported by operational investment. At Morgan Lewis, a newsroom-style editorial process supports contributions from hundreds of partners. Substantive legal review remains with practitioners, while professional editors focus on clarity, tone, and consistency. The system balances scale with quality control, ensuring compliance while maintaining a unified voice.

"Our editorial team does much more than check for typos," notes Zeiberg. "They're offering substantive edits with fresh eyes, helping shape the substance and sharpen the message. Partners often tell us, 'This is better than when I started', and that's the type of collaboration we aim for."

Goodwin Procter also relies heavily on a dedicated editorial team led by a former *McKinsey Quarterly* editor and staffed with experienced journalists. Rather than repurposing traditional marketing roles, the firm invested in professional storytellers capable of elevating ideas and shaping narrative arcs. The team is coached to use AI to streamline routine alerts, preserving their editorial bandwidth for distinctive, higher-value projects.

The team's pedigree, skills, and work send a strong message as powerful as any speech from leadership – original thinking is not an afterthought. It is an institutional priority worthy of professional support.

Without passionate leaders and empowered editorial teams, average results can persist. When one Am Law 100 firm found that average page read times hovered around 40 seconds, its communications leadership introduced a "Smart Brevity" style to help readers quickly grasp key points and explore deeper layers if desired. The adjustment was tactical, but the mindset was strategic – respect the audience's time, and compete on clarity.

Firms may differ in how they approach their teams, but the key is to unleash a passion and drive conversations around the news and how best to deliver it. By fostering psychological safety in a dedicated group of professionals with a clear aim, law firm leaders can send a strong message about the importance of serving clients.

Recognizing and rewarding what counts

If thought leadership is going to thrive at any firm, it needs to be visibly validated and rewarded.

Every month, lawyers at Goodwin receive an internal newsletter called *The Lead*. It highlights the month's "bestsellers" – the top ten articles produced by the firm based on metrics such as page views and email opens. It also links to what the editorial team has been reading that month and an invitation for lawyers to submit ideas for collaboration.

"We spend a lot of time explaining what we produce and the impact and the results from it," he says. "*The Lead* is a way of saying, 'Here's how we can help you. Get in touch.'"

Newsletters like *The Lead* reaffirm a firm's values by spotlighting successful editorial contributions. It's crucial that firms think through what they choose to highlight. Metrics help evaluate content performance because they are easy to understand. But an overreliance on them can kill the culture of experimentation and usefulness that firms are trying to create. That's why firms need to provide space to celebrate wins beyond pageviews, likes, and impressions.

In a daily briefing email, Morgan Lewis includes a dedicated thought leadership section that highlights instances in which a client found a piece of content particularly interesting or helpful.

Recognizing editorial success creates a self-fulfilling cycle of motivation and opportunity. Shishkin recalls a time when a partner at the firm asked a member of the editorial team to share byline credit on an article they had collaborated on because of its extraordinary quality.

"It makes the team feel like they're really a part of the firm's success, not just a person doing stuff in the background," he notes. "And success begets success. The more we do this, the more we get resources and permission to try new things."

To truly cement a culture, Coffey strongly advises involving financial incentives. His suggestion – include the chief marketing officers in compensation discussions for attorneys. This ensures that the attorneys' concrete contributions to growing the practice through thought leadership are financially recognized and rewarded.

Making it easy to leverage content

Most law firm content suffers from a single-use syndrome. It's written, published, and forgotten. The fix is not content. It is systems. If thought leadership is to become a competitive asset, it needs to be easy to repurpose and share. The first step, then, is to remove all barriers and friction from sharing.

It's what Orrick's business development team had in mind when it created "relationship partner toolkits", notes the firm's former chief marketing officer, Jon Brewer. The toolkits included skeleton emails to make client outreach as frictionless as possible for the attorneys. Instead of just blasting out generic thought leadership to a mailing list, lawyers were asked to select high-value targets and use these skeleton emails to easily craft a customized message.

The goal of these templates was to help lawyers proactively reach out to clients and explain how new market developments would directly impact their clients' businesses. By providing these pre-written, highly targeted drafts, the firm made it much easier for lawyers to spark meaningful conversations with their clients.

"Instead of sending a generic news blast that 50 other law firms were also sending, lawyers were able to proactively add value by using the content to spark a meeting and connect their clients with the right firm experts," notes Brewer, now a senior executive with Intapp.

Leveraging content is deeply ingrained in Morgan Lewis's culture as well. A webinar with a large slide deck, for example, will become a summary post on its website with quick "key takeaways".

They stretch core themes by producing large, collective-thought pieces on broad topics (such as the impact of new SEC regulations), while also spinning out highly specific, niche content tailored to individual states (such as New Jersey or California employment law) or regions such as Puerto Rico.

Partners are also prompted to send content to specific clients with a personalized note (e.g., "I saw this, and I thought of you"), highlighting exactly what they should pay attention to. In some cases, content bypasses mass distribution entirely and is published as a "client-directed piece" for a discrete list of clients impacted by a specific development.

Beyond reducing friction for lawyers, these efforts at leveraging open new opportunities for meaningful metrics. Instead of simply tracking pageviews, open rates, and downloads, firms can track client meetings triggered by content, speaking invitations, inbound inquiries, and cross-selling opportunities.

Many firms treat publishing as marketing. The real leverage happens when it becomes a reason to call a client, a credibility marker in RFP responses, or a conversation starter in dormant relationships. When insights are reused, cited, and used to deliver client work, lawyers see tangible impact. Tangible impact reinforces participation.

Great expectations

A culture of thought leadership is not defined by the number of articles published or webinars hosted. It is defined by an ambition and impulse to interpret, synthesize, and clarify the implications of relevant developments for clients' businesses. It is a shared belief that insight is part of the job – not an extracurricular activity delegated to marketing or reserved for a few enthusiastic partners.

When leadership consistently signals that ideas matter, lawyers respond. When strategy clarifies which ideas matter most, effort sharpens. When infrastructure makes it easier to develop and distribute insight, and recognition and incentives reinforce the behavior, momentum compounds. In a market where competence is assumed, firms that create cultures of original thinking can do what is so crucial today – stand out.

The authors wish to thank all the interviewees cited in this chapter for their comments.

References

1 https://law-disrupted.fm/
2 www.goodwinlaw.com/en/resource/forces-of-law

Chapter 7:
Embedding a BD mindset – making it part of your professional identity

By Trish Lilley, chief marketing and business development officer, Barnes & Thornburg

While the legal industry has transformed significantly over the past several decades, lawyer attitudes and firm approaches to business development have been slower to evolve. Certainly, we're past the days when sales was a "bad word" and we've seen sophisticated client relations initiatives implemented at many firms. Great strides have been made and plenty of firms are engaged in advanced client development. However, the industry norm hasn't yet fully integrated business development into the ethos of lawyering.

At the core of that challenge is "purpose". Individuals pursue careers as lawyers for myriad reasons. Developing a book of business doesn't top the list. The law school experience doesn't move the needle much. Very few law schools devote much of the curriculum to the business of law – or even basic client service principles. Emphasis is on absorption and memorization that then morph into knowledge and performance with a bit of intellectual agility, oration, and strong writing icing the cake.

That emphasis follows grads into their legal careers. As lawyers traverse their professional paths, they spend years perfecting the craft, investing hours in ensuring pristine deliverables, adopting best-practice research and writing skills, and focusing on providing timely service to both internal and external clients. The message? Your professional value proposition lies in intellectual rigor, technical expertise, sophisticated analysis, risk mitigation, and zealous advocacy.

While there's a boatload of truth to that takeaway, it's not enough. Unfortunately, the industry's traditional professional development model does a disservice. With nearly 1.4 million lawyers in just the United States, competition for clients is fierce across almost all practice areas and in all segments of the industry. Solid training and technical prowess are givens. Excellent lawyering is table stakes. Clients want, and expect, far more – and they'll walk if they don't get it.

Given this competitive reality, both an understanding of, and a commitment to, business development are crucial for career success and longevity. The emphasis on practical skills training both in law school and continuing well into mid-stage career development keeps BD out of the realm of consideration for lawyers and deemphasizes some of the skills that most effectively fuel it, such as relationship building, competitive analysis, business operations, and horizon-scanning to identify opportunities and emerging trends. While some of these skills are complementary and even transferable, the lack of emphasis on applying them in the context of business development can create a disconnect, or misalignment, within a lawyer's professional identity.

When juxtaposed with the industry's highly competitive quest for clients and their loyalty, this disconnect in professional identity surfaces as a major Achilles' heel that can significantly hamper a lawyer's and a firm's success. That challenge underscores the importance of revisiting how BD is viewed by lawyers and firms and shifting the ways in which they understand and approach it. Impactful business development can be achieved only if it's sustainable, and BD becomes sustainable only when it's embedded in one's identity in a meaningful, authentic way.

Institutional efforts are key to the cultural shift that needs to occur around BD, but they cannot succeed until lawyers themselves embrace business development as a key component of their profession and their practices, recognizing it as a factor as essential to their client service as the actual legal work they perform. The most effective business development cultures emerge not when firms teach tips, techniques, and tech, but when they educate and empower lawyers, so those practitioners come to understand that business development is inseparable from professional excellence, practice mastery, and true client service.

So how do we get there?

Speak a new language

Shifting ingrained mindsets takes work, both big and small. While it may seem a "small" piece, retooling the language we use around business development is important and a key first step. Words matter. They may matter even more in this industry than in others, given how many lawyers make their living from them – selecting, analyzing, interpreting, critiquing, and debating them. Phrasing and nomenclature are no small matter in this sector!

As part of the reframing effort, firms can benefit from abandoning the traditional characterization of relevant activities. Put "rainmaking" and "selling" to the side. Recast in a client-focused way. Doing so fosters a more direct connection with lawyers' "day jobs" – and likely casts these activities in a more familiar light for most of them. Client development, client expansion, sector penetration, and even revenue generation can be more effective ways to present the efforts and objectives that firms want to encourage. At the end of the day, it comes down to service, so let's adopt language that reflects that.

Know what we're up against

To combat or eliminate resistance to incorporating business development into a lawyer's personal and professional identity, we need to delve a bit deeper into the ingrained resistance many have. Understanding objections provides a clear path to dispelling them and paving a new way forward.

Essentially, resistance stems from a few predictable barriers. The core one is the identity-conflict issue we are focused on altering. As noted, lawyers invest years in honing their craft and becoming top-notch practitioners. They don't view themselves as salespeople and often have no desire to engage in "sales". There's a sense that superb work product and advice should "be enough" and speak for themselves. Excellent work should lead to an impeccable reputation in the market, client loyalty, and repeat business. But, as we know, excellent work just isn't enough.

There are two more common concerns related to business development that also impact lawyer objections – fear of rejection and fear of the unknown. Business development introduces uncertainty into an otherwise fairly regimented and predictable professional arena. The qualities that influence successful relationship building can seem amorphous. Rolling the dice on an overture to a new contact or discussing an expanded service offering with an existing client doesn't offer a guaranteed outcome. The unknown is uncomfortable, unpredictable, and very different from relying on precedent, laws, and regulations. These aren't the rules of engagement that most lawyers welcome. And we know that these overtures and discussions don't always succeed – which is tough for goal-oriented achievers, who are wired to win.

Resistance is rarely personal. It's largely structural and cultural. Lawyer pushback or even lack of engagement are often compounded by institutional issues such as poor training and incentive misalignment. Many lawyers have only a loose understanding of what business development means and, therefore, how to integrate it into their professional lives at all, let alone effectively.

They often think BD means suffering through awkward dinners with strangers or uncomfortably asking casual contacts for work. They don't know that it can and should be much more natural and involve listening, sharing insights, and serving as a business partner.

Institutional obstacles can sabotage efforts to integrate BD into a lawyer's professional identity. Firms often say they want lawyers to engage in business development without truly recognizing the full landscape of what activities that encompasses. Many reward high hours, technical excellence, and activities that fuel internal visibility, but they offer only anemic recognition and rewards for behaviors that contribute to strong client relationship development. This cultural disconnect can exacerbate pre-existing lawyer resistance to valuing business development at the same level as technical skills or hours billed. Rather than compound the problem, firms should look to shift their approaches.

To move the needle and reduce the disconnect between what behaviors are incentivized and what behaviors are desired, strategic firms look to retool their strategies and fundamental structures. For instance, a few simple questions can begin to shift the institutional mindset. Firm leaders should ponder:

- Do our lawyers view BD as a component of professional excellence?
- Do we reward relationship stewardship? Do we recognize it at the same level we reward hours billed?
- Do we train lawyers to understand clients' businesses and industry? Do we educate them on our own?
- Do we foster a cohesive team model of support for our clients and reward collaboration among our professionals, at all levels and in all types of roles?
- Do our leaders model client engagement behavior to demonstrate authentic institutional commitment to nurturing relationships?
- Do our tools and systems make relationship cultivation and nurturing easy or difficult?

Firms need to help lawyers redefine success. Historically, being a great lawyer has equaled demonstrating technical excellence, achieving high billable hours, and developing a positive internal reputation. A new model should shift what success looks like. In this version, success translates to a great lawyer being a professional who serves as a trusted client partner, developing and offering industry insights while focusing as much on "lawyering" as on acting as a collaborative and strategic relationship builder.

Certainly, the quickest way to demonstrate tangible commitment to these goals is to institute a compensation system that rewards desired behaviors. Nothing shapes culture as effectively as strategically aligned compensation systems. Without that alignment, any articulated commitment will fail to ring true.

Beyond aligning comp – for more on which see chapters four and five – firms need to establish and showcase more holistic success models that emphasize client leadership, relationship stewardship, and business-focused partnership. Workshops, coaching, and resources are excellent components to support client development. But culture does not change through training alone. Cultural shifts require the imprimatur of leadership on new models of professional success and identity.

In championing this sort of cultural shift, leadership needs to demonstrate, endorse, and reward behaviors it wants emulated, repeated, and woven into the fabric of the client care and relationship development its attorneys provide across the entity. Managing partners and practice heads should demonstrate curiosity about clients, proactive relationship management, and collaboration across the enterprise. Firms should celebrate relationship expansions, client insights, and forward-thinking, opportunity-focused practice-growth efforts as well as lauding traditional success metrics such as originations and positive major-matter outcomes.

Recasting business development as a core professional responsibility

If we reframe business development effectively, we can more easily move beyond the pushback, the resistance, and the fear and apprehension. Many lawyers associate business development with networking or PR or promotional activity. Clients and contacts, however, experience it differently. Clients value lawyers who understand their businesses and industries, who anticipate, and red-flag challenges, and who offer practical, business-driven insights. These aren't "marketing" activities – they are professional behaviors that fuel meaningful engagement and relationship development. They build trust and camaraderie and a sense that "we're in this together" and "you have my back".

The shift is not about learning to sell. The shift is about expanding one's role – taking it from executing work to shaping outcomes. The most effective lawyers think beyond the matter and look deeper. They dig into their clients' businesses. The move from legal technician to business partner. The turning point occurs when lawyers understand that business development is fundamentally about the care and keeping of clients.

The most effective BD is fueled by understanding client needs, anticipating risks and opportunities both for the client and for oneself, and helping clients succeed, so the relationship and the trust deepen consistently over time. This aligns perfectly with legal professionalism, and, in fact, it mirrors many of the primary ethics guidelines in the American Bar Association Model Rules of Professional Conduct,[1] which focus a great deal of attention on client communication and relationship hygiene.

The best lawyers and business developers already are engaging in white-glove client care. They learn their clients' products and services, develop fluency in their industries, follow related news and developments, understand their corporate structures, and know their competitors. By doing those things, those lawyers are best equipped to advise their clients and tailor their guidance to clients' unique needs and situations. Their bespoke advice optimizes their clients' positions and cements those lawyers' roles as true business partners. And that is BD. Just as lawyers must remain competent, communicate with clients, and protect client interests, they must also ensure the client relationship thrives.

A business partner understands the client's day-to-day role, knows the company, anticipates issues, provides contextual judgments (not just answers), and maintains long-term relationships. When a lawyer immerses themselves to that level, BD emerges naturally. If done right, client service extends into client development. Why? Because business partners stay close to clients and expand those relationships organically. Trust and reliance deepen as relationships evolve. Firms can institutionalize this view by adopting the narrative. Instead of asking lawyers to "do more business development", firms should challenge them to become true business partners with their clients and equip them with the knowledge and tools to support that objective while incentivizing and rewarding those who engage.

Making the shoe fit – authenticity as strategy

Thankfully, there is no single BD model. Writers, connectors, educators, introverts, extraverts – come one, come all, there's a method for everyone! When lawyers approach client development in ways that align with their talents, their interests, their life stages, and their priorities, they position themselves for success. Their actions, overtures, and interactions will ring true, feel natural, and ultimately resonate more meaningfully with clients, connections, and prospects because they'll be obviously authentic, and authenticity builds trust.

How does one determine that authentic path? Most lawyers haven't spent considerable time indulging in self-analysis or, as noted, exploring best practices for building business. A basic self-assessment is really all that's needed. Sure, there are fancy systems, digital tools, and even old-school, color-coded schematics in which they can invest to explore their deepest selves. But a few simple questions really should do the trick or, at least, prime the pump enough to start the journey.

In taking those initial steps toward exercising BD muscles and determining how to weave it into one's professional DNA, lawyers should consider:

- What do you enjoy doing? Are you the proverbial "people person"? Is networking your thing?
- Or are you an orchestrator? Does that interest in others and ease with connection translate better into a people-intensive yet somewhat behind-the-scenes role?
- Are you a "connector", to use Malcolm Gladwell's term,[2] who is adept at professional matchmaking and facilitating introductions and relationships for others beyond your own?
- Does the above sound like a nightmare? Would you far prefer a quiet office, some hefty research hours, and the satisfying production of a cerebral tome with serious heft that could become an indispensable guide for in-house counsel operating within your service sector or practice area?
- Maybe that research and writing has appeal but you're less about heft and more about pith. Blogging, or quick despatches shot directly to contacts or shared on social media platforms may be more your speed.
- Do you dig into client industries and horizon-scan for issues in the markets they're prioritizing and sectors in which they operate? Do you enjoy taking your wonk-level industry immersion to the podium and speaking at conferences?

It could be that your fires are lit by none or all or some of the above. The point, though, is to give intentional thought to your personal drivers and preferences so you can more readily identify activities with which you are most comfortable and conversant. Those activities are the ones into which you can most easily settle, the ones that will most seamlessly integrate into your day, and the ones that will most effortlessly weave into the ways in which you interact with existing clients, professional contacts, and new acquaintances. Like Cinderella's slipper or Goldilocks' choice of chair, fit is key. Natural inclinations and talents are crucial to determining which client development activities will feel "just right".

Sustainability – embedding BD in behavior

Business development becomes manageable when it is integrated into daily habits. The most effective business development approach is the one lawyers will actually commit to taking. BD muscles need to be exercised regularly. Like wins in the gym, client development success is built through consistent, small actions – sharing insights, following up, asking targeted questions, initiating an introduction, reaching out regularly. These behaviors compound over time. Curiosity leads to engagement. Engagement creates value. Value builds trust. Trust creates opportunity. Opportunity strengthens reputation. The cycle perpetuates.

Once attorneys refine their thinking on what types of activities best align with their personalities, their talents and their interests, they can use that knowledge to inform their approach to client development. Whether solo or with marketing professionals at their firms, lawyers can develop a personal strategy suited for them. Once the overall strategic approach is identified, lawyers are better positioned to craft a plan that will gain traction and be sustainable. A personal client development plan should include activities compatible with strengths and inclinations and identify specific and measurable goals, benchmarks, and outcomes. The greater the specificity, the easier the execution – and the easier it is to see what works best and where to invest time and energy most effectively.

Initiating the type of activity that can lead to professional transformation isn't all that complicated. With just some small steps, lawyers can begin to move from technicians to partners, from order-takers to issue-identifiers, and from risk assessors to true business partners engaging in industry and company-specific opportunity, threat, and development discussions with their clients. Lawyers can exercise their relationship-building muscles by regularly "next-stepping" from their daily interactions and engaging in deeper dives into their clients' businesses. They should regularly explore their clients' industries, determine how current economic and political developments might impact, follow clients' established and emerging competitors, and synthesize that information so to position themselves as business partners, proactively identifying key developments, opportunities, and risks and suggesting mechanisms and routes to approach them optimally. Actions flowing from this client-care strategy can involve things such as sending an article relevant to a client's industry, introducing two professional contacts to each other, touching base with a client after a major event or development, and asking about upcoming challenges. This isn't sales – this is relationship building.

Integrating this type of client development activity into professional responsibilities means it needs not only to be aligned with personality, strengths and interests but also in sync with logistics. BD activity must be woven into the fabric of lawyers' days or it will fall by the wayside. Client development isn't something "done" at 3pm on a Thursday or only when at a business lunch or when networking with clients. To truly make it a part of who and what one is as a professional, lawyers need to incorporate that mindset across the board. Lofty goals and ambitious aspirations can sound great, but if they aren't realized, they're just fluff. The rubber meets with road when one consistently commits.

With this in mind, it's important to note that client development will likely look different at various life stages, both from the perspective of what activities might fit with a certain schedule and the level of sophistication with which one performs various types of activities. In determining how and in what ways they can incorporate BD into their lives, lawyers may want to consider issues along the lines of:

- How many hours a week am I prepared, or able, to devote to client development efforts? Do I need to try to structure those hours within certain days or timeframes? What flexibility do I have?
- Have I assessed or assigned priority levels to my professional relationships to assist in allocating my time to its highest and best use?
- Which activities and interactions with clients and professional contacts will I prioritize? If I am newer in my career or newer to a firm, should I incorporate internal marketing and relationship building into prioritized activities?
- Are there commitments and activities I have in my personal life that I can leverage for, or in support of, client development so I can optimize my time by marrying the personal and professional? For instance, if an attorney is coaching a child's sports team or serving on a condo residents' board, can the associated relationships and interactions further their client development efforts in any way?

Client development done well, as noted, is highly personal. As such, these types of questions and the commitments and activities they drive very much need lawyer input and direction. Only the lawyer can truly determine what will fit into a schedule or be sustainable from a time-management standpoint or be compatible with family commitments.

With that said, some general guidelines easily apply to the nuts-and-bolts of client development. The golden rule of these is that if it's not scheduled, it's not happening. Leveraging basic tools like an Outlook calendar can take lawyers a long way toward staying on course with their BD plans. Of course, there are events and commitments that need to be slated, but, just as importantly, scheduling a weekly BD check-in with oneself is critical. At that weekly touchpoint, lawyers should review the past week's activities, handle follow-up outreach and action, and prioritize the coming week's client development goals. Amidst the busy days of a demanding legal career, a week can pass in the blink of an eye, and a month can quickly whiz past. Intentionally carving out an hour a week for a BD check-in helps to avoid the predicament many lawyers end up in when they realize it's been six months since they touched base with a prospect or sent an article they'd mention they would share with a client, for example.

A simple routine will keep lawyers on track and accountable. Those regular check-ins are also an effective way to track the efficacy of various investments (of time and/or funds) as lawyers can note outcomes such as whether a particular event was worthwhile or if an article they published received expected traction. Measuring impact and value along the way makes it easier and more manageable. Another solid practice is to slate and undertake a quarterly assessment of plan status and return-on-investment from various activities. This is an excellent opportunity to recalibrate an annual BD plan as needed and institute any course corrections required.

Firms can further individual lawyer efforts with a host of programs. From client feedback and listening programs to key client initiatives to industry teams to BD coaching, firms have a broad universe from which they can choose in order to promote client development and bolster attorney engagement. Technology platforms integrating relevant firm and client data play an important role in supporting these efforts as well. A CRM (client relationship management system), an ERM (electronic relationship management system), and business intelligence tools that provide market intelligence paired with firm data are essential to assessing, informing, expanding, and solidifying client relationships. Marketing and BD teams can also direct and support these efforts as facilitators, coaches, and strategists, providing insights, connecting dots across the firm, and conceptualizing meaningful client-facing activity from thought leadership to educational programming. Even if firms do a poor job of showcasing the tools and resources available, lawyers should take it upon themselves to investigate what is on offer and avail themselves of the support on offer.

The nutshell

The firms that succeed in coming decades won't be those with the most aggressive marketing strategies or the highest-volume PR hits. Rather, the firms that thrive in this ever-evolving legal landscape will be those where the lawyers understand something deeper – that serving clients fully means investing in building and nurturing relationships, immersing themselves in clients' industries, anticipating client challenges and needs, and extending themselves authentically to help clients succeed.

Firms seeking to embed client development holistically into lawyers' professional identities should:

- Change the language around business development;
- Recast BD as an organic and expected extension of top-notch client service and sophisticated lawyering in keeping with the RPC and professionalism expectations;
- Align compensation systems to incentivize and reward desired behaviors and outcomes;
- Provide training on the business of law and industries relevant to the firm's client base;
- Offer business development coaching to support individualized planning for lawyers;
- Integrate client development skill-building and milestones into career progression and performance assessment;
- Provide tools and resources for client relations activities such as client feedback and key client teams; and
- Laud and recognize relationship success stories and client relations wins.

Client development is not a discipline separate from the practice of law. BD is excellent lawyering, practiced intentionally and stemming from bespoke, attentive client service. It is a mindset. Lawyers who are curious, consistent, and client-focused build stronger relationships – and practices. When lawyers see business development as part of their professional identity, growth becomes a natural by-product of their excellent lawyering.

References

1 ABA Model Rules of Professional Conduct: www.americanbar.org/groups/professional_responsibility/publications/model_rules_of_professional_conduct

2 Malcolm Gladwell, *The Tipping Point: How Little Things Can Make a Big Difference* (Abacus, 2002)

Chapter 8: From knowing and doing to being – how lawyers become effective, wholeperson practitioners

By Diane Rosen, EdD, JD, MBA and Natalie Loeb, MS

The legal profession has changed dramatically in recent decades. There are more laws and regulations, new practice areas, exceedingly complex transactions and disputes, and increased specialization – complicated by the fact that more legal issues are multi-disciplinary. Lawyers are expected to be available around the clock, but clients want to decrease legal bills. Technology has sped up the pace of work, communications, and the ability to generate work product while automating some practice areas, making room for other professionals not practicing law to deliver certain services. The advent of artificial intelligence and its role in generating documents, analysis and strategy has further muddled how and what to learn.

Law is considered a 'practice' – a continual work in progress where ongoing learning is fundamental to keep current and develop the skills critical to law practice. However, the substantive law studied in law school is not sufficient to produce competent lawyers. Dynamic, complex modern law practice requires learning to act, work, and feel like a lawyer to become a professional with a strong professional identity. The process by which lawyers actually become effective practicing lawyers, however, remains something of a mystery.

The underlying assumption is that somehow, by osmosis or magic or grit, these qualities and abilities will manifest after law school. Magical thinking is not a viable strategy, so how does this transformation occur? The informal and incidental learning that takes place in the course of law practice fuels the process of moving from knowing the law to acting like a lawyer to being one.

Old school law school

Legal education is perceived as a form of traumatic intellectual hazing – an intensive, inhospitable, academic experience where mere mortals are transformed into lawyers. Law school teaches students to work hard (putting aside personal life) and compete for and value external rewards (grades, law review, high-paying jobs). In the course of legal training, they become habituated to competition, excessive workloads, and stress, where fatigue and anxiety may replace enthusiasm.[1]

American law schools immerse students in the study of the law (doctrinal learning) and its application to fact patterns through the study of cases and statutes to teach students the vocabulary and methodology of legal analysis and concepts. Legal education tilts toward a cognitive bias that ranks knowledge of law, rational analysis, reason, and detached and unemotional objectivity over exploring the emotional, human, and contextual dimensions of case law or how to make meaning from and then apply what is learned. Law school produces graduates who may think more like law professors than practicing lawyers, often with inaccurate senses of actual lawyering.[2]

There is much written about the need for law school to address more than thinking like a lawyer. It must also address skills and practice; professional values and identity; support students' self-reflection; lifelong and self-regulated learning; and honor, justice, rule of law, integrity, and fair play.[3] Law schools have experimented with various ways to improve and humanize legal education to build emotional intelligence, social, and communication skills, empathy, and reflection, and teach practical skills (document drafting, discovery, business basics, trial logistics, etc.) but this remains a work in progress.

Legal education, however, generally leaves newly minted lawyers, fresh from law school and a grueling bar exam, with little to guide them in navigating their careers as they transition from students to practitioners. New hires jump into work without specific preparation for the practice area, organizational culture, client interaction, practical skills, or a clear indication of how to become competent lawyers. The idealized apprenticeship model, where young lawyers learn from their elders, has, for the most part, diminished as the practice of law has transformed to the legal business.[4]

If law school does not graduate practice-ready attorneys who are prepared to meet the demands of the profession, then how do lawyers move from knowing the law to actually becoming capable, effective attorneys?

Professionalism, professional identity, professional formation

Lawyers are not just professionals – they are people who function in multiple roles, one of which is being a lawyer. Becoming a lawyer requires absorbing and orienting to the norms of the profession throughout one's career. The

Best Practices Report[5] sums up professionalism as the values, behaviors, attitudes, and ethical requirements of the profession, encompassing the formal rules of professional conduct plus meeting the expectations of the public and best traditions of the profession.

Professionalism contemplates being a trusted adviser, commitment to client service, self-directed professional development, doing not only what is legally permissible but what is right, and technical expertise, being an effective leader, and meeting ethical responsibilities to clients, firms, the rule of law, and civil society.[6]

Professionalism in the law has also been framed as professional identity formulation – moving from outsider through growth in skill and knowledge to become an engaged member of the professional community in a process of socialization, learning what it means to be a lawyer, cultivating a sense of self as a member of the profession, and seeing oneself and being seen as a lawyer.[7]

Despite the ambitious characterizations of professionalism and creating a professional identity, adherence to these standards within the legal community is hard to measure and even harder to enforce. That is left to individual lawyers to self-orchestrate while they also develop a broad array of practical skills.[8] These behaviors strengthen professionalism for lawyers and legal administrators, enabling them to handle pressure, improve interpersonal dynamics, and build stronger leadership, management, emotional intelligence and communication skills to be successful as a lawyer.

What competencies and characteristics do lawyers need?

Lawyers must juggle multiple roles and tasks as they toggle between abstracting doctrine and applying it to facts in a context of uncertain outcomes, relying on experience and analysis. Lawyers need to cultivate specific competencies and characteristics. Multiple studies and legal scholars have identified an array of competency factors for lawyers, including:

- Ability to interpret, explain, persuade, and categorize;
- Accountability and judgment;
- Being able to deal with uncertainty;
- Business development;
- Business/technology competence;
- Client and business relations;
- Conflict resolution;
- Emotional intelligence;

- Leadership;
- Mathematical abstract thinking;
- Planning, project management, and organizing;
- Research and information gathering;
- Resilience;
- Selecting practice areas and job contexts that align with values, strengths, skills, and preferences;
- Social proficiency;
- Speaking and writing skills; and
- Working with others.[9]

Learning to be a lawyer

Becoming an effective lawyer is built on iterative experiences. Learning from experience is an intuitive, appealing concept. We process where we have been, thought, felt, and acted, and make choices and decisions (conscious/unconscious) that direct (in)action, which affects future thinking and behavior in an ongoing, mutually reinforcing feedback loop. Learning has been defined[10] as knowledge creation resulting from processing experience through a cycle of feeling, reflecting, thinking, and doing.

Each attorney must chart his/her own course by watching, doing, and learning, figuring out the hierarchies, how to comport oneself, how to get advice and help as needed, what it takes to advance and succeed, and constantly recalibrating in a fast-paced high-stakes environment. The learning cycle that supports this can happen in a flash or evolve over time and operates on the micro level (in the moment) and macro level as the practitioner builds an archive of experiential learning on which to draw in real time and in planning for next steps. The experiences from which lawyers learn range from content-driven formal instruction, self-study, observation and vicarious experiences, dialogue, mentorship, and other informal and/or incidental learning.

Via interactions with, and observation of, others, lawyers learn skills, knowledge, strategies, rules, consequences, etc., and what is useful and appropriate. They then base their actions on their beliefs about themselves and the outcomes they expect from their efforts. Thus, while individuals process experiences via an internalized learning cycle, the valence and impact of those experiences exist within social structures and environments that affect each touchpoint in the learning cycle and further inform what those experiences mean. The interconnection of the internal and external in making sense of experiences and what to do with that information contributes to one's experience of oneself, how one is situated in one's environment, and ultimately to the professional evolution of each lawyer.

Lawyers have a heavy lift post-law school. Lawyers primarily work autonomously, figuring things out, making factual and legal determinations, and responding to and generating questions and solutions in real time. Much time is spent alone drafting, researching, on calls, in meetings or court, often with limited time to discuss ideas with others in the moment or get meaningful supervision. However, to become effective practitioners, lawyers must be agile, creative, and focused, and be able to use their skills and knowledge in service of client representation.

Informal learning (IL) is something everyone experiences outside of formal education. IL is not particularly conscious, systematized, organized, or structured. It is natural, anecdotal, and can result from trial and error or problem solving, as well as learning through experience, social interaction, and networks. IL is enhanced by critical reflection, meaning-making, analysis, and questioning. It is not always visible or easy to measure. IL may be integrated with work, emerge from communities of practice, mentoring, or coaching, or may be an internal experience. In the workplace, IL thrives in a learning culture and is crucial in constantly and rapidly changing environments where people are dealing with complex issues.[11]

Legal training to issue-spot and find patterns may uniquely position lawyers to sort, capitalize on, and operationalize IL. Becoming an autonomous, self-directed learner does not rest on agency and self-efficacy beliefs in noticing and optimizing opportunities expanding autonomy. Cues, feedback, goals, priorities, strategies, and perceptions come from reflection, intention, and interaction with others.

Becoming a professional[12] requires various propositional and practical knowledge, as well as familiarity with practices. In developing this knowledge base, professionals cycle through four dimensions of expertise – unconscious incompetence, conscious incompetence, conscious competence, and unconscious competence. The role of IL in professional formation – particularly where there is no formal instruction in place – has been developed into a taxonomy of informal professional learning methods,[13] with a shorthand acronym of PROFESSIONAL:

Practice and repetition
Reflection
Observation and copying

Feedback
Extra-occupational transfer
Stretching activities
Switching/perspective changing
Interaction with mentors/coaches
Osmosis/unconscious absorption
Neurological/psychological devices or techniques
Articulation
Liaison/collaboration

Organizations can create settings that facilitate IL. The factors most critical to early-stage career professionals are the challenge and value of the work, feedback and support, and commitment and personal agency.[14] Implementation of such practices can potentially improve confidence, provide support and feedback, and create more opportunities to learn through interactions and having appropriate challenges.[15] In designing organizational practices, beware common pitfalls such as assuming one-size-fits-all development, not building in ownership and accountability for relevant parties, and equating substantive skill with soft skill development.

Organizations can promote practices that can support development and informal learning. These include:

- Allocating and structuring assignments to encourage individual participation and collaboration.
- Clearly articulating firm values, pathways for advancement, and performance, behavioral, and other expectations.
- Creating processes that enable group work activities, working alongside others, tackling challenging tasks, and working with clients.
- Deliberately and intentionally promoting and reinforcing critical thinking, emotional intelligence, self-regulation and self-efficacy, and self-advocacy.
- Designing staffing models that expose lawyers to a broad array of matters, lawyers, and clients and ensure equitable access to high-value work.
- Emphasizing autonomy plus support for lawyers to maximize opportunities for learning via a balance of hands-off and hands-on management, constructive/timely feedback and coaching, and formal and/or substantive learning as needed.
- Establishing infrastructure for meaningful formal and informal

mentorship to connect with others in the firm and reinforce an apprenticeship model.
- Moving from performance management (hitting metrics to inform advancement and compensation decisions) to performance sustainability (to enhance engagement, provide meaningful feedback and assistance for development), clarify expectations of performance and progress, and make feedback routine and in real time whenever possible.
- Providing coaching resources at all levels and at transition points (e.g., associate to counsel/partner).
- Prioritizing offering chances to be in the room and in the trenches with colleagues, clients, and others.[16]

How individuals can maximize and self-direct their learning

Ongoing learning occurs at all ages and stages during a career. Being mindful of seeking and taking advantage of opportunities is a sure way to optimize professional growth and development, expanding competencies, and developing the soft skills that support effective law practice.

Learn by doing. Direct experiential learning.	• Break tasks into components, get immediate feedback, and repeat with adjustments. • Seek progressively harder assignments that isolate target skills. • Use after-action debriefs to capture lessons before they fade.
Learn by observing. Vicarious learning.	• Ask for specific opportunities to be in the room. • Harness peer learning via case rounds, mock negotiations, and cross-practice clinics. • Observe skilled practitioners in meetings, negotiations, and court.

continued on next page

Reflective practice. Reflect in-action (while doing) and on-action (after doing).	• Build reflection rituals to convert experience into durable learning (e.g., debriefs, at regular intervals). • Keep short learning logs detailing what went well, what went less well, what you might do differently. • Periodically review learning logs to track growth and patterns.
Self-awareness/self-direction. Seek and respond to coaching and feedback (formal and informal).	• Set measurable, actional behavioral goals and accountability mechanisms. • Solicit 360-style input on observable behaviors. • Translate insight from coaching/feedback into habit.
Visibility. Opportunities to be seen and self-advocacy.	• Be intentional about building relationships that expose your work to decision makers and clients. • Demonstrate reliability and impact so advocates have evidence to champion you. • Seek sponsors who are willing to who advocate on your behalf for assignments, introductions, and promotions.

Becoming a lawyer is not a solo endeavor

While lawyers may do much of their work independently, they are rarely working in a vacuum. For those working in organizations (firms, in-house, public sector) the success of the organization, as well as that of individuals, is built on interdependence, collaboration, and synergy among members at all levels. Coaching, mentoring, and sponsorship are all tools that can support professional development. They can be initiated within organizations, in some cases via established programs, or by individuals themselves outside of their workplaces.

Coaching

Executive coaching can serve as a resource through which an individual can identify strengths, develop and amplify interpersonal skills and relationships, build on previous success and learn from mistakes, increase self-awareness and emotional intelligence, improve self-regulation, and clarify and articulate personal and professional goals together with action plans in pursuit thereof. Lawyers can be encouraged to feel better about (and more committed to) their work, more connected to others, and primed to make thoughtful and deliberate career and personal decisions.

At the heart of executive coaching is a confidential, collaborative relationship between coach and client built on trust, the primary purpose of which is for the coach to assist the client with moving toward personally valued objectives developed and articulated by the client, and to reach his or her potential and optimize capabilities and talents. The process includes identifying goals and intentions and exploring pathways to reach those. Depending on the needs of the client, coaching can focus on myriad matters including a current position/situation, transition, skills acquisition/development, specific or general learning, and/or behavioral matters, all in service of improving the client's performance, wellbeing, and satisfaction in connection with the client's desired outcomes. Through the process, clients can challenge self-limiting beliefs and thoughts, imagine new possibilities, and experience insights to move in a desired direction with intentionality and commitment while being kept accountable.

Lawyers are excellent candidates for coaching because, as is integral to the practice of law, they tend to be self-motivated, results-oriented, and focused on creating and implementing plans. Lawyers are trained to issue spot, and once aware of the issue, to seek solutions. This process aligns well with situation analysis and formulation of action plans. As achievers, lawyers want to be proactive to get to the desired outcome, a critical element in the coaching process.

As a group,[17] lawyers typically score high on personality traits such as skepticism and autonomy but low on sociability, and since effective coaching is personalized, self-directed, requires critical thinking, has clients taking the lead, analyzing the situation, finding one's own solutions and asking questions, lawyers and coaching are a good fit.

Although there are many areas where lawyers can benefit from coaching, getting lawyers to a coach may be complicated. Within the profession, the need to seek help may be considered as a weakness and impediment to advancement. To the extent that working with a coach is framed primarily as a remedial action rather than an opportunity for learning, growth and development, and a positive antecedent to advancement, lawyers may resist coaching. This challenge can be addressed by promoting coaching as a career enhancement tool, emphasizing the confidentiality of the process, and working with coaches who have credibility.

Mentorship

Mentorship is another tool that can help lawyers develop professionally. Traditionally, mentors are more experienced individuals who focus primarily on the career development of mentees. The emphasis of mentorship is on the mentee – coaching, providing visibility and helping the mentee advance his/her career, professional identity, and competencies. Individual lawyers can identify formal and/or informal mentors at their places of work or outside of the workplace who can help them both with technical legal skills relevant to their practice area or more generally to grow as professionals.

In organizational settings, there may be formal mentoring programs, the stated objectives of which may also include helping mentees understand organizational and professional expectations, as well as providing aspirational role models for younger employees. Meaningful mentorship programs require an overarching, mission-driven intention to promote organizational and individual success. It can and should have an impact beyond merely advancing a junior level individual within the organization by providing an opportunity to showcase and operationalize organizational values, as well as fostering relationships among employees at different career stages. The positive impact of *effective* mentoring programs includes improving talent retention, recruitment advantages, grooming employees for success, and clarifying business goals and enhancing communication. The process translates firm culture into action – how to navigate within the company and the business and the passing on of nuanced organizational norms.

Although most mentorship programs are anchored in fostering mentee career advancement, an alternative model for a mentorship program is one that focuses on the reciprocal nature of the relationship itself. In this construct, while traditional mentee career advancement components are incorporated into the program, mentorship transcends the purely teacher/student relationship and is based on mutual growth and learning where both parties have something to gain. It is a more holistic, and less transactional, model where the parties are encouraged to meet each other's needs without expectation of repayment and assumes that "mentorship" is not uni-directional but rather runs in all directions. The value lies in the relationship itself. Relational-oriented mentorship is focused on "power with" (the ability to operate effectively, interdependently, and with connection) rather than "power over" (the exercise of authority). Mentors and mentees are encouraged to think broadly and creatively about transferring and sharing knowledge (in both directions and from multiple perspectives) to learn from each other about substance, organizational (and industry and professional) context, and strengthening interpersonal skills.

Sponsorship

Sponsorship is similar to mentorship but with a different intention. Mentors share knowledge and guide the mentee while sponsors actively promote the sponsee through introductions, opening doors, and providing access to opportunities and resources. Essentially, mentors are advisors and sponsors are advocates. Sponsors are typically senior to, and more experienced than, their sponsee. There are organizations that have formal sponsorship programs, but many sponsorship relationships develop organically or informally.

Coaching, mentorship, and sponsorship are all valuable in the creation of professional identity and growth. Having the opportunity to connect with others in the profession, who are profession adjacent, or just wise and experienced people who have insights to share perhaps more generally than related to lawyering, and/or professionally trained individuals who can help with goal development and execution and increasing self- and other-awareness, all contribute to moving from doing to being.

The whole-person lawyer – integrating identity, skills, and relationships

Individuals create their own careers. In the best case, there are supportive lawyers, at one's place of work or otherwise, who can model competence, effectiveness, excellent lawyering, and provide advice and counsel. Developing as a lawyer is more than skill acquisition. It involves forming a professional identity. Lawyers can and should, with regularity, ask themselves, What kind of lawyer do I want to be? Is my practice aligned with my strengths and preferences? How do I want clients and colleagues to experience me? How can I align my daily habits (time management, communication, interfacing with colleagues, clients, counterparties, pro bono choices, work-life integration) to promote coherence and reduce career friction?

Lawyers can operationalize their professional development with specific strategies as set forth below. These are a sampling of ideas that should be tailored and augmented as appropriate and viable.

Junior lawyers:

1. Articulate a "development plan" that is shared with a mentor or supervisor.
2. Prioritize learning goals – pick two or three skills to improve each quarter and request tasks that target them.
3. Request structured feedback after key matters; propose short debriefs.

Mid-level lawyers:

1. Begin formal mentoring of juniors to sharpen coaching and delegation skills.
2. Convert accumulated experience into leadership – run matters, supervise juniors, lead internal projects.
3. Seek a sponsor by consistently demonstrating impact and making ambitions known to decision makers.
4. Use coaching to enhance personal hard and soft (e.g., delegation, giving feedback).

Senior lawyers:

1. Create stretch opportunities for others and be deliberate about diversifying who gets them.
2. Invest in executive coaching to refine leadership presence, partner management, and business development.
3. Model resilience and work-life integration norms so rising lawyers learn sustainable practice.
4. Sponsor high-potential lawyers publicly – in pitches, staffing, and promotion forums.

Putting it together

In the vernacular, the practice of law is primarily about knowing and applying substantive law. However, it is also about practicing to 'be' a lawyer. Assuming the professional identity of a lawyer and developing a wide range of competencies is like putting on new clothes and finding the right fit to be confident and comfortable. Even for seasoned lawyers, learning continues as new situations arise with a novel matter, a client situation, or even intra-firm politics. Lawyers can always benefit by observing how colleagues, clients, and counterparties communicate, comport themselves, address sensitive issues, manage relationships, etc., while also understanding the ever-evolving norms and expectations within their firms (their practice group, working with other groups, interfacing with clients, staff, and counterparties, etc.).

Becoming an effective lawyer is a process that combines deliberate practice, relationships, behavioral change, and reflective identity work. Mentoring, sponsorship, and coaching are powerful levers within that process that can accelerate the conversion of technical learning into dependable client outcomes, leadership capacity, and career satisfaction. Firms and legal departments that view development as a system – integrating experience, feedback, advocacy, and support – create not only better lawyers, but contribute to the health and resilience of their lawyers and, writ large to the profession.

Portions of this chapter were drawn from Diane Rosen's doctoral dissertation, "Learning from Experience to Build Psychological Capital: A Journey to Wellbeing among Big Law Partners" (2023) Degree: 2023, Columbia University URL: https://doi.org/10.7916/x9qq-kx80

References

1 Krieger, L. S. (2002). Institutional denial about the dark side of law school and fresh empirical evidence for breaking the silence. *Journal of Legal Education 52* (1, 2), 112-129.

Krieger, L. S. (2005). The inseparability of professionalism and personal satisfaction: Perspectives on values, integrity and happiness. *Clinical Law Review*, 11, 425-445.

2 Rosen, D. (2023). *Learning from Experience to Build Psychological Capital: A Journey to Wellbeing among Big Law Partners.* (Doctoral Dissertation). Columbia University. Retrieved from https://doi.org/10.7916/x9qq-kx80

3 American Bar Association, Section of Legal Education and Admissions to the Bar. (1992). *Legal education and professional development – An educational continuum* (MacCrate Report). www.americanbar.org.

American Bar Association, Committee on The Professional Education Continuum. (2013). *Twenty years after the MacCrate Report: A review of the current state of the legal education continuum and the challenges facing the academy, bar, and judiciary.* www.americanbar.org.

Stuckey, R. (2007). *Best practices for legal education: A vision and a road map* (Best Practices Report). Clinical Legal Education Association.

Sullivan, W. M., Colby, J., Wegner, J. W., Bond, L. and Shulman, L. S. (2007). *Educating lawyers: Preparation for the profession of law* (Carnegie Report). The Carnegie Foundation for the Advancement of Teaching.

4 Rosen, D. (2023). *Learning from Experience to Build Psychological Capital: A Journey to Wellbeing among Big Law Partners.* (Doctoral Dissertation). Columbia University. Retrieved from https://doi.org/10.7916/x9qq-kx80

5 Stuckey, R. (2007). *Best practices for legal education: A vision and a road map* (Best Practices Report). Clinical Legal Education Association.

6 Heineman, B. W., Lee, W. F. and Wilkins, D. B. (2014). *Lawyers as professionals and as citizens: Key roles and responsibilities in the 21st century.* Harvard Law School, Center on the Legal Profession. https://clp.law.harvard.edu/assets/Professionalism-Project-Essay_11.20.14.pdf.

7 Fruehwald, E. S. (2015). Developing law students' professional identities. *University of LaVerne Law Review.* https://ssrn.com/abstract=2599057

8 Loeb, N. and Sarnoff, D. B. (2026) *Beyond the Courtroom: Proven Strategies from the Legal Field for Leadership, Emotional Intelligence, and Well-Being in the Modern Workplace.* www.loebleadership.com/beyond-the-courtroom-book

9 Rosen, D. (2023). *Learning from Experience to Build Psychological Capital: A Journey to Wellbeing among Big Law Partners.* (Doctoral Dissertation). Columbia University. Retrieved from https://doi.org/10.7916/x9qq-kx80

10 Kolb, A. Y., & Kolb, D. A. (2005). Learning styles and learning spaces: Enhancing experiential learning in higher education, *Academy of Management Learning & Education*, 4(2), 190212.

11 Marsick, V. J. and Watkins, K. E. (1990). *Informal and incidental learning in the workplace.* Routledge.
Marsick, V. J. (2009). Toward a unifying framework to support informal learning theory, research and practice. *Journal of Workplace Learning*, 21(4), 265-275.
Watkins, K. E., Marsick, V. J. and Faller, P. G. (2018). Transformative learning in the workplace: Leading learning for self and organizational change. In E. W. Taylor and P. Cranton (Eds.), *The handbook of transformative learning: Theory, research, and practice* (pp. 373-387). Jossey-Bass.

12 Cheetam, G. and Chivers, G. (2005). *Professions, competence and informal learning.* Edward Elgar.

13 *Ibid.*

14 Eraut, M. (2004). Informal learning in the workplace. *Studies in Continuing Education*, 26(2), 247-273.
Eraut, M. (2007). Learning from other people in the workplace. *Oxford Review of Education*, 33(4), 403-422.

15 *Ibid.*

16 Rosen, D. (2023). *Learning from Experience to Build Psychological Capital: A Journey to Wellbeing among Big Law Partners.* (Doctoral Dissertation). Columbia University. https://doi.org/10.7916/x9qq-kx80

17 Pladziewicz, C. (2009). *The Value of Coaching in the Law Firm.* Eagan: Thomson Reuters. Retrieved 4 January 2018,
http://nawl.timberlakepublishing.com/files/White+Paper.pdf

Chapter 9:
How internal communications impact morale and firm cohesion

By Allan Schoenberg, chief communications officer, and Renate Wagner, director of internal communications, Vinson & Elkins

Culture as the operating system

Business development in law firms is often framed through individual performance and origination, compensation structures, and formal training. Those elements matter. Yet they do not fully explain why some firms sustain growth across market cycles while others plateau despite strong talent, brand strength, or favorable demand. Sustainable business development is not merely transactional, it is cultural.

A firm's culture determines how effectively professionals collaborate, how knowledge moves across practices and offices, how quickly the organization adapts to evolving client expectations, and whether strategy translates into consistent behavior. Culture shapes whether lateral hires integrate or remain siloed. It influences whether client relationships are institutionalized across teams or concentrated among a handful of partners. It determines whether learning is shared or guarded. In professional services firms, culture decides whether expertise compounds or fragments.

Culture is the operating system through which strategy becomes action. Internal communications is what keeps that system calibrated and connected.

Law firms are distinct. Authority is distributed. Partnership governance diffuses decision making. Professionals are trained to value autonomy and precision. Teams form and dissolve matter-by-matter. Hybrid work reduces the serendipity of hallway conversations. And in most firms, the individuals closest to clients have the strongest influence on priorities. In this environment, internal communications is not a downstream function. It is an imperative leadership discipline. It shapes how professionals interpret firm priorities, how they align around direction, and how they respond to change for forward momentum.

Recent data underscores the urgency of effective internal communications. After peaking in 2020, US employee engagement has declined steadily.

Gallup reports engagement of employees across industries averaged 31 percent in 2025, well below the 2020 peak, alongside declines in clarity of expectations and perceived opportunities to develop.[1] This is not merely an HR concern. In professional services, disengagement erodes collaboration, inhibits knowledge-sharing, reduces discretionary effort, and weakens the consistency of client experience. Internal communications sits at the intersection of clarity, engagement, and performance.

Internal communications strategy directly influences behavior, and behavior drives business development outcomes. When leadership, behaviors, and communication align, firms build trust, engagement, and collective ownership. When they do not, even well-designed business development strategies struggle to take hold.

The culture–communication–leadership loop

Culture is often described as intangible, but research consistently shows that it is measurable and linked to performance. McKinsey & Company's work on organizational health argues that healthier organizations tend to outperform less healthy ones, and that organizational health is a strong predictor of long-term performance and value creation.[2] Trust research reinforces the same point from another angle. Edelman's Trust Barometer findings[3] repeatedly emphasize that trust is fragile and must be earned through credible leadership, consistency, and communication that aligns words with actions.

For professional services firms, these insights point to a reinforcing loop (Figure 1):

- Leadership drives culture.
- Behaviors reinforce culture.
- Communication circulates culture.

Leadership sets direction and models expectations. Behaviors, rewarded or tolerated, signal what truly matters. Communication ensures those expectations are understood across offices, practices, and roles. In law firms, this loop is uniquely fragile. Partnership autonomy can create variability in interpretation. Lateral mobility introduces competing norms and "prior-firm muscle memory". Layer in hybrid work, which reduces informal information flow. In the absence of disciplined internal communications, coherence and cohesion erode quickly.

When leadership, behaviors, and communication align, culture becomes strategic infrastructure. When they diverge, fragmentation follows.

Figure 1: The culture–communication–leadership loop.

Fragmentation shows up in predictable ways – inconsistent client service standards, uneven lateral integration, "information hoarding" by practice groups, internal competition that undermines cross-selling, and a lack of shared language about what the firm is building and why.

Internal communications is not the only lever that shapes culture – it is the system that sustains it, especially in distributed organizations where leaders cannot be everywhere at once.

Translating strategy into shared language

Strategy cannot influence performance unless it is understood. *Harvard Business Review* has written about the gap between strategic intent and execution, emphasizing that organizations often unravel at the point where priorities are not translated into clear, actionable guidance.[4] In law firms, this translation challenge is compounded by the partnership model – professionals are sophisticated, skeptical, and busy; they are not looking for slogans. They are looking for clarity about priorities, expectations, and how their work fits into the larger whole.

Consistent and thoughtful internal communications transforms strategy into shared vocabulary. It reinforces priorities through cadence and repetition. It connects macro-objectives (sector focus, geographic growth, technology investment, client service standards) to daily behavior. The goal is not to "broadcast strategy" once – it is to create shared language that makes strategic priorities clear and usable.

At Vinson & Elkins, a firmwide culture and engagement survey conducted in 2022 captured perspectives across lawyers and business professionals on workplace culture, values, and beliefs. The survey served as a listening mechanism and a mirror showing where the culture was strong, where it was inconsistent, and what professionals valued most. That listening process led to the development of *What Connects Us*, a branded cultural framework articulating four core values, as shown in Figure 2.

Figure 2: What Connects Us.

The framework is deliberately simple. It is not meant to compete with legal work for attention – it is meant to create a common reference point. What matters is not the words on the page – it is whether leaders and teams use those words consistently to reinforce expectations.

Culture gains credibility when it emerges from listening. It gains traction when it is reinforced through communication and modeled by leadership behavior.

For law firm leadership, this is a core insight – business development becomes durable when the culture has shared language for collaboration, service, and growth. When professionals can articulate "how we do work here and why it matters" in consistent terms, institutional client relationships become easier to build, protect, and expand – and top talent easier to recruit and retain.

An important and effective way to express shared language and coalesce organizations and teams is through storytelling. In 2025, Vinson & Elkins landed an extensive profile in *Law360*,[5] highlighting the firm's strong culture – both collaborative and competitive – brought to life through a 25-year-plus running "chili cook-off" tradition. What started as a spirited competition has become an annual, firmwide, cross-departmental ritual that captures the firm's vibrant history and collegial spirit. The result is more than a fun event – it's a living story that connects offices and teams, reinforces shared identity, and gives people something memorable to rally around year after year.

Leaders understand the power of a great story and that human emotions are stirred and inspired by shared narratives. Stories are a way to reinforce culture and turn strategy into something people understand, remember, and act on. McKinsey suggests that leaders should be the Chief Storytellers[6] to articulate and champion the organization's culture and values, translating the abstract into real world behaviors.

Transparency – honesty, consistency, and judgment

Transparency is one of the most cited and least precisely defined concepts in internal communications. It is often confused with volume or immediacy. Transparency is not "sharing everything in real time". It is intentional communication grounded in honesty, consistency, and judgment.[7]

- Honesty builds credibility. People do not expect perfection – they expect truth, and they want authenticity.
- Consistency builds trust over time. When people know where and how they will hear important information, they are less likely to fill gaps with speculation.
- Judgment ensures that communication is contextual, responsible, and aligned with the organization's needs.

The modern environment raises the stakes. Decision windows have collapsed. Conversations happen in real time across multiple channels. Information spreads quickly, often without context. AI has increased both capability and risk – accelerating misinformation, impersonation, and content velocity. Edelman's Trust Barometer research highlights how trust remains scarce and fragile – leaders who appear inconsistent, evasive, or reactive can lose credibility quickly.

Gagen MacDonald's work on human-centric leadership and change underscores this reality – during restructuring, transformation, and AI adoption, clarity and trust become decisive factors. Poorly communicated change increases disengagement and voluntary turnover.[8] In law firms, where professionals value autonomy and are sensitive to ambiguity, communication gaps are filled fast, often by rumor, assumption, or worst-case interpretation.

Transparency is not a single message. It is a system that is created by:

- Predictable cadence (so people know when to expect updates);
- Clear channel roles (so people know where to look); and
- Follow-through (so people trust that what leadership says leads to action).

When transparency is executed with honesty, consistency, and judgment it stabilizes morale, increases engagement, and creates a firmer foundation for collaboration, especially across offices and practices.

Listening as a leadership discipline

Internal communications without listening is incomplete. Listening is not a "nice-to-have" – it is the mechanism that keeps communication grounded in reality.

Gallup research consistently finds that employees who feel heard are more likely to be engaged. More broadly, Gallup emphasizes that leaders play an outsized role in engagement outcomes, meaning that listening must be both systemic and locally embedded in leadership routines, not confined to annual surveys.[9]

A law firm's listening system should include multiple layers:

1. Firmwide listening (surveys, audits, pulse checks, feedback mechanisms) to identify patterns.
2. Leader listening (town halls, open Q&A, office visits) to build credibility.
3. Partner and manager listening (team meetings, 1:1s, structured feedback loops) to convert insight into action.
4. Signal listening (channel analytics, intranet search trends, Q&A themes) to spot friction early.

At Vinson & Elkins, the 2022 firmwide culture and engagement survey provided a broad baseline on values and beliefs, and a communications audit in 2025 evaluated how, where, and when people find information. The audit served as both diagnostic and symbolic infrastructure – it identified friction points (overload, duplication, channel confusion) while signaling that clarity is a strategic priority.

Listening also builds psychological safety. Amy Edmondson's work defines psychological safety as a shared belief that people can speak up without fear of punishment or humiliation.[10] In professional services, psychological safety enables learning, innovation, and cross-practice collaboration. It also enables better client service – professionals ask for help sooner, surface concerns and risks sooner, and share ideas sooner.

A strong culture doesn't just invite input – it converts it into visible action. Around 2010, a Vinson & Elkinsjunior partner felt comfortable pitching a brand-new idea for a client event the firm had never tried – a festive, activity-filled holiday gathering for clients' children. That simple suggestion grew into the large-scale annual Gingerbread Party, now a signature tradition enjoyed by hundreds of clients and their families each year – and a tangible way to deepen client relationships.

When professionals see their feedback reflected in executing events, channel improvements, leadership messaging, or operational changes, trust increases. And trust is the precondition for engagement and successful business development.

Communications architecture – channels, cadence, and governance

A common reason why internal communications is ineffective in professional services firms is not lack of effort, but lack of architecture. Messages proliferate. Channels multiply. Leaders communicate in different styles. Department emails compete with firmwide priorities. It becomes clutter and noise, and people feel overloaded yet uninformed.

To avoid this, firms need a clear communications architecture that defines:

- Which channels exist;
- What each channel is for;
- Who owns each channel;
- How frequently it is used; and
- What standards apply (tone, clarity, audience, actionability).

A mature architecture often includes a mix of the following:

- Leadership messages (strategy, direction, priorities, tone-setting).
- Town halls (context, Q&A, accountability).
- Frequent firmwide email or newsletter (timely updates, predictable cadence).
- Intranet (easily searchable and regularly maintained reference information, policies, evergreen content).
- Internal podcasts/videos (storytelling, culture reinforcement, accessibility).

- Collaboration platforms (Teams, Slack; and increasingly, AI-enabled tools such as Copilot and legal AI assistants).
- Business development and matter-tracking systems (opportunity visibility, coverage, coordination).
- Client and alumni interaction tracking systems (touchpoints, engagements, preferences, newsletter opens).
- Knowledge management systems (easily accessible institutional information).
- Onboarding and continuous learning platforms (integration, early clarity, cultural expectations, ongoing skill development, shared baseline for growth).
- Department and targeted communications (from talent, technology and data services, etc.; audience-targeted communications – i.e., BD Lab,[11] office-specific, etc. – all aligned to firm direction).
- Emergency communications (mechanism for urgent and crisis messaging).

External channels such as a firm's website, client portals and extranets, social media platforms, earned and placed media should all reinforce the internal communications messages.

What really matters is not the number of channels, however – it is the clarity of roles and consistency of messaging. People should know, "If it's urgent, I'll see it here. If it's strategic direction, it will come from leadership here. If it's reference content, it lives here." A channel ecosystem without clear roles produces noise.

Governance by leadership of the communications function is the enabling mechanism to serve as the rudder. Governance does not mean control – it means steering in a coordinated, forward direction with mechanisms such as:

- A shared editorial calendar.
- Standards for clarity, tone, voice, and branding.
- Rules about when to use firmwide channels vs department channels.
- A defined escalation path for urgent updates.
- Metrics ownership (what "success" looks like for each channel).

A robust internal communications ecosystem is directly relevant to business development culture. When communication is coordinated, professionals spend less time searching and more time collaborating. When priorities are clear, professionals align their energy with firm goals. When knowledge is discoverable, teams reuse insight instead of reinventing it. This is how communication becomes a growth lever rather than a productivity drain.

Knowledge-sharing as a growth engine in an era of uncertainty

Business development in law firms depends on institutional knowledge. Sector insight, regulatory experience, litigation strategy, deal and case precedents, and market intelligence must circulate across offices and practices to compound in value.

A firm's advantage is not only what any one partner knows – it is what the firm knows collectively, and how quickly that knowledge can be mobilized to serve clients.

Research links collaboration to performance. McKinsey's work on organizational health points to the value of organizations in sustaining performance over time and through uncertainty.[12] In law firms, this matters because many of the most valuable opportunities are cross-disciplinary – energy and infrastructure deals with regulatory and tax components; disputes that require industry nuance and novel solutions; data and cybersecurity matters that require coordinated advice across practices.

Knowledge sharing is also a cultural question. When professionals believe collaboration is risky or unrewarded, they hoard. When they believe it is valued, and safe, they readily share more.

Legal industry research reinforces this point. BTI Consulting Group's *Client Service A-Team* research shows that corporate clients reward firms that deliver consistent, integrated client service and operate as cohesive teams across practices and geographies.[13] When clients experience the firm as "one team" rather than a set of disconnected individuals, relationships deepen and expand. That is the foundation of institutional client coverage and cross-selling.

Similarly, Thomson Reuters' *Sharplegal* research and related Institute reports point to clients' growing expectations for coordinated, multidisciplinary advice and deeper understanding of the client's business environment.[14] In a world of complex and ever-evolving risk, clients increasingly buy confidence and coordination, not isolated expertise.

Uncertainty heightens the need for knowledge sharing. Decision cycles compress. The pace of change increases. Information overload rises. In these environments, internal communications must do more than inform. It must create meaning so professionals can interpret priorities and act consistently.

This is where internal communications and business development culture converge:

- Morale influences discretionary effort and collaboration.
- Cohesion reduces friction in cross-practice work.
- Clarity aligns behavior with strategy.
- Knowledge sharing improves speed-to-solution and client responsiveness.
- Trust reduces internal competition and increases teamwork.

See Figure 3.

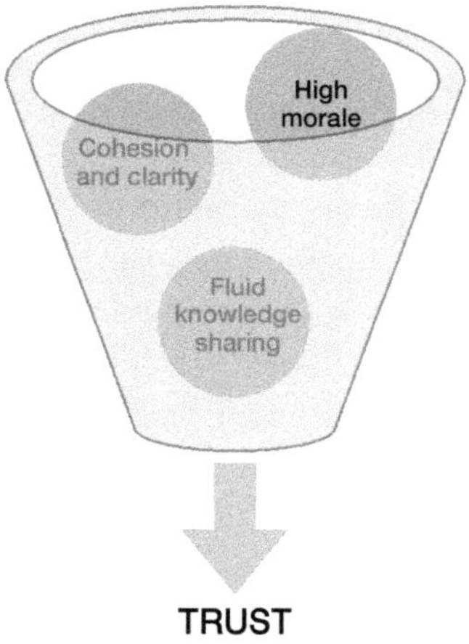

Figure 3: Trust.

The business development implication is straightforward – firms that create systems for institutional knowledge-sharing reduce duplication, increase responsiveness, and deliver more consistent client outcomes. That consistency becomes a differentiator.

Recognition and learning – making culture visible

In law firms, culture is communicated as much by what is recognized as by what is said. Recognition is not simply "congratulations". It is behavioral reinforcement. Celebrating wins tells the organization what to repeat.

Recognition systems that support business development culture often highlight:

- Cross-office collaboration;
- Cross-practice teaming;

- Client service excellence;
- Knowledge sharing and mentoring;
- Business professional contributions; and
- Innovation and improvement efforts.

When recognition is aligned to strategy, it becomes an engine for growth. It signals that business development is not only origination, it is service delivery, responsiveness, teamwork, and institutional contribution.

Learning is the companion to recognition. Firms that create safe spaces for learning and experimentation build stronger cultures. Those safe spaces can be formal (training programs, learning systems, apprenticeships, post-matter debriefs) or informal (manager routines, mentoring, communities of practice, regular feedback). What matters is that learning is normalized and not penalized.

Psychological safety is a key precondition.[15] Without it, professionals refrain from asking questions and admitting uncertainty, avoid reaching across practice boundaries and seniority levels, and hesitate raising new ideas. With it, knowledge flows faster, innovation thrives, and the organization adapts more quickly.

Internal communications can support learning by:

- Sharing practical insights from matters (without breaching confidentiality);
- Highlighting "how we did it" examples;
- Creating recurring formats for knowledge exchange (short interviews, internal podcasts, quick case studies); and
- Surfacing lessons learned during high-pressure moments (post-crisis reviews).

This is also where AI-enabled tools and collaboration platforms can help. When internal knowledge is curated, searchable, and usable, professionals become faster and more confident. Tools do not replace judgment, but they can reduce friction, especially for new joiners and cross-practice teams.

The manager cascade – where strategy becomes real

One of the most overlooked components of internal communications in law firms is the manager cascade. Even the best firmwide message, no matter how well written, rarely translates into behavior unless it is reinforced locally, in the routines where work actually happens.

Gallup's research on engagement consistently reinforces that managers shape how people experience an organization day-to-day.[16] In law firms, "manager" is often broader than a formal title. It includes practice group leaders, office leaders, matter leads, senior lawyer mentors, client relationship partners, and senior business professionals who set the tone within their teams. These leaders are the interpretive layer between firm strategy and individual action.

A strong manager cascade does three things well.

First, it translates strategy into relevance. A firm may prioritize a client sector, cross-selling, innovation, or a culture theme like *What Connects Us*, but people need to understand what that means in their world. A cascade equips leaders to answer practical questions: What should we start doing? What should we stop doing? What does "team-first" look like on our matters? Where are the collaboration opportunities right now?

Second, it creates shared meaning through dialogue, not broadcast. Messages land differently in different practices and geographies. Teams need space to ask questions and test understanding. This is where safe learning spaces are built. Managers normalize "we don't know yet," invite thoughtful skepticism, and surface concerns early rather than allowing quiet disengagement.

Third, it builds feedback loops. Cascades should not be one way. They should generate structured upward feedback (recurring questions, misunderstandings, hotspots, and resistance points) so leadership can adjust messaging, clarify decisions, and address genuine friction.

Operationally, strong cascades are supported by simple tools – short manager briefs with talking points and FAQs, "What this means for your team" prompts, and 10-15-minute discussion guides for practice group meetings. Timing matters. If managers do not discuss key messages within a week, momentum disappears and informal narratives fill the gap.

When the cascade is strong, culture travels faster, strategy becomes actionable, and business development priorities become embedded. When it is weak, firms are left with a familiar problem – a clear plan at the top and inconsistent behavior everywhere else.

Measurement and accountability

If internal communications is positioned as a strategic lever, it must be measurable without turning measurement into an exercise in vanity metrics. Leaders don't need dozens of dashboards. They need credible signals that communications are improving clarity, enabling alignment, and influencing behavior in ways that support performance, client needs, and business development.

The most useful approach is a balanced measurement model – communication effectiveness metrics, paired with behavioral indicators and business-relevant outcomes.

Communication effectiveness includes reach and engagement measures such as email and newsletter open and click rates (directional, not definitive), town hall attendance, intranet traffic and search queries, survey completion rates, podcast listens, and participation in collaboration platforms. These metrics help identify what people are consuming, what they are ignoring, and where they are actively looking for information. The real value is diagnostic – if search queries spike around "strategy", "compensation", or "restructuring", the firm has a clarity gap to close.

Behavioral indicators are where communications begin to show its strategic value. In law firms, these can include cross-practice matter participation, usage of BD or deal tracking systems, participation in onboarding and learning platforms, and measurable patterns of knowledge-sharing (for example, increased contributions to internal playbooks, communities of practice, or training sessions). On the people side, retention risk indicators – especially among mid-level associates and key business professionals – often correlate with clarity and managerial effectiveness.

Finally, business development-adjacent outcomes can be tracked without forcing communications to "own revenue". These include growth in institutional client coverage (more partners and practices engaged with key clients), increased internal referrals, improved lateral integration timelines, and stronger participation in client feedback or account planning processes. In other words – are teams behaving more like a coordinated platform?

Accountability is not about proving that a single email drove a new matter. It is about demonstrating that communications is reducing friction, strengthening cohesion, and increasing the likelihood that the firm executes strategy consistently. Done well, measurement also improves trust – it shows that leadership is listening, adapting, and investing in the operating system of the firm: its culture.

If the firm measures what matters, shares results transparently, and adjusts based on what it learns, internal communications becomes a visible engine of engagement and a practical driver of a stronger, more institutional business development culture.

Culture as competitive advantage in law firms

In law firms, culture is structural.

Partnership governance distributes authority. Practices operate semi-autonomously. Lateral mobility introduces variability. Hybrid work reduces informal information exchange. Cultural coherence is both difficult and essential.

Internal communications becomes a foundational integration.

A strong culture, clearly articulated and reinforced through disciplined communications, creates the conditions for fluid and institutional business development. It does so by reducing friction and increasing alignment. It creates shared language for collaboration and service. It makes expectations visible. It builds trust through transparency executed with honesty, consistency, and judgment. It creates listening systems that keep leadership grounded. It uses recognition and learning to reinforce the behaviors the firm wants to repeat.

The business development and client relationship benefits are tangible:

- More teamwork, because collaboration is normalized and rewarded.
- More sharing, because knowledge is treated as an institutional asset, not a personal advantage.
- More safe spaces for learning, because psychological safety enables questions and innovation.
- Better client relationships, because clients experience the firm as a cohesive, coordinated platform.

Industry research supports this direction. BTI's client service survey underscores that corporate clients reward firms that operate as integrated teams and deliver consistent service across practices and geographies.[17] Thomson Reuters' research similarly reflects rising expectations for coordinated expertise and deeper understanding of client business needs.[18] When clients experience a firm as "one firm", relationships deepen. When they experience it as fragmented, relationships stay narrow.

Business development cannot rely solely on individual rainmakers. Clients increasingly evaluate firms based on cohesion and coordination. Institutional growth depends on institutional behavior. Culture shapes behavior. Behavior shapes collaboration. Collaboration shapes client outcomes. Client outcomes shape growth.

Internal communications is not ancillary to business development. It is the nexus.

Firms that recognize this, and invest accordingly, do not merely communicate more effectively. They compete more effectively.

Practical recommendations for law firm leaders and top communicators

For managing partners and executive leaders:

1. *Treat internal communications as a leadership discipline.* Your messages are not just information; they are cultural signals that reinforce business goals.
2. *Prioritize clarity over volume.* More messages do not equal more transparency. Honesty, consistency, and judgment build trust.
3. *Invest in listening systems – and act on what you learn.* Surveys and audits create value only when they lead to visible improvements.
4. *Model the collaboration you want to see.* Cross-practice behavior starts with leadership behavior.

For communications leaders:

1. *Build a communications architecture.* Define channel roles and reduce noise through governance.
2. *Strengthen the manager cascade.* Strategy becomes real in team conversations, not firmwide broadcasts.
3. *Use recognition as behavioral reinforcement.* Recognize collaboration, knowledge sharing, execution, and client service excellence.
4. *Measure what matters.* Align metrics to business outcomes and cultural indicators, not only engagement statistics.

For practice leaders and managers:

1. *Translate strategy locally.* Help teams understand what priorities mean for their work.
2. *Create safe spaces for learning.* Encourage questions, debriefs, and cross-practice knowledge exchange.
3. *Reinforce the firm's core values through daily decisions and actions.* Culture is what people experience, not what the firm publishes.

References

1 Jim Harter, "U.S. Employee Engagement Declines From 2020 Peak," Gallup, 28 January 2026 www.gallup.com/workplace/701486/employee-engagement-declines-2020-peak.aspx

2 Aaron De Smet et al., "Organizational health is still the key to long-term performance," McKinsey & Company, 12 February 2024 www.mckinsey.com/capabilities/people-and-organizational-performance/our-insights/organizational-health-is-still-the-key-to-long-term-performance

3 Edelman, 2025 Edelman Trust Barometer: www.edelman.com/trust/2025/trust-barometer

4 Donald Sull, Rebecca Homkes, and Charles Sull, "Why Strategy Execution Unravels – and What to Do About It," *Harvard Business Review*, March 2015 (reference listing) https://hbr.org/2015/03/why-strategy-execution-unravelsand-what-to-do-about-it

5 Lynn LaRowe, "V&E Heats Up 'Ridiculous Fun' With Annual Chili Cook-Off," Law360 Pulse, 28 February 2025 https://connect.velaw.com/69/4805/uploads/chili-cook-off—-law360.pdf

6 McKinsey & Company, "The CEO's Role as Chief Storyteller," 30 June 2025 www.mckinsey.com/capabilities/strategy-and-corporate-finance/our-insights/the-ceos-role-as-chief-storyteller

7 Allan Schoenberg, "You Keep Using That Word: Transparency in Internal Communications," *Global Legal Post*, 21 May 2025 www.globallegalpost.com/news/you-keep-using-that-word-transparency-in-internal-communications-1055766540

8 Gagen MacDonald, "Five Priorities in 2026 for Human-Centric Leaders," 14 January 2026 www.gagenmacdonald.com/blog/white-paper-five-priorities-in-2026-for-human-centric-leaders

9 Jim Harter, "U.S. Employee Engagement Declines From 2020 Peak," Gallup, 28 January 2026 www.gallup.com/workplace/701486/employee-engagement-declines-2020-peak.aspx

10 Amy C. Edmondson, "How Fearless Organizations Succeed," 14 November 2018 www.strategy-business.com/article/How-Fearless-Organizations-Succeed

11 Law360, "V&E Is Training Associates To Think Like Business People" https://media.velaw.com/wp-content/uploads/2025/09/03140516/VE-Is-Training-Associates-To-Think-Like-Business-People.pdf

12 McKinsey & Company, "Organizational health: A fast track to performance improvement," 7 September 2017 www.mckinsey.com/capabilities/people-and-organizational-performance/our-insights/organizational-health-a-fast-track-to-performance-improvement

13 BTI Consulting Group, "BTI Client Service A-Team 2023" (and executive summary PDF)
https://bticonsulting.com/bti-client-service-a-team-2023; see also https://bticonsulting.com/wp-content/uploads/2023/03/BTI_Client_Service_A-Team_2023_Executive_Summary.pdf
14 Thomson Reuters Institute, 2023 Report on the State of the Legal Market www.thomsonreuters.com/en-us/posts/wp-content/uploads/sites/20/2023/01/2023-State-of-the-Legal-Market.pdf
15 Amy C. Edmondson, "How Fearless Organizations Succeed," 14 November 2018 www.strategy-business.com/article/How-Fearless-Organizations-Succeed
16 Jim Harter, "U.S. Employee Engagement Declines From 2020 Peak," Gallup, 28 January 2026
www.gallup.com/workplace/701486/employee-engagement-declines-2020-peak.aspx
17 BTI Consulting Group, "BTI Client Service A-Team 2023" (and executive summary PDF)
https://bticonsulting.com/bti-client-service-a-team-2023; see also https://bticonsulting.com/wp-content/uploads/2023/03/BTI_Client_Service_A-Team_2023_Executive_Summary.pdf
18 Thomson Reuters Institute, 2023 Report on the State of the Legal Market: www.thomsonreuters.com/en-us/posts/wp-content/uploads/sites/20/2023/01/2023-State-of-the-Legal-Market.pdf

Chapter 10:
Wellbeing as business infrastructure – why BD cultures fail without psychological safety

By Renee Branson, MA, RB Consulting

The pitch meeting looked perfect on paper.

Six partners from different practice areas gathered in a conference room to prepare for a major opportunity – a long-standing corporate client was expanding internationally and needed coordinated legal support across employment, regulatory, tax, and litigation risk. The firm had the talent. It had the client relationship. It had the opportunity to deepen its role as trusted advisor. But the meeting never quite clicked.

The employment partner spoke first, outlining her approach to the client's workforce expansion. The tax partner offered a few observations but seemed hesitant to elaborate. The litigation partner nodded politely but largely stayed quiet. When the business development director asked whether the team should propose an integrated client strategy, the conversation shifted. Someone asked how origination credit would work.

Another partner noted that the client had historically hired lawyers individually rather than through formal teams. A third suggested that perhaps the firm should "keep the pitch simple". The meeting ended with a plan to submit separate proposals from each practice group. No one openly disagreed. No one argued. But something important had just happened – the opportunity for collaboration quietly evaporated.

From the outside, the meeting looked professional and collegial. Internally, however, subtle dynamics shaped the outcome. Partners hesitated to risk stepping into each other's territory. Questions about credit and ownership lingered beneath the surface. The result was not conflict. It was caution. And caution – when it becomes the default posture – can quietly undermine business development culture.

The hidden infrastructure of business development

Business development asks people to do their most human work in systems that often reward the opposite. We expect lawyers to build trust, collaborate across silos, and bring forward new ideas, while operating in cultures shaped by scarcity, zero-sum credit structures, and chronic cognitive overload.

From a neuroscience perspective, this creates a predictable problem. When the brain perceives threat (whether to status, reputation, or security) it shifts into self-protection. Cognitive resources narrow. Creativity, learning, and interpersonal risk-taking decline.

When psychological safety is absent, business development behaviors don't disappear – they go underground. People hoard relationships, avoid collaboration, and default to self-protection. What leaders often label as disengagement or lack of initiative is, in fact, a neurobiological safety response. Understanding this distinction changes everything about how leaders design BD culture. Harvard Business School professor Amy Edmondson, whose research first popularized the concept, defines psychological safety as a shared belief that a team is safe for interpersonal risk-taking.[1]

Law firms invest millions in business development strategy – training programs, CRM systems, cross-selling initiatives, compensation tweaks. Yet many of these efforts stall or fail outright. The missing ingredient is rarely ambition or intelligence. It is psychological safety.

Business development is inherently relational and risky. It requires people to speak up, ask for help, share credit, admit uncertainty, and tolerate short-term discomfort in service of long-term growth. These behaviors only emerge when the brain registers that interpersonal risk will not result in punishment or loss of standing. None of that happens consistently in environments where fear, internal competition, or reputational risk dominate daily decision making.

This chapter makes a simple but often overlooked case that wellbeing – and specifically psychological safety – is not a "nice-to-have" cultural benefit. It is the operating condition that enables the brain to support the very behaviors business development depends on. It is core business infrastructure for sustainable BD performance.

In psychologically safe environments, people feel comfortable speaking up, asking questions, sharing ideas, and admitting uncertainty without fear of embarrassment or punishment. These behaviors may sound unrelated to business development. In reality, they are central to it. Business development requires lawyers to do things that feel risky:

- Invite colleagues into client relationships.
- Share credit for work.
- Ask for help outside their expertise.

- Propose new approaches in front of peers.
- Admit they may not be the best person to solve a client problem.

When psychological safety is strong, these behaviors feel natural. When it is weak, lawyers instinctively protect their position.

The neuroscience of professional risk

Understanding why psychological safety matters requires a brief look at how the human brain processes threat. The oldest part of our brain, evolutionarily speaking, includes the amygdala. Its job is to avoid danger and it is excellent at it. To do its very important job, it must first power down our prefrontal cortex. That's where our cognition lives. For those of us in knowledge and critical thinking-based careers, it's our money maker. In situations of physical danger, we don't need our pre-frontal cortex. Case in point: if I am out for a swim in the ocean and I see a fin making its way toward me, I don't need my prefrontal cortex getting inquisitive about what kind of shark that might be, at what speed it is traveling, or what it may or may not have already eaten that day. No. I need my amygdala firing on all cylinders, telling me to get the hell out of the water as fast as I can. That's also why we often have clouded memory about an event that triggers our amygdala – physically dangerous or not.

The brain is constantly scanning the environment for cues that signal danger or safety. In professional settings, threats are rarely physical. Instead, they tend to involve social or reputational risk. "Am I walking into a meeting where I am going to be ganged up on or humiliated?" "Will working with this person end up costing me something?"

Research in organizational neuroscience shows that the brain processes social threats – such as status loss, exclusion, or public embarrassment – in ways similar to physical threats. Again, the amygdala is great at what it does, but it is not very good at nuance. When people perceive these risks, the brain shifts into a more defensive posture. Curiosity narrows. Creativity declines. People become more cautious about sharing ideas or exposing vulnerabilities.

In law firms, these dynamics often appear in subtle ways. A partner may hesitate to introduce a colleague to a client if credit allocation is unclear. A junior lawyer may avoid asking questions in front of senior partners. A practice group leader may discourage open debate in order to preserve harmony. None of these behaviors are inherently unreasonable. In fact, they often reflect rational responses to perceived risk. The operative word being "perceived". It is only rational if the perception is correct. If the perception is incorrect, those behaviors become widespread and collaboration suffers.

Why lawyers hesitate to cross-sell

Many law firms assume that cross-selling fails primarily because lawyers lack incentives or awareness of opportunities. In reality, the barriers are often relational. Consider what cross-selling actually requires.

A partner must:

- Trust that bringing in another lawyer will benefit the client.
- Believe the colleague will perform well and protect the relationship.
- Feel confident that credit and recognition will be fairly allocated.

If any of these elements are uncertain, hesitation naturally follows. The stakes are particularly high in professional services, where client relationships often define a lawyer's status and compensation. Even firms that encourage collaboration can unintentionally reinforce protective behavior if credit systems are opaque or inconsistently applied. One recent client shared an experience that illustrates this dynamic. She was considering bringing another partner onto a matter because he had technical expertise that would benefit the client. What should have been a straightforward conversation about how best to collaborate quickly turned into something else.

During their first meeting, the discussion devolved into a negotiation over how to divide credit for the work, an issue the firm left entirely to individual lawyers to resolve among themselves. Instead of spending that time mapping out strategy for the client or exploring how their skills could complement each other, the conversation became a contentious debate about compensation and ownership.

The partner ultimately did move forward with the collaboration, but she acknowledged that the interaction had already shaped her perception of the relationship. "I don't think it will affect the work we do for the client," she reflected afterward, "but it definitely makes me less likely to work with him again in the future."

Moments like these raise an important question – at what point does a low-trust environment begin to quietly influence not only internal relationships, but the quality of service delivered to clients?

The result is a pattern many firm leaders recognize. Lawyers express support for cross-selling in principle, but in practice they hesitate – or avoid it altogether.

The cost of performative collaboration

When psychological safety is limited, firms often develop what might be called performative collaboration. Performative collaboration occurs when organizations adopt the language and structures of teamwork without the trust required to make those structures effective. Client teams may exist on paper but rarely meet. Practice groups agree to share opportunities but continue operating independently. Lawyers attend BD trainings but hesitate to implement what they learn.

This dynamic can also appear in pitch meetings. A carefully assembled group of lawyers, diverse across practice areas, backgrounds, and demographics, delivers a polished presentation to a prospective client, emphasizing the firm's commitment to collaboration and inclusion. The message is clear – this is a firm where different perspectives come together to serve the client. Yet one client later remarked about such a presentation, "Half of those lawyers – maybe three-quarters of them – I never saw or heard from again".

Moments like this reveal the difference between symbolic representation and operational reality. The pitch communicates collaboration and diversity, but the day-to-day work may remain concentrated among a much smaller and less integrated group. When that happens, the organization risks falling into a pattern of performative collaboration and, at times, performative diversity.

Both stem from the same underlying issue – when psychological safety is limited, organizations may showcase collaboration rather than truly practice it. Diverse teams are assembled for visibility, but the trust and openness required to sustain meaningful collaboration over time never fully materialize.

From a leadership perspective, the organization appears aligned. From a behavioral perspective, little changes. The costs of this dynamic are significant.

Lost revenue opportunities

Integrated client service is increasingly important in complex legal matters. Corporate clients rarely experience their challenges through the neat categories that exist inside law firms. A regulatory change may have employment implications. A cross-border transaction may trigger tax, compliance, and litigation exposure. Cybersecurity issues may quickly evolve into governance and reputational risk. From the client's perspective, these issues are interconnected, and they expect their outside counsel to recognize those connections.

When firms fail to coordinate expertise across practices, they leave substantial value on the table. Opportunities to address adjacent legal risks go unexplored. Matters that could deepen the client relationship remain narrowly scoped. The firm may solve the immediate legal issue while missing the broader strategic role it could play.

Fragmented client experience

Clients may receive excellent service from individual lawyers but lack a cohesive strategy across the firm. Clients notice this fragmentation. Increasingly, sophisticated legal departments are selecting outside counsel not simply for technical excellence within a specialty, but for their ability to assemble teams that understand the client's business holistically. Firms that can seamlessly bring together lawyers from different disciplines are better positioned to anticipate issues, offer proactive guidance, and build long-term strategic partnerships with their clients.

By contrast, when collaboration breaks down internally, clients may experience the firm as a collection of highly skilled individuals rather than an integrated advisory team. The work may still be excellent, but the opportunity to deliver greater value – and to strengthen the relationship – has been diminished.

Internal frustration

Business development professionals often sit in a unique vantage point within law firms. Because they work across practices and client teams, they frequently see opportunities for collaboration that individual lawyers may not fully recognize. They can identify complementary expertise, emerging client needs, and strategic connections that could strengthen relationships and expand the scope of work.

Yet recognizing these opportunities and activating them are two very different things.

In many firms, BD professionals must navigate complex internal dynamics when attempting to bring lawyers together around a client opportunity. Encouraging collaboration may require raising sensitive questions about client ownership, credit allocation, or team leadership. Even when those issues are not explicitly discussed, they can shape how lawyers respond to suggestions about expanding a client team.

This places BD professionals in a difficult position. Their role is to facilitate growth and connection across the firm, but they often lack the authority to resolve the structural or cultural issues that make collaboration difficult. As a result, they may spend significant energy trying to broker introductions, coordinate conversations, or encourage participation in client development initiatives – only to encounter quiet resistance or reluctance.

Over time, this dynamic can lead to frustration and inefficiency. BD professionals may feel they are repeatedly identifying valuable opportunities that never fully materialize because the internal conditions required for collaboration are not in place. Meanwhile, lawyers may view BD initiatives as additional pressure rather than as a resource that helps them serve clients more effectively.

When this pattern persists, the firm risks underutilizing one of its most valuable strategic assets – professionals whose role is specifically designed to help lawyers connect their expertise in ways that strengthen client relationships.Top of FormBottom of Form

Cultural cynicism

When leaders repeatedly launch business development initiatives without addressing the underlying cultural barriers that inhibit collaboration, a quieter but equally damaging dynamic can begin to take hold – cultural cynicism.

Many lawyers already approach new initiatives with a degree of skepticism. Research by psychologist Dr Larry Richard,[2] who has studied lawyer personality traits for decades, consistently shows that lawyers score significantly higher than the general population on measures of skepticism. This trait serves an important professional function – lawyers are trained to question assumptions, identify risks, and probe for weaknesses in arguments. In legal analysis, skepticism is a strength.

Inside organizations, however, that same trait can amplify doubts about whether new programs will truly change anything.

When lawyers observe a pattern in which leadership introduces successive BD initiatives (new cross-selling campaigns, client team structures, or collaboration incentives) without addressing the deeper cultural dynamics that shape behavior, skepticism can quickly turn into cynicism. Lawyers begin to view these initiatives less as meaningful strategic shifts and more as temporary management trends.

Comments such as, "We've tried this before" or, "Let's see how long this lasts" begin to surface quietly in hallways and practice group meetings.

Over time, this erosion of confidence makes each new initiative harder to implement than the last. Even well-designed programs may struggle to gain traction because lawyers assume that the underlying dynamics of credit, competition, and risk will remain unchanged.

Eventually, collaboration itself begins to be framed less as an operational expectation and more as an aspirational ideal – something the firm talks about publicly but that lawyers do not fully expect to see consistently practiced.

Case example – a firm that changed the dynamic

The following composite example reflects patterns described by multiple law firm leaders and business development professionals.

For years, the firm had invested heavily in business development infrastructure – CRM platforms, client team structures, and cross-selling incentives. Yet collaboration remained inconsistent across practice groups. Leadership initially assumed the issue was execution. They introduced additional BD training and created more detailed client development plans. The results remained uneven.

Eventually, the firm conducted an internal culture and wellbeing assessment and discovered something revealing. Partners were not resisting collaboration out of stubbornness or lack of interest. They were navigating uncertainty and interpersonal risk.

Many lawyers expressed concerns about:

- Losing control of client relationships;
- Inconsistent application of credit policies; and
- Fear of appearing less capable when seeking help.

None of these concerns had been openly discussed in prior BD initiatives.

In response, the firm shifted its approach. Rather than launching another training program, leadership focused on strengthening psychological safety. They clarified credit-sharing policies and communicated them transparently. Practice group leaders began modeling collaborative behavior by inviting colleagues into their own client relationships. Meetings were redesigned to encourage candid discussion about client strategy rather than polished updates.

Within two years, cross-practice collaboration increased significantly.

The firm did not abandon its BD tools or programs. Instead, it strengthened the cultural infrastructure that allowed those tools to work.

Psychological safety as strategic infrastructure

Infrastructure rarely receives much attention when it functions well. Yet without it, everything else slows down.

Psychological safety plays a similar role in professional services organizations. It supports the behaviors that make business development possible:

- Sharing client insights across practices.
- Testing new ideas for client service.
- Asking colleagues for expertise.
- Coordinating complex matters across teams.

Research across industries consistently shows that teams with higher psychological safety are more innovative, more collaborative, and more adaptable. A widely cited Google study known as Project Aristotle[3] examined hundreds of internal teams and found that psychological safety was the single most important predictor of team effectiveness. In professional services environments where knowledge sharing and collaboration drive value, this finding is particularly relevant.

Psychological safety readiness for BD initiatives

Before launching major business development initiatives, leaders can assess whether their firm's culture supports collaborative behavior.

The following checklist can help identify potential barriers.

Leadership behavior

- Do leaders invite dissenting views during discussions?
- Are mistakes treated as learning opportunities rather than sources of blame?
- Do leaders openly acknowledge uncertainty?

Credit and compensation

- Are origination and matter credit policies transparent?
- Do lawyers trust that collaboration will not harm their compensation?
- Are joint client successes visibly rewarded?

Meeting dynamics

- Do practice group meetings allow for candid debate?
- Are junior lawyers comfortable asking questions?

- Do business development professionals feel empowered to challenge assumptions?

Client ownership culture

- Are client relationships viewed primarily as firm assets or individual assets?
- Do lawyers regularly introduce colleagues to clients?
- Are there clear pathways for expanding client teams?

If leaders encounter hesitation across multiple areas, strengthening psychological safety may be a prerequisite for successful BD initiatives.

Red flags leaders should watch for

Several patterns often signal that psychological safety is limiting collaboration.

Siloed client relationships

This dynamic often emerges subtly. A partner may continue to manage a long-standing client relationship independently even as the client's needs evolve beyond that lawyer's primary expertise. For example, a corporate partner handling transactional work may be aware that the client is facing emerging employment or regulatory issues but hesitate to introduce colleagues out of concern about losing control of the relationship or diluting origination credit.

From the client's perspective, the firm may appear less proactive than competitors that regularly bring multidisciplinary teams to the table. Internally, other lawyers may hear about opportunities only after the matter has already developed, when it is too late to contribute strategically. Over time, valuable expertise remains underutilized and the firm's collective capabilities are never fully visible to the client.

Overly polished meetings

Practice group discussions that lack disagreement or exploration of alternative approaches appear efficient and harmonious at first glance. Partners provide updates, leaders outline priorities, and discussions move quickly from one agenda item to the next. What is missing, however, is meaningful debate.

For example, when discussing strategy for a key client, no one challenges assumptions or raises potential risks. Junior lawyers remain silent even when they have relevant information. Business development professionals may hesitate to suggest new approaches if they sense that disagreement could be interpreted as criticism.

While the absence of conflict can feel productive in the moment, it often signals that participants are withholding candid perspectives. Without open discussion, teams may miss opportunities to rethink client strategy, identify emerging risks, or experiment with more innovative approaches to service.

Reluctance to share information

An ideal example of this are lawyers who hesitate to enter meaningful insights into CRM systems.

Many firms invest heavily in CRM platforms designed to track client interactions, identify cross-selling opportunities, and support coordinated business development. Yet these systems often remain underutilized.

Lawyers may enter only minimal information (basic contact details or high-level meeting notes) while withholding deeper insights about client strategy, upcoming projects, or potential vulnerabilities. In some cases, this hesitation stems from concerns about confidentiality. In others, it reflects a quieter concern that sharing too much information could expose valuable relationships or opportunities to internal competition.

The result is a system that functions more as a directory than a strategic resource. Without robust information sharing, the firm loses one of the key advantages that CRM systems are meant to provide – visibility into how the organization can bring its collective expertise to bear for the client.

BD fatigue

Business development professionals can feel they are constantly pushing reluctant lawyers toward collaboration. A Sisyphean task.

When cultural barriers persist, the responsibility for driving collaboration often falls disproportionately on business development professionals. They may spend significant time encouraging partners to attend client team meetings, coordinating introductions between practice groups, or persuading lawyers to participate in cross-selling initiatives.

In some firms, these efforts begin to feel like an uphill battle. BD professionals repeatedly identify promising opportunities for collaboration, only to see them stall because lawyers are reluctant to share relationships or unsure how credit will be allocated.

Over time, this dynamic can lead to frustration on both sides. Lawyers may perceive BD outreach as pressure rather than support, while BD professionals feel their strategic role is reduced to repeatedly prompting behavior that the firm's culture has not yet fully embraced.

These signals do not necessarily indicate resistance to business development. They may instead reflect underlying uncertainty about interpersonal risk.

Leader behaviors that lower threat

Psychological safety is shaped primarily by leadership behavior. Small actions repeated consistently can dramatically influence how safe people feel taking interpersonal risks.

Model curiosity

Leaders who ask thoughtful questions rather than immediately offering answers create space for broader participation. For some leaders – particularly lawyers – this can feel counterintuitive. Research shows that lawyers tend to score higher on traits like skepticism and perfectionism, which can reinforce the belief that leaders should have the answers rather than ask the questions. In reality, modeling curiosity signals intellectual openness and invites others to contribute ideas, raise potential risks, and explore solutions together. These are the conditions that strengthen both problem solving and collaboration.

Normalize learning

Leaders who treat mistakes as opportunities for reflection rather than occasions for blame create an environment where people feel safer experimenting, raising concerns, and sharing ideas. In professional cultures that prize expertise and precision – such as law firms – mistakes can carry a strong stigma, which can discourage lawyers from taking risks or admitting uncertainty. When leaders openly acknowledge that complex work inevitably involves learning, they help shift the focus from fault-finding to problem solving. This approach encourages teams to surface potential issues earlier, learn from setbacks, and continuously improve how they serve clients.

Share credit publicly

Highlighting collaborative successes reinforces the value of teamwork and signals that shared effort is recognized and rewarded. When leaders publicly acknowledge matters that involved multiple practices, offices, or lawyers working together, they help shift the narrative away from individual "rainmaker" achievements toward collective impact for the client. This recognition not only validates the lawyers involved but also demonstrates to others that collaboration is both valued and expected. Over time, consistently celebrating joint successes helps normalize partnership across the firm and encourages lawyers to seek out opportunities to work together rather than operate in isolation.

Clarify expectations
Transparent credit policies and decision processes reduce the uncertainty that often undermines collaboration. When lawyers are unsure how origination credit, matter leadership, or compensation will be allocated, they may hesitate to bring colleagues into client relationships or share opportunities. Clear and consistently applied policies help remove this ambiguity by establishing fair expectations about how contributions will be recognized. When lawyers trust that collaboration will not jeopardize their standing within the firm, they are far more likely to invite others into client work and pursue opportunities that benefit both the client and the organization.

Invite diverse voices
Encouraging input from across seniority levels signals that expertise is distributed rather than purely hierarchical. When leaders actively invite contributions from associates, junior partners, and business professionals (not just the most senior voices), they create space for ideas and insights that might otherwise remain unspoken. This practice not only broadens the range of perspectives considered in client strategy and business development but also reinforces that thoughtful contributions are valued regardless of title. Over time, it strengthens engagement, surfaces emerging talent, and helps teams make more informed decisions.

Over time, these behaviors create an environment where collaboration becomes easier.

The economics of psychological safety

Beyond cultural benefits, psychological safety has clear economic implications. In professional services firms, value is created through knowledge sharing and coordinated expertise. When lawyers collaborate effectively, firms can deliver more comprehensive solutions and deepen client relationships.

When collaboration stalls, firms experience:

- Lost cross-selling revenue;
- Inefficient duplication of effort;
- Reduced innovation in client service; and
- Increased internal friction.

Conversely, organizations that cultivate psychological safety unlock new forms of value.

Lawyers are more willing to bring colleagues into conversations earlier. Client teams develop integrated strategies rather than fragmented advice. Firms can pursue larger and more complex matters that require coordinated expertise.

In this sense, psychological safety is not simply a wellbeing initiative. It is a driver of organizational performance.

From initiative to culture

Many law firms approach business development primarily through initiatives. They introduce programs, systems, and incentives designed to encourage collaboration. These tools are important. But they function best within cultures that support interpersonal risk-taking.

When psychological safety is present, BD initiatives gain traction quickly. Lawyers share information more freely, client teams become more dynamic, and collaboration accelerates. Without that foundation, even well-designed programs struggle. The difference lies not in strategy but in culture.

A framework for BD culture – the collaboration infrastructure model

Leaders can think about business development culture as resting on four interconnected layers.

1. *Psychological safety.* This is the foundation. Lawyers feel safe asking questions, sharing ideas, and inviting colleagues into client relationships.
2. *Trust and transparency.* There exist clear expectations around credit, compensation, and collaboration.
3. *Collaborative behavior.* Lawyers actively share opportunities, expertise, and client insights.
4. *BD systems and strategy.* CRM platforms, training programs, and structured initiatives all help scale collaboration across the firm.

Many firms attempt to strengthen the top layer – systems and strategy – without reinforcing the layers below it. When that happens, initiatives often underperform. But when the foundation is strong, tools and strategies become powerful accelerators.

The infrastructure leaders cannot ignore

The legal profession is entering a period where collaboration is no longer optional. Clients increasingly expect integrated solutions that draw on expertise across disciplines, jurisdictions, and industries. Meeting those expectations requires more than talented lawyers and sophisticated BD programs. It requires an environment where collaboration feels safe.

Psychological safety may not appear on traditional business development dashboards, yet it quietly determines whether those dashboards improve. When lawyers trust that sharing opportunities, inviting colleagues into relationships, and asking for help will strengthen rather than threaten their position, collaboration becomes real rather than performative. And when collaboration becomes real, business development becomes far more powerful. In that sense, wellbeing is not a peripheral concern for law firm leadership. It is the infrastructure that allows business development culture to function at all.

References

1 Edmondson, A. (1999). Psychological safety and learning behavior in work teams. *Administrative Science Quarterly*, 44(2), 350–383.

2 Richards, L. (2002). Herding Cats: The Lawyer Personality Revealed. *Report to Legal Management*, 29(11).

3 Google. (2015). *Guide: Understand team effectiveness (Project Aristotle)*. Google re:Work.

Chapter 11:
Leveraging AI as a strategic partner in business development

By Jennifer Leonard, founder, Creative Lawyers

Artificial intelligence is already reshaping how professionals work, compete, and grow. It offers unprecedented opportunities to leverage data, relationships, and a firm's experts to understand historical trends related to the firm's past BD efforts, focus directly on the activities that lead to the best BD outcomes, and strengthen business generating activities such as RFP pitches, thought leadership creation, and client alerts. For law firm leaders navigating this transformation, the question is how to harness AI to grow revenue in a time when the billable hour and leveraged labor models are under intense pressure in large part because of AI. So how can we turn AI from a threat to an opportunity?

AI represents something more profound than another technology tool to be deployed or managed. It offers a new form of co-intelligence because it can serve as a strategic thought partner that can fundamentally reshape how firms identify opportunities, articulate their value, understand their clients, and tell their stories. The firms and lawyers who will thrive in this era are not necessarily those with the largest technology budgets or the most sophisticated IT departments. They are those whose leaders foster a culture of creative experimentation and who understand AI as a catalyst for strategic thinking, rather than merely a mechanism for efficiency.

What follows is not a technical manual. You do not need to understand machine learning algorithms or large language models to benefit from this chapter. Instead, we will explore a practical framework leveraging AI across five dimensions of competitive advantage, called VOICE – Value proposition, Opportunity intelligence, Insight generation, Creative storytelling, and Empathetic engagement. Along the way, we will examine how different types of firms – ranging from solo practitioners and boutiques to mid-size firms and global giants – can deploy these approaches in ways tailored to their particular circumstances and aspirations.

The AI moment in legal business development

Before diving into frameworks and applications, it is worth pausing to understand why this moment is different from previous waves of legal technology. Law firms have weathered many technological shifts. Lawyers have adopted word processing, email, online research, and e-discovery platforms. Each met fierce internal resistance and an insistence that things had to be done the way they'd always been done. Each was eventually absorbed into the fabric of practice without fundamentally altering how lawyers build relationships and win work.

AI is different. Its general-purpose nature means it touches every aspect of professional work, including business development. Unlike specialized tools designed for discrete tasks, AI systems can engage with the full complexity of human communication, analysis, and creativity. They can draft a pitch letter, analyze a competitor's public filings, identify patterns in client feedback, help develop thought leadership content, and suggest questions for a client interview. And it can do all of this in the same conversation. AI agents move beyond just chatting with us. They are increasingly capable of actually *doing* the work for us.

This general-purpose capability creates both opportunity and uncertainty. For leaders accustomed to evaluating discrete technology investments with clear ROI calculations, AI presents a different kind of challenge. Its value emerges through experimentation, iteration, and creative application rather than through deployment of a fixed solution. The firms gaining ground during these early days are those whose leaders have created space for their people to explore, fail safely, and discover unexpected applications.

Our team has spent the last year supporting firms in reframing questions whose original form forces them to retreat to an increasingly outdated model. For example, instead of asking, "How can we ensure our junior associates continue to meet their billable hour requirements?", firms could instead ask, "How do we ensure our junior associates continue to generate revenue for the firm while building valuable skills?". This reframe opens a path to new possible solutions, including deploying associates to support their practice groups and partners in pursuing business development opportunities in a much more sophisticated and informed way.

This reframe also illustrates an important point – the value of AI in business development often emerges from engaging different stakeholders in the firm to think creatively about their roles through experimentation and sharing, not from top-down implementation of predetermined solutions.

The leader's role is to create the conditions for this experimentation to flourish.

The VOICE framework – five dimensions of AI-enhanced business development

To provide structure for thinking about AI in business development, I propose the VOICE framework. Each letter represents a dimension of competitive advantage that AI can help amplify.

V: Value proposition

Every firm believes it offers distinctive value. Few can articulate that distinctiveness in ways that resonate with clients and feel truly different from another firm. Redact a firm's name on its website and see whether you can actually name the firm or if it sounds like dozens of other similar firms. But AI can serve as a rigorous thinking partner in the work of clarifying and sharpening value propositions.

The process begins with honest examination. What do we actually do better than our competitors? What patterns exist in our most successful engagements? What do clients say about us when we are not in the room? AI can help analyze client feedback, matter histories, and outcomes to identify themes that might not be apparent from internal perception alone.

Using AI to analyze win rates, client retention, and matter complexity across years of engagements might reveal, for example, that a firm's true strength is not what it has been marketing, but could lead to knowledge that a particular expertise in a niche area other firms may be undervaluing. Insights like these could completely reposition the firm's marketing approach to attract exactly the kinds of matters where it excels.

AI is also increasingly capable of blending data analytics with knowledge of client relationships and lawyer talent. This nuanced specificity makes BD efforts more targeted and more effective than the prior era's focus on innate great networking skills.

AI can also help stress-test value propositions. By role-playing skeptical clients or competitors, AI can identify weaknesses in positioning and help refine messaging until it can withstand rigorous scrutiny. This kind of iterative refinement, carried out through conversation with an AI partner, can accomplish in hours what might take weeks of internal workshops and external consultant engagements.

O: Opportunity intelligence

Market intelligence has always been valuable for business development, but it has traditionally been time-consuming and expensive to gather systematically. AI dramatically changes this equation by enabling sophisticated analysis of public information at scale.

Opportunity intelligence encompasses several applications. First, AI can help identify emerging trends and regulatory developments that will create client needs. By analyzing news, regulatory filings, industry publications, and academic research, AI can surface patterns that suggest where legal demand will grow. A corporate practice might use this capability to anticipate which industries will face increased M&A activity or regulatory scrutiny.

Second, AI can assist with competitive intelligence. Understanding what competitors are doing, including their practice areas of focus, recent hires, thought leadership themes, and pricing approaches can help firms position themselves more effectively. AI can systematically and continuously monitor competitor activities and synthesize insights that would be impractical to gather manually.

Third, and perhaps most powerfully, AI can help identify specific opportunities. By analyzing public filings, news coverage, and industry developments, AI can flag companies that may be facing legal challenges or opportunities aligned with a firm's capabilities. A restructuring practice might use AI to identify companies showing early signs of financial distress. An employment practice might track companies announcing expansions into new jurisdictions where they would need employment law guidance.

The key is using AI to focus human energy on the tasks that have the greatest likelihood of leading to business. AI can surface hundreds of potential opportunities – human professionals must evaluate which are worth pursuing and how to approach them authentically.

I: Insight generation

Understanding clients deeply and knowing their businesses, challenges, aspirations, and concerns is the foundation of effective business development. However, many lawyers approach client relationships with assumptions rather than genuine insight. AI can help develop richer, more nuanced understanding of client needs.

Voice of the client research is an area where AI excels. By analyzing client communications, feedback, and public statements, AI can identify themes that reveal what clients truly value and where they feel underserved. This goes beyond simple satisfaction surveys to uncover latent needs that clients themselves may not have articulated.

For example, a global firm could use AI to analyze transcripts of client interviews conducted over several years. The comprehensive analysis that emerges could reveal that clients consistently mention wanting lawyers who could help them think through strategic implications, not just legal risks. Yet the firm's pitches and marketing emphasize technical expertise and jurisdictional coverage. This insight could lead to a fundamental shift in how the firm presents itself and trains its lawyers to engage with clients.

Predictive analytics represent another frontier. By analyzing patterns in client behavior, including engagement frequency, matter types, and industry developments, AI can help identify which clients may be at risk of defection, which may be poised to need additional services, and which relationships merit investment. This allows business development efforts to be targeted where they will have greatest impact.

Perhaps most importantly, AI can help prepare for client interactions. Before a pitch meeting or client review, AI can synthesize information about the client's business, recent developments, competitive landscape, and potential concerns. It can also help with understanding a general counsel's perspective and the latent concerns that may be left off the formal RFP but lie in wait as the true service opportunity for lawyers who understand how to work with AI. This preparation ensures that conversations are substantive and demonstrate genuine understanding rather than generic relationship-building and a focus on the firm's lawyer instead of the client's problem.

C: Creative storytelling

Lawyers are trained to present arguments and marshal evidence. They are often less educated about the importance of storytelling – the art of crafting narratives that engage, persuade, and inspire. But storytelling is fundamental to effective business development. And it's deeply human. Clients choose lawyers they trust, and trust is built through compelling stories that demonstrate understanding, experience, and values.

AI can be a powerful creative partner in developing these narratives by augmenting human creativity. By engaging in iterative dialogue with AI, lawyers can develop pitches, thought leadership content, and client communications that are more compelling than what they might produce alone.

Consider the pitch process. Rather than starting with a blank page or recycling language from previous pitches, a lawyer can engage AI in conversation about what makes this opportunity unique, what the client truly needs, and how the firm's experience addresses those needs. Through this dialogue, a distinctive pitch emerges that would not have developed through either the lawyer or the AI working alone. At one point in my career, I was in the client's shoes and I reviewed plenty of RFP responses from various firms that clearly used copy and paste boilerplate, a rushed and inauthentic recitation of the problem the firm thought we had, and a comprehensive description of the experiences and credentials of the firm's lawyers. It was very rare to receive a response that felt like the firm truly "got it" and spoke to us in a way that focused on us as the client rather than focusing on their lawyers.

Thought leadership is another area ripe for AI collaboration. Many lawyers have valuable insights but struggle to translate them into compelling articles, presentations, or social media content. AI can help structure ideas, suggest angles that will resonate with target audiences, and refine language until it achieves the right balance of substance and accessibility.

Imagine how powerful this unlock could be for a solo practitioner. AI could offer a single lawyer doing everything herself the chance to work with a thoughtful and tireless content creator for next to nothing. That lawyer can now publish a client alert more than twice a year, because the writing process consumes much less time. With AI as a collaborative partner, the same lawyer could produce weekly content that establishes her as a leading voice in her niche. The content could reflect her expertise and voice. She would never publish something that does not feel authentically hers, but AI helps her develop and refine ideas far more rapidly than she could alone.

E: Empathetic engagement

The final dimension of the VOICE framework addresses perhaps the most important aspect of business development – building genuine human connections at scale. The objection to AI in relationship-building is understandable, as nothing can replace authentic human connection. But this objection misunderstands how AI can be deployed.

AI enables empathetic engagement by freeing human attention for what matters most. When AI handles research, preparation, and follow-up tasks, lawyers can be fully present in client conversations rather than mentally composing to-do lists. When AI helps personalize communications at scale, lawyers can maintain meaningful touchpoints with larger networks than would otherwise be possible.

Consider how AI can enhance the client check-in. Rather than a generic "just following up" email, a lawyer can use AI to prepare a personalized message that references recent developments in the client's industry, asks thoughtful questions about challenges they may be facing, and offers relevant insights. The communication is still authentically from the lawyer because they review and personalize it before sending, but AI helps make each touchpoint substantive rather than perfunctory.

AI can also help lawyers prepare for conversations by suggesting questions that might uncover client needs, anticipating objections that might arise in a pitch, or role-playing difficult conversations. This preparation allows lawyers to approach interactions with greater confidence and deeper empathy for the client's perspective.

The goal is to deepen relationships. AI handles the cognitive labor that might otherwise distract from genuine human connection, allowing lawyers to bring their full attention and care to the relationships that matter most.

Applications across firm types

The VOICE framework applies across all firm types, but its specific applications vary depending on organizational context. What follows are considerations for three different firm configurations.

Solo practitioners and boutique firms – punching above your weight

For smaller practices, AI represents an unprecedented opportunity to compete with much larger organizations. Tasks that previously required dedicated staff or expensive consultants – such as market research, competitive analysis, content creation, and pitch preparation – can now be accomplished with AI assistance.

The solo practitioner or small firm leader should focus on applications that provide the greatest leverage. Whereabouts in the firm is the lack of people to do the task causing the real bottleneck? If the activity provides value and if the firm has no plans to hire someone, AI could be a great fit. Opportunity intelligence is particularly valuable because it allows small practices to identify and pursue prospects that larger firms might overlook or find inefficient to target. A boutique with deep expertise in a particular niche can use AI to monitor industry developments and identify companies entering that space who will need specialized counsel.

Creative storytelling also offers tremendous leverage. Small firms often have compelling stories of founding partners, of notable representations, or of unique approaches, but they get lost in generic marketing materials. AI can help craft these stories in ways that resonate with target audiences and differentiate the practice from larger competitors.

Mid-size firms – differentiation in a crowded market

Mid-size firms face a particular challenge – they are too large and generalized to claim the boutique's specialized expertise but too small to match the global reach and resources of BigLaw. AI can help them find and exploit a differentiated position.

For mid-size firms, insight generation is often the most valuable application. Understanding clients deeply and in ways that go deeper than larger competitors who may treat them as smaller fish allows mid-size firms to compete on relationship quality rather than scale. AI can help synthesize client information, identify unmet needs, and prepare partners for conversations that demonstrate genuine understanding.

Mid-size firms can also use AI to respond to RFPs with unprecedented speed and customization. Rather than recycling boilerplate language, they can use AI to analyze the RFP requirements, identify what the prospective client truly cares about, and craft responses that speak directly to those concerns. This responsiveness and customization can differentiate them from larger competitors who may approach RFPs more mechanically.

If you are in a mid-size firm, consider using an upcoming RFP response as a chance to use "AI-enhanced pitch sprints". When a significant opportunity arises, a team spends a concentrated period using AI to research the prospect, analyze competitors, develop tailored messaging, and prepare for the pitch. The intensity of preparation this enables, which is far beyond what is practical with traditional approaches, could result in a marked improvement in pitch success rates. And it carries the added bonus of building the firm's muscle for using AI.

Large law firms – maximizing strategic advantage

Large firms have resources that smaller practices lack – significant client relationships, global reach, talent depth, and existing data infrastructure. The challenge is deploying AI in ways that maximize these advantages rather than merely automate existing processes.

For BigLaw, the most powerful applications often involve firm-wide intelligence systems. By aggregating insights across client relationships, practice areas, and geographies, large firms can identify cross-selling opportunities, anticipate client needs, and coordinate business development efforts in ways that smaller competitors cannot match.

Predictive analytics offer particular value at scale. With large datasets of client interactions and matter histories, AI can identify patterns that predict which relationships are at risk, which clients are likely to need additional services and which pitch approaches are most effective with different types of prospects. These insights can be deployed across the organization to focus business development resources where they will have greatest impact.

Large firms can also create new approaches to thought leadership. Rather than relying on individual partners to generate content, they can use AI to identify emerging topics, synthesize expertise from across the firm, and produce integrated perspectives that draw on their full range of capabilities. This institutional voice can establish the firm as a leader on complex issues that span multiple practice areas.

A global firm could create an "AI client intelligence hub" – an AI-powered system that synthesizes information about key clients from across the firm, identifies opportunities for deeper engagement, and suggests connections between client needs and firm capabilities. Partners may find that the system surfaces opportunities they would never have identified on their own and enables conversations with clients that demonstrate unprecedented understanding of their businesses.

Building a culture of creative experimentation

The frameworks and applications discussed above are only valuable if people throughout the organization actually use them. This requires building a culture where experimentation with AI is encouraged, safe, and rewarded.

The first requirement is leadership engagement. Partners and firm leaders must visibly experiment with AI themselves, not merely delegate it to marketing departments or technology committees. When a managing partner shares how they used AI to prepare for a client pitch or develop a strategic insight, it signals that experimentation is valued and expected.

Second, firms must create psychological safety around experimentation. AI applications will not always work as expected. Early attempts will produce results that are mediocre or miss the mark. If people fear criticism for experiments that fail, they will not experiment. And if they do not experiment, they will not learn. Leaders must communicate clearly that thoughtful experimentation is valued even when particular applications do not succeed.

Third, successful experiments must be shared and celebrated. When someone discovers an effective AI application, that knowledge should spread through the firm. Regular forums for sharing AI experiments create collective learning and inspire others to try new approaches.

Fourth, experimentation should be resourced. This might mean dedicated time for exploring AI applications, access to tools and training, or internal consultants who can help people develop their ideas. The specific resources will vary by firm, but the principle is clear – experimentation that is merely permitted but not supported will not flourish.

Finally, firms must think carefully about how AI experimentation relates to quality and ethics. Clear guidelines about what applications are appropriate, how client confidentiality is protected, and how AI outputs are reviewed and validated allow people to experiment with confidence. Without such guardrails, caution will stifle creativity.

Identifying your highest-value opportunities

As you consider how to apply the VOICE framework in your own context, the following questions may help identify where to focus initial efforts:

- *On Value proposition:* Can you articulate what makes your practice distinctive in one sentence? Would your clients describe your value the same way you do? When did you last test your positioning with a skeptical audience?
- *On Opportunity intelligence:* How do you currently learn about emerging trends that will affect client needs? What would it mean for your practice if you could identify opportunities three months before your competitors?
- *On Insight generation:* How deeply do you understand what your clients truly value? What patterns exist across your successful engagements that you have not yet articulated? Which client relationships deserve deeper exploration?
- *On Creative storytelling:* What stories do you tell about your practice? Are those stories compelling to the audiences you most want to reach? How might AI help you develop and refine those narratives?
- *On Empathetic engagement:* How do you prepare for important client conversations? Are your touchpoints substantive or perfunctory? What would it mean to bring greater attention and care to your most important relationships?

The answers to these questions will vary by firm and individual. What matters is honest assessment of current capabilities and genuine openness to how AI might enhance them.

Seizing the moment

We are in the opening days of the AI era in law. The tools available today will seem primitive within a few years, just as early websites and email now appear quaint. The professionals who engage now by experimenting, learning, and developing intuitions for how AI can enhance their work will carry advantages that late adopters will struggle to match.

This is ultimately not a technology conversation but a leadership one. The firms that will win in the AI era are those whose leaders foster cultures of creative experimentation, who understand AI as a strategic thought partner rather than merely an efficiency tool, and who have the courage to reimagine how they compete and grow.

The VOICE framework offers a structure for this exploration – sharpening your Value proposition, developing Opportunity intelligence, generating deeper Insight into client needs, crafting Creative narratives that differentiate your practice, and enabling more Empathetic engagement at scale. Each dimension offers opportunities for AI to amplify human capabilities in ways that create genuine competitive advantage.

AI *will* transform business development in law. Will your firm be among those who lead that transformation or among those who follow?

Chapter 12: Budgeting and ROI measurement – ensuring marketing investments deliver measurable value

By Monica Rodriguez Kuniyoshi, principal, MRK Strategies

A 2024 report from BTI Consulting found that while 79 percent of law firms have written strategic plans, only 18.6 percent implement all or most of their planned initiatives.[1] Lest readers despair at such statistics, these outcomes are not for lack of trying – and they are not unique to the legal industry. In diagnosing the root cause of this issue, researchers at McKinsey & Company found that the poor performance rests in lack of resources, misalignments, and execution difficulties.[2] It does not have to be this way.

Budgeting and ROI measurement sits at the heart of building sustainable business development culture. ROI measurement is the way you find out whether the "road" you have built for business development – the plan, the structure, the initiative, and its goals – will take the firm where it needs to go. It is the discipline that tests whether the firm's carefully constructed initiative works in practice, not just on paper. In that sense, ROI measurement functions as the firm's GPS – it tells leadership if they are on the right track toward their destination, pointing to trouble up ahead, recommending recalculated routes, and where to make refinements rather than simply driving on and hoping for the best.

Therefore, this chapter asserts a simple principle – success starts with measurement, not money. It positions budgeting and measurement not as isolated exercises, but as strategic and interrelated tools for steering law firm investments toward measurable value, despite the reality of lean teams, limited data, and uneven attorney engagement. The approaches and insights shared in this chapter will be useful to any law firm of any size undergoing the important work of building a business development culture, whether they are trying to change behavior among a small group of partners, shift the mindset of entire practices, or measure a large-scale initiative across hundreds of attorneys.

This chapter makes extensive use of a ladder framework, allowing the reader to develop ROI measures and a budget that aligns with what is most practical for where they are in their data journey. While advanced analytics are the gold standard, most law firms are not at that level. That's OK. By taking a measurement-first approach, any firm can improve clarity, use its resources wisely, and make better decisions next quarter than could be made before.

Reducing risk by taking a measurement-first approach

Why begin a budget conversation with measurement? Firms understand that a successful BD culture is the engine of growth. Using the GPS metaphor, firms can identify their desired destination. But how exactly they get there is often where the rubber meets the road.

Without ROI measures, it is like driving with the GPS's volume turned off. The driver knows they are moving but are unable to navigate effectively. Worse yet, most law firms define their destination but not their starting point.

Marketing budgets developed without clear and objective ROI measurement face several risks, including:

- *Decision making that defaults to tradition and internal politics.* Funds flow to the most influential voices, the most persistent complainers, or the partners with the most ideas, regardless of whether those ideas are aligned with firm strategy. They get outsized support because no one can point to objective signals that would justify steering the wheels in a different direction.
- *Legacy line items are routinely renewed without a disciplined review of their impact.* There is no structured way to decide whether a conference, training or other BD initiative should be continued, refined, or retired.
- *Partner needs and the resources to satisfy them are misaligned.* The marketing or BD team is too lean and bandwidth-constrained to successfully execute on expectations. They want to make the initiative successful but do not have the necessary tools, skills, experience, or influence to effectively guide the process.

On the other hand, when ROI measurement systems are working well, the future state is as visible in behavior as it is in spreadsheets. Decisions become more focused and more neutral. Leaders can see progress throughout the journey, not just when they look at quarterly revenue. They can reward long-term progress and improved behavior and results, as well as short-term collections. Further, because leaders are not reliant on instincts or "sacred cows", conversations around effort and outcomes can be less politically charged, leading to better decision making and more patience with the process.

Measurement-first as a tool for alignment, credibility, and decision making

Defining success before you budget is like turning on the GPS before you start driving. The budget is the car, success is the destination. The exact route may change and there will be detours and traffic along the way, but everyone benefits from knowing where they are headed. That clarity allows the firm to use its most constrained resource – attorney time – as efficiently as possible rather than scattering effort across too many loosely related initiatives.

From a leadership perspective, pursuing a measurement-first approach has three additional advantages:

1. *Alignment*. Explicitly stating where the firm is now and where it wants to go – whether for one attorney, a cohort, a practice, or the entire firm – produces durable alignment. When stakeholders articulate their current state and desired future state together, they are more likely to "get in the car" heading toward the same destination.
2. *Credibility*. When marketing and BD leaders bring rigor and discipline to defining success and metrics, they position themselves as partners in helping attorneys focus on what they do best, rather than as administrators pushing generic programs.
3. *Decision making*. Using a measurement-first approach, leaders naturally create milestones where they can come back to attorneys with updates, insights, and refinements. Instead of setting a budget once and ignoring it for a year, they build a rhythm of a review where the GPS is checked and decisions are refined.

Importantly, defining success at the outset is not a set of handcuffs. Success measures can and should evolve as the firm learns from early signals. The point is to agree on a direction and initial markers so that course corrections are intentional, not reactive. When leaders explain that this upfront work will save time later and will allow them to reallocate attention toward the highest-yield activities, skeptical audiences are more willing to engage.

Understanding the starting point – the measurement ladder

Where to start? The first question leaders should ask is, "How will we know that it worked?". Defining success before any money is allocated helps to right-size the budget, focus limited time and energy, and clarify which investments truly support the firm's strategic goals.

Using the GPS metaphor, in addition to knowing its desired destination, the firm needs to know its origin or starting point. ROI measurement is about tracking movement from a baseline state to a future state, not just checking whether a revenue target was hit. Without that journey in mind, initiatives work to some degree, but leadership cannot tell how much, why, or how to make them more effective next time.

The measurement ladder shown in Table 1 gives leaders a framework for understanding their firm's starting point. The ladder moves the conversation away from "who gets budget" and toward a more strategic sequence – what metrics the firm can track, what behaviors drive those outcomes, and what is the smallest set of investments that will move the system. It helps leaders avoid over-promising, name limiting factors openly, and identify which future investments will unlock better measurement and better decisions.

Table 1. Measurement ladder – assessing the starting point

Level and goal	Data available	Questions to ask	Where to focus
1.0 – Visibility Primary goal: Create clarity and discipline	– Basic revenue and activity data available (i.e., revenue, matters, participation) – Early CRM or ERM usage – Agreed definitions for core BD terms – Progress can be reviewed quarterly	– Where does revenue data live? Who maintains it? – What activity is already tracked, by who and where? – Who can run reports? – What definitions differ between departments?	– Five consistent definitions across departments – Stronger data hygiene and consistent reporting discipline – Two or three outcome metrics (i.e., revenue, score) – Two or three desired attorney behaviors – Initial mapping of the client journey and identification of stages – Quarterly review cadence – Leadership alignment on what the data can and cannot tell you

continued on next page

Level and goal	Data available	Questions to ask	Where to focus
1.0 – Connection Primary goal: Inform timely decision making	Add: – Ability to connect effort to outcomes (i.e., conversion rates, cross-selling, follow-up consistency) – Track pipeline stages – See correlations – Can adjust mid-quarterly based on signals	Add: – Do we have clarity at each stage of the pipeline? – Is CRM adoption consistent? – Is the reporting cadence regular and streamlined?	Add: – Key definitions by stage and more robust journey-mapping – More consistent and structured follow-up workflows – Increased CRM rigor and better aggregate signals – Monthly and quarterly review cadence
3.0 – Optimization Primary goal: Refine and scale	Add: – Clean integrated data (i.e., client lifetime value, share of wallet, etc.) – Forecasting capability – Investment comparisons possible – Predictive modeling and insights	Add: – Do we have integration across systems? – Do we have advanced segmentation capability? – What is the quality of our predictive analytics? – Is there data governance discipline?	Add: – Ongoing governance and data quality discipline – Continued data integration and quality improvements across all systems – Forecasting models and predictive analytics – Transparency that empowers attorneys to use data for their own decisions – Continuous dashboards and monthly review cadence

Because data availability varies widely between firms, ROI metrics work best when they align with what the firm can easily and consistently measure. Many firms have access to excellent software with the ability to track myriad metrics. Even then, deriving regular and consistent insights from them requires attention to shared definitions, data hygiene, and ease of reporting. Therefore, often the most transformational growth happens when a firm moves from 1.0 (Visibility) to 2.0 (Connection) because of the necessary change in habits, behavior, and data infrastructure. That is the foundation for future growth.

Behavioral data to measure progress

Outcome data alone does not tell you whether your BD initiative is creating the behavior change that drives long-term performance. Attorney attitudes, habits, and participation levels are the single biggest determinant of success. Business development is emotional and identity-linked, and attorneys (like all humans) avoid what feels uncomfortable, risky, unclear, or punitive, even when they intellectually agree that the outcome matters. For that reason, ROI measurement benefits from capturing and rewarding progress and momentum alongside outcomes.

Further, many meaningful BD outcomes take time to bear fruit and if leaders look only at outcome metrics, they risk mistaking "not yet" for "not working". Returning to the GPS metaphor, behavioral measures provide directional signals that often come before revenue. They show that the vehicle is still moving, even if the destination has not yet appeared on the screen.

Understanding the attorneys' starting point, including how confident they feel about BD, what they already do, and what they resist, allows the firm to tailor both support and metrics. Behavioral metrics might include measures such as meaningful touch points, meetings held, pitches made, and client nurturing activities, as well as self-reported confidence and habit scores from surveys or diagnostic tools. Because so much BD activity is offline, especially conversations and relationship building, the goal should not be perfect capture from day one. Instead, firms can aim for modest improvement (say, ten percent better tracking) and build more robust capture as attorneys and systems adjust.

To capture qualitative and subjective baselines efficiently, firms can use short surveys, supplemented by coaching conversations. Well-designed surveys can help attorneys reflect on their current behaviors, confidence levels, and emotional barriers. They can also reveal patterns that allow leaders to group "like with like" into more meaningful attorney cohorts. This grouping can significantly improve both the quality of data and the effectiveness of the initiative because the firm is no longer trying to run one monolithic initiative for attorneys who are all at vastly different starting points.

Art of the possible – aligning ROI measures to the firm's current level

With your baseline assessment in place, it is easier to define the minimum viable ROI data needed to begin. A practical way to organize these measures is in three categories:

1. *Outcome measures (what the firm wants to see).* Most firms have access to robust financial data such as matter intake, revenue by client, realization, and other indicators used by the CFO to assess firm health. Similarly, outcome data is embedded in email marketing, CRM, and ERM platforms. The task at this stage is not to catalog every metric available. Focusing on the few outcome metrics that directly reflect the firm's BD goals is far more powerful.
2. *Leading indicators (signals that predict outcomes).* These metrics show whether the work that precedes revenue is happening. It helps leaders intervene early, before underperformance shows up in lagging outcome measures.
3. *Adoption measures (evidence of culture shift).* When taking the measurement-first approach, adoption is not a "nice to have". It is the mechanism that makes other ROI claims plausible.

A guiding principle is to start with the smallest, lightest-weight set of measures that can create observable evidence that something is changing, without demanding a massive shift in behavior or infrastructure. Again, the measurement ladder is a useful tool for deciding what is possible depending on the firm's stage. Change in law firms is a journey, and measurement systems should be designed with the expectation that rigor will increase over time. See Table 2.

Table 2. Measurement ladder – outcome measures, leading indicators, and adoption measures

Level and goal	Outcome measures	Leading indicators	Adoption measures
1.0 – Visibility Primary goal: Create clarity and discipline	– Revenue growth – Increase in matter count – Increase in matter value	– Increase in BD meetings/presentations to prospects and targets – Higher pitch volume – More content sharing that advances BD conversations	– Documented target list – Regular participation in coaching – Engagement with a system for regular BD activity
2.0 – Connection Primary goal: Inform timely decision making	Add: – Improved conversion rates – Outcomes from cross-selling	Add: – Increased cross-selling effectiveness – Improved follow-up after BD activities – Clear indicators of client nurturing by stage in the CRM	Add: – Consistency of follow-up – Frequency of client listening – Quality of opportunity notes in the CRM
3.0 – Optimization Primary goal: Refine and scale	Add: – Increase in client lifetime value – Increase in share of wallet – More reliable forecasting	Add: – Higher scoring at different pipeline stages – Frequency of client listening – Increase speed of responsiveness to inquiries – Supporting predictive analytics	Add: – Regular review of dashboards and other reporting

These categories allow leaders to tell a coherent ROI story without claiming precision that the data cannot support. Further, because these categories run on different timelines, they should be reviewed on different cadences:

- Outcome measures often require quarterly or semi-annual review because results take time to show up.
- Leading indicators are best viewed monthly because they allow for timely redirection and intervention.
- Adoption measures should be reviewed weekly, because participation and follow-up can fall off quickly without regular touchpoints.

Defining these cadences in advance reduces the risk of panicking too early when outcomes lag, or for declaring victory before the initiative has matured.

The risks of over-relying on data

Lest leaders fall into the trap that data alone will improve decision making, a sober assessment of the risks is necessary. Below are some risks to consider:

- *False precision*. Otherwise known as the illusion that, because you have numbers, you have the whole story. Data tends to smooth out nuance. This is helpful for spotting outliers but can obscure the "messy middle" where many real-world decisions live. For example, a report might suggest that sponsoring a particular conference "always" leads to new clients, but contextual factors such as the reputation of the partners involved plays a significant role. Not considering those contextual factors could lead to assuming the same result when a different partner chooses to take part.
- *Gaming the metrics*. When attorneys understand which metrics are used to assess compensation, status, or leadership attention, the risk is that some will focus on ways to achieve them with the least friction or effort. Given their training, attorneys are excellent at finding loopholes and many bristle at being tracked. If the initiative only rewards what can be easily measured, some people will gravitate toward activities that generate favorable metrics – not necessarily those that best serve clients or build sustainable books of business.
- *Erosion of trust*. If attorneys feel reduced to a series of numbers, without recognition for the qualitative aspects of their work and relationships, they may disengage from firm initiatives and lose a sense of shared purpose. Leveraging their unique insights and judgement in the context of the initiative is a key way to preserve trust.

- *Analysis paralysis.* In Level 1.0 or 2.0 firms where the data infrastructure is still developing, insisting on complete information before acting slows decision making. Leaders must be able to act on "good enough" data, using metrics as guardrails and directionally useful signals, rather than the only source of truth.

An effective measurement-first approach needs to have as its guiding principle that a law firm is a human enterprise that uses data to help focus attention on what is most likely to move the needle, not replace the richness of nuance and human intelligence.

Expanding your field of view – budgeting for technology, internal resources, and external support

While financial systems force budgets into line items and departments, it is strategically useful to design budgets first around three levers – technology, internal resources, and external support. Think of these three levers as the gauges in a car's dashboard, helping the driver understand if there is enough "gas in the tank" to get the firm to its destination.

Applying the three levers while building the budget supports better sequencing because leaders can see how each lever must be pulled differently as the firm's measurement capacity matures. The measurement ladder in Table 3 highlights minimum capacity at each level.

Table 3. Measurement ladder – technology, internal resources and external support

Level and stage	Technology investment	Internal resources	External support
1.0 – Visibility Primary goal: Create clarity and discipline	– CRM data cleanup – Consistent fields – Simple reporting	– Behavioral support – Focus team time on tracking and quarterly review	– Advisory or pilot support – One-to-one coaching

continued on next page

Level and stage	Technology investment	Internal resources	External support
2.0 – Connection Primary goal: Inform timely decision making	Add: – Pipeline tracking – Stage definitions – AI tools – Reporting refinement	Add: – Internal coaching and "connecting the dots" – Project management – Analytics discipline	Add: – Structured BD initiative or cohort coaching
3.0 – Optimization Primary goal: Refine and scale	Add: – Data integration – Sophisticated BI tools – Predictive dashboards	Add: – Dedicated analytics capability	Add: – Advanced modeling or optimization advisory work

Leaders do not need perfect data to lead well. They do not need advanced analytics to build discipline. They need clarity about what "enough" looks like at their stage, a cadence for reviewing it, and the willingness to strengthen it over time. Firms that are at the 1.0 Visibility stage have a solid foundation. From there, moving toward 2.0 Connection and eventually 3.0 Optimization becomes a natural next step rather than an expensive leap.

Lever 1: Technology evaluation checklist

First, identify what data is available today and where it resides. If key outcome metrics live in financial systems, determine how reliably and how often the team can access them. Will they be available via dashboard or will someone in another department need to run periodic reports? Understanding the mechanics of access prevents ambitious measurement plans from collapsing under the weight of manual reporting.

Second, consider the technology that already supports attorneys' BD efforts day-to-day. What tools (e.g., CRM, ERM, pipeline platforms, or other systems) are already in place to surface insights, capture activities, and prompt action? Do the firm's existing technologies have additional features that haven't been purchased yet, but could support this initiative? Which tools do the attorneys already use? The answers will heavily influence which behavioral and outcome metrics you can track without adding excessive friction. A measurement plan that assumes behavior tracking and systems that attorneys barely use is unlikely to succeed.

If the decision is to purchase new technology, the following practical evaluation checklist helps leaders visualize the full cost of technology necessary to support BD across its lifecycle and avoid the trap of selecting tools based only on the initial purchase price.

Resources required for development, reporting and maintenance:

- *Data capture.* How easy is it to capture only the data needed to make credible ROI claims (not "curiosity data")?
- *Integrations.* Does the tool integrate with other systems so the team is not wrangling multiple reports? If not, can middleware or APIs address the issue?
- *Reporting.* Are reports easy to run, interpret, and present as signals (your "GPS") for leaders and attorneys?
- Attorney workflow fit. Does it align with how attorneys already work (e.g., email-centric, mobile)? Does it minimize tool-switching?
- *Administrative burden.* What people-time is required for ongoing maintenance, data hygiene, support, reporting and system updates?

Resources required for onboarding and integration:

- *Development and implementation.* Who owns development and implementation (IT or marketing)? Will outside consultants be necessary to facilitate implementation?
- *Governance.* Who owns changes, definitions and fields? How will cross-department consistency be maintained? Does it require headcount and in which department?
- *Training.* Is training provided by the vendor and is it supportive of adoption across all levels of users (attorneys, staff and administrators)? Is that an add-on cost?

One practical tactic is to document "known limitations" explicitly at the outset. In addition to identifying what data is available and what you can credibly measure now, you name what's not yet possible and why. Socializing those limitations early sets the expectation that data will be imperfect, that it requires qualitative insights and that the measurement approach will evolve as the firm strengthens data capture and governance over time.

In addition, there are also situations where it is wise to pause and fix "the plumbing" before committing to ROI measures that the firm cannot reliably support. Two flags to be on the lookout for:

1. *Conflict over data sources, consistency, or ownership*. This is especially important when access to financial data requires collaboration with leaders who have reasons to be sensitive about how their data is used. If basic questions about access and ownership trigger defensiveness or misalignment between department heads, leaders should align first so that measurement doesn't turn into a political battle.
2. *Severely inconsistent or incomplete data*. This is often because definitions differ across groups (for example, a "proposal" means different things to different people) or because the information is not consistently applied. Clean up the data first, focusing on the smallest possible effort to get the metrics that are needed.

Lever 2: Internal resources checklist

It is the rare firm where "change agent" is a role on the organization chart. Attorneys should own the aspects only they can do, such as client interactions, relationship follow-up, and real-world engagement. The marketing BD team should own what they are expert at – connecting dots across the firm, supporting consistent follow through, keeping the "GPS volume" on, and helping recalibrate the initiative when signals suggest refinements are needed. Marketing and BD professionals often have broader context than individual attorneys and can leverage the full weight of the firm to support relationship-building efforts.

Because internal teams are often bandwidth-constrained, it can be tempting to outsource the initiative to an external consultant or coach. But internal teams are critical for success and bring significant benefits, especially in partnership with external support. Before considering whether and how to leverage outside resources, evaluate the firm's internal capacity.

Back-office capabilities:

- *Data hygiene and analytics*. Ensuring data quality and generating actionable insights.
- *Content development/enablement*. Materials, templates and resources that support consistent messaging and support relationship-building efforts.
- *Project management*. Coordination, scheduling, accountability and reporting.
- *Training facilitation*. Delivery of individual or group learning experiences.

Attorney-facing capabilities:

- *Coaching.* One-on-one and small group support to build attorney skills and confidence.
- *Partner advising.* Senior-level consulting to practice leaders and rainmakers.

Many teams are strong in some areas and not in others. Even light but consistent internal support can compound returns because it provides consistency, reinforcement, and accountability that sustains attorney habits. Further, attorneys are more likely to participate when expectations are organized, follow-through is dependable, and participation does not feel optional. Therefore, codifying internal support in the budget (even as fractional allocations only on spreadsheets) helps make the initiative feel real to both staff and attorneys, reducing the likelihood that the initiative fades under day-to-day pressure.

Lever 3: External support

As noted, external resources can be highly effective when paired with internal capability. They tend to generate high ROI when the goal is skills transfer, acceleration, and neutrality, especially:

- When the firm needs to get over the hump of launching a new initiative, including by aligning language or building credibility quickly;
- Because they accelerate progress when internal team members can only allocate limited time; and
- When external coaches transfer skills not only to attorneys but also to the internal team so that everyone is working from a shared approach.

That said, the marketing and BD team benefit from being clear drivers of the initiative, leveraging external support to make the initiative more effective, not as a replacement for their leadership. Therefore, when evaluating external providers, leaders benefit from adding to the standard RFP questions to assess fit with the firm's measurement-first approach. Useful considerations include:

- Will the external vendor align with the firm's definitions and measurement ladder, or will they push a one-size-fits-all ROI story because that's what they're familiar with?
- To support change, how will they collaborate with the internal team and technology, rather than operating as a standalone solution?
- Do they have a measurement plan that aligns with the firm's ladder level and ROI goals?

- What enablement will they provide to the firm's internal team, so capabilities transfer over time?
- Does their approach fit with the firm's culture and the starting point of the initiative's actual participants?

Budgeting through the ladder – pilot, improve, scale, and refine

This approach favors sequencing over scattershot tactics. Rather than funding a dozen disconnected activities, leaders fund the few components that create a functioning system – definitions, workflows, accountability, and reporting. In the GPS metaphor, the budget is the car, but the system is the engine that makes the car move. Once the system works on a small scale, incremental spending becomes less risky and leaders can see where additional investment compounds results. This compounding effect is much harder to see when budgets are built as one monolithic block.

In addition to piloting the initiative before scaling, budget should also follow measurement maturity. Buying 3.0 Optimization-level tools when the firm is at the 1.0 Visibility stage often creates complexity and misaligned expectations. When you can clearly articulate where your firm sits on the ladder, what you can measure, and what capability the next investment unlocks, budgeting becomes a strategic conversation with the CFO, not a defensive one. See Table 4.

Table 4. Measurement ladder – budgeting

Level and stage	What can be measured today	Budget priorities	CFO framing
1.0 – Visibility Primary goal: Create clarity and discipline	– Revenue – Basic participation	Improve data, clarify definitions, consistent reporting	"We can see revenue and participation, but we cannot yet connect effort to outcome. Our budget priority is strengthening definitions and reporting so future investments can be evaluated more precisely."

continued on next page

Level and stage	What can be measured today	Budget priorities	CFO framing
2.0 – Connection Primary goal: Show which activities correlate with which results	Add: – Pipeline movement – Leading indicators related to results and progress	Strengthen pipeline tracking, coaching, regular and transparent review cadence	"We now see correlations between effort and results. Our budget priority is reinforcing those behaviors and refining what we can see so we can allocate more strategically."
3.0 – Optimization Primary goal: Refine and scale	Add: – Integrated analytics – Forecasting – Modeling and comparing ROI across initiatives	Data integration, analytics capability, forecasting tools	"We have the infrastructure to compare ROI across initiatives. Our budget focus is refinement and scaling what performs the best."

In litigation, attorneys understand that outcomes rarely hinge on a single fact. Rather, they depend on patterns of evidence. ROI measurement operates the same way. In law firms, isolating single-point causation is rarely realistic. Business development outcomes are the result of numerous factors, including market timing, attorney reputation, client need, collaboration, pricing, and execution. The question is not whether one initiative alone "caused" revenue growth, but whether the pattern of evidence supports continued investment.

Making progress – strategy meets stage

By starting with measurement rather than money, leaders shift the conversation from "who gets budget" to "what outcomes do we want, what behaviors drive those outcomes, and what is the smallest set of investments needed to move the needle". This approach creates alignment, builds credibility, and keeps initiatives on track.

The measurement ladder provides a realistic framework for firms at any stage of their data journey, from foundational tracking to advanced analytics. The three budget levers (technology, internal resources, and external support) offer a structured way to translate measurement needs into concrete investments. The emphasis on behavioral metrics alongside outcome measures ensures that initiatives remain grounded in the human realities of a law firm.

Ultimately, a measurement-first approach does not replace the instincts and relationships that make attorneys successful. It focuses those instincts on the highest-value opportunities, providing the GPS to navigate towards shared goals and the discipline needed to refine and scale what works. For law firms committed to building a sustainable business development culture this is where strategy meets execution and where the rubber meets the road.

References

1 https://bticonsulting.com/themadclientist/dissecting-law-firm-strategic-planning-11-take-aways

2 www.mckinsey.com/capabilities/strategy-and-corporate-finance/our-insights/how-strategy-champions-win

Chapter 13: Lateral integration and onboarding – using marketing strategy to accelerate success

By Jessica Grayson, chief growth officer, Stradley Ronon

Reframing lateral hiring as a growth strategy

Lateral partner hiring sits at the center of most law firm growth strategies. Done well, it accelerates market entry, builds practice depth, and refines competitive positioning.

Many firms still treat lateral acquisitions as a recruiting function, focusing on identifying candidates, negotiating compensation, and drafting offer letters, assuming that talented lawyers will slide right into place.

What if law firms treated lateral hiring as a firm-wide integration effort?

Marketing and business development professionals are a critical missing piece in lateral hiring. These teams are routinely left out of the process, yet they are among the people best positioned to make it succeed.

These professionals already help partners build and execute growth strategies as part of their daily roles. They understand markets, clients, positioning, and competitive dynamics and have the frameworks to accelerate lateral integration that complements a recruiting team's work.

Most firms involve marketing and business development teams too late in the lateral hiring process, if at all. By the time these professionals are informed, decisions are finalized, announcements are prepared, and there is an assumption that client transitions and new business will occur seamlessly. It rarely works that way.

A different model

This chapter makes the case for a different model – one where marketing and business development professionals are embedded in the lateral hiring process from start to finish.

Consider how insights from these professionals can inform each stage of the process – before the search, during recruitment, between signing and day one, throughout the first 90 days, and beyond. Each phase offers an opportunity to reduce risk, set expectations, and build momentum. This approach can determine whether a lateral hire becomes a long-term success or an expensive misstep.

A note to managing partners and practice group leaders: this chapter is written for you as much as it is for your marketing and business development colleagues. The recommendations described require leadership decisions, including inviting the right professionals in search conversations before identifying candidates, allocating resources for pre-arrival planning, and holding the firm accountable for structured integration support. As you read, consider not just whether these ideas are sound, but whether your firm's current structure allows for implementation.

The frameworks here are drawn from real-world experience with law firms navigating these challenges. The firms that get lateral integration right treat it as a comprehensive, firm-wide process.

The decision to hire is often where firms make their first mistake.

Before the search – aligning laterals with growth strategy

Key insight: Costly lateral acquisition failures often result from skipped steps, not flawed candidates. When firms prioritize urgency over strategic alignment, they can create avoidable challenges that talent alone cannot resolve.

Marketing and business development teams are uniquely positioned to ask the right questions at the right time. These professionals can help firm leadership address foundational questions before a search begins:

- Will a lateral advance a strategic priority for the firm?
- What specific outcomes will define success in 12 to 24 months?
- Are the success outcomes realistic given the market, the lateral's practice profile, and the firm's existing infrastructure?
- What resources will a lateral need to succeed, and does the firm have the will and capacity to provide them?

These questions sound simple but often are not. Marketing and business development professionals are positioned to facilitate probing conversations with practice group leaders and firm management. They can also help the hiring team pressure-test assumptions (for instance, that clients come with the lateral) before they become expensive commitments.

Put it into practice: Hold a strategic alignment session with recruiting, marketing and business development, practice group leadership, and other key stakeholders. If the group cannot provide clear, specific answers, postpone launching the search.

Market intelligence as a screening tool

Key insight: Many firms evaluate laterals on credentials and revenue projections, yet few consider whether their practices align with the firm's market position and strategic goals.

Marketing and business development teams often possess market intelligence, such as client interview feedback, competitive market analysis, emerging practice-area demands, and an understanding of their firm's differentiators.

This intelligence can be used to build a "fit screening assessment" to serve as a framework for strong lateral hiring. A well-designed fit assessment goes beyond credentials and portable book size, and could include questions such as:

- Does the lateral's practice align with documented client needs or unfilled gaps in the firm's service offering?
- Is the lateral's target client profile consistent with the types of clients we are positioned to serve and retain?
- Are there market dynamics (such as regulatory changes, industry consolidation, emerging practice areas) that make the lateral's expertise more or less strategically valuable right now?
- What does our competitive intelligence tell us about market perceptions of the lateral?

This approach is not intended to create unnecessary bureaucracy. Its purpose is to ensure lateral searches are strategically guided, enabling firms to select the right hires and avoid costly mistakes before making investments.

Put it into practice: Collaboratively build a lateral fit screening assessment template. Incorporate data from client feedback, competitive analysis, revenue, and market trends. Require this assessment before advancing any lateral candidates beyond initial discussions.

Recruitment phase – using brand and experience to compete

Key insight: The lateral recruiting process is a two-way evaluation. The materials, meetings, and messages a candidate encounters are not formalities. They are the firm's audition.

Lateral candidates evaluate your firm with the same rigor you evaluate them. They are reading your website, following your thought leadership, asking their networks about your culture, and forming judgments with every interaction.

Many firms overlook this aspect of the process and underestimate the impact of their brand.

Marketing and business development professionals understand that an authentic brand is a strategic asset. They know how to tell a compelling, differentiated story about a firm's market position, practice strengths, client relationships, and culture. Yet in the recruiting process, this team is often left out of the conversation.

Crafting a well-executed, bespoke recruiting brand strategy is a differentiator. The best-performing recruiting collateral includes:

- Candidate-specific content that speaks directly to a lateral's practice area and client profile. It also proactively addresses likely questions about the firm's capabilities and market position.
- Authentic storytelling from current partners who speak credibly about their own experience joining the firm. You may opt to include what delighted them and how the firm helped them integrate successfully.
- A clear explanation of what differentiates the firm. Avoid generic statements about "collegiality" or "entrepreneurial culture". Instead, highlight specific attributes that will resonate with experienced lateral candidates.

Put it into practice: For each serious lateral candidate, prepare a one-page summary of the firm's strengths, directly relating them to the candidate's practice, client base, and potential concerns. Include partner stories that align with the candidate's background to help them envision themselves at the firm.

Designing the candidate experience

Key insight: Every candidate who walks away from your process carries a story about your firm. You don't get to choose what they say, but you can influence it.

The recruiting process itself is a branding exercise that shapes how candidates perceive the firm. Marketing and business development teams are skilled in curating experiences that define how candidates feel, regardless of the outcome. Establish a positive experience using:

- Well-prepared meetings with clear agendas and purposefully selected participants who can guide the right conversations.

- Thoughtful follow-up that demonstrates genuine interest and attention to what the candidate expresses throughout the process.
- Personalized materials that are prepared specifically for the candidate's practice and clients.
- Consistent, coordinated processes to exhibit that candidates are dealing with a sophisticated, client-focused law firm.

Candidate experience is important even if they do not join the firm. Attorneys who decline an offer may refer colleagues or clients, or may consider joining in the future. Their recruiting experience, whether positive or negative, will influence how they speak about the firm long-term.

Put it into practice: Create a candidate experience checklist that covers pre-meeting preparation, participant selection, materials development, follow-up, and post-process communication.

Vetting beyond the portable book

Key insight: Self-reported portable books of business deserve careful scrutiny. Candidates are rarely dishonest, but can often walk a fine line between realistic and aspirational client portability and personal versus team utilization, particularly with institutional clients. Marketing and business development professionals are trained to interpret that line and report the reality.

Perhaps the most valuable contribution these teams can make during lateral recruiting is assessing a candidate's realistic business potential.

This is a delicate but essential conversation, and marketing and business development professionals are skilled at navigating it. They know how to identify opportunities that may be clouded by perspective, looking beyond a self-reported book of business and asking probing questions such as:

- What is the profitability of the book of business? Revenue figures can be misleading. Rate structures, billing realization, and collection rates tell a more complete story.
- Who controls the client relationships? Is the lateral the primary relationship holder, or are other attorneys at their current firm integral to client retention?
- How dependent is the book on the current firm's infrastructure, leverage, brand, or existing relationships? Some work is genuinely portable; some is far more tied to institutional context than the lateral may realize.

- How did they initially win the business? How likely are clients to go out to RFP rather than follow the lateral? Understanding how work is awarded to the lateral currently is critical to understanding how portable the work actually is.
- Is there client overlap with the firm's current clients? Discussions about how client relationships will potentially be shared once a lateral joins should happen during the recruiting process – not after a lateral joins.
- What business development support will this lateral need to adequately service the book of business, and does the firm have the infrastructure to provide it?

Put it into practice: Add a book-of-business analysis to the lateral evaluation process, asking a business development professional to review client concentration, relationship depth, rate sensitivity, platform dependency, and realistic transition rates.

Between signing and day one – building the launch plan

Key insight: The time between acceptance of the offer and the start date is an important window for driving integration success.

Most firms treat the period between signing and starting as administrative – paperwork, office setup, and the like. These tasks are necessary, but this window is also valuable for integration planning. When a lateral gives notice to their current firm, marketing and business development teams need to begin working directly with the lateral, creating a personalized 90-day launch plan, addressing:

- *Client transition strategy.* Which clients are coming, and who needs to be personally contacted? What is the sequencing and messaging for these conversations? What do the clients need to see and hear to confirm they've made the right decision to transfer?
- *Key introductions.* Which partners does the lateral need to meet and when? Which external relationships (such as referral sources, industry contacts, and former colleagues) should be activated immediately?
- *Firm and practice positioning.* How will the lateral speak about the firm? How will their practice be positioned within the firm's overall narrative? What do clients and the market need to know about this addition?
- *Initial business development goals.* What specific business develop-

ment tactics need to be launched in the first 90 days, and who is responsible for supporting this process?

A launch plan should be thoughtful and supported by appropriate resources, though it does not need to be complex. A straightforward document outlining tasks, responsible parties, timelines, and goals is sufficient. The lateral's arrival should signal the execution of a prepared plan, not the start of planning.

Put it into practice: After a lateral gives notice to their current firm, schedule a planning session with the lateral, practice group leaders, and marketing and business development professionals.

Market messaging and announcements
Key insight: Make arrival announcements a strategic moment to build momentum and launch lateral success from day one.

Announcing a lateral hire is a strategic decision, not a communications checkbox. Done well, it signals strength and provides a platform. An effective announcement strategy includes:

- *Internal communications first.* Those who will be working with the lateral should hear the news first, before they read it in a press release.
- *Time market announcements appropriately.* An announcement that goes out the day a lateral arrives can create complications. The new partner may still be working through client outreach, meeting new colleagues and learning the firm's tools and processes.
- *Customize outreach to different audiences.* Not everyone should get identical outreach. The message to existing firm clients should differ from that directed to the lateral's professional network, which in turn differs from the general market announcement. Craft each of these messages appropriately, positioning the news for each audience segment.
- *Make it a platform, not a press release.* Consider how content, speaking opportunities, and client events coincide with the lateral's arrival. Amplify the lateral's arrival announcement with substantive events that dovetail with practice development strategies.

Put it into practice: Develop an announcement sequencing plan for each lateral hire, aligning actions with key audiences.

Aligning expectations before day one

Key insight: The most common source of lateral failure is not poor performance by the lateral, but misaligned expectations on both sides. The pre-arrival period is the safest time to have the hardest conversations.

One of the most common and costly sources of lateral failure is misaligned expectations. The firm expected X, the lateral expected Y, and nobody explicitly discussed the gap until both sides were frustrated. These conversations are uncomfortable, but they are far less so when they happen early.

During the pre-arrival period, bridge both sides by facilitating conversations that address:

- The firm's expectations of the lateral in the first year (or documented time period). These are not aspirational numbers, but realistic targets with clear definitions.
- The specific resources and support that the lateral can count on to meet expectations, and whether the firm has the capacity and willingness to provide it.

Put it into practice: Before the lateral starts, hold a structured discussion with the lateral, practice group leaders, and marketing and business development to establish clear expectations for both parties. Document the results and schedule a follow-up in 90 days.

Onboarding and integration – the first 90 days

Key insight: True lateral integration requires business development infrastructure, cultural embedding, and practice growth.

There is a critical distinction between orientation and integration. Orientation happens in the first week – the office tour, systems introduction, and policy reviews. It's necessary, but it's not integration.

Integration is the process by which a lateral becomes embedded in the firm's culture, client relationships and partnership dynamics. True integration takes months, not days, and it requires intentional design.

Marketing and business development teams are essential to building an effective integration system. They facilitate meaningful internal relationships and enhance external visibility that drives revenue. Integration should be intentional, with a well-designed system that addresses:

- *Business development support.* Provide access to business development professionals, tools, intelligence, and visibility-building resources.
- *Internal relationship building.* Intentionally facilitate relationships that the lateral needs to succeed inside the firm.
- *Practice group integration.* Share key insights on how the lateral's practice fits within existing infrastructure, client relationships, and the market narrative.
- *Client introduction strategy.* Craft a deliberate plan for introducing the lateral to firm clients and to the partners who already serve those clients.

Put it into practice: Before a lateral attorney's first day, assign a marketing and business development professional to serve as their integration point of contact and help them integrate smoothly.

The first 90 days framework

Key insight: A 90-day integration plan is most effective when structured into three distinct 30-day phases, each built around specific goals.

Working through a 90-day plan may look something like this.

Days 1-30: Foundation setting

The first 30 days of a lateral's integration should focus on getting oriented. The lead integration contact will facilitate internal and external introductions to drive the lateral's success:

- *Orchestrate internal introductions.* Be purposeful in making introductions, provide context about why the relationship matters, and follow up to answer questions and confirm interactions.
- *Business development infrastructure setup.* Provide access and training for tools such as the CRM, pitch materials, client intelligence, and business development processes.
- *Client transitions.* Facilitate outreach to the lateral's clients, referral sources, and networks by drafting communications, preparing materials, and managing logistics.
- *Early quick wins.* Identify specific, achievable business development actions the lateral can undertake in the first 30 days to build momentum and confidence.

Days 31-60: Building momentum

In the second 30 days, shift from foundation-building to active engagement:

- *Launch market-facing business development.* Facilitate the lateral's inaugural client meetings at the firm, coach them on their quick pitch, craft personalized materials, and follow up on next steps to provide excellent client service.
- *Host events for client touchpoints.* Coordinate small client gatherings to create opportunities for the lateral to introduce new colleagues.
- *Begin cross-selling conversations.* Identify firm clients who should meet the lateral, orchestrating introductions through existing partner relationships.
- *Check-in and course-correct.* As the lateral settles in, check in to be sure expectations are still aligned. This is the time to address and resolve unexpected obstacles.

Days 61-90: Long-term sustainability

In the final 30 days of the formal integration period, establish the lateral's identity as a firm partner through sustainable, ongoing business development efforts:

- *Cement an ongoing business development cadence.* Coach attorneys to build routine in regular client outreach, content development, and events with the goal of bringing in new work from both existing and prospective clients.
- *Evaluate early results.* Open a dialogue about what is working, what needs adjusting, and what needs to be added to support strong business development outcomes.
- *Transition identity.* By day 90, the lateral should feel and be perceived as an integrated partner, giving them room to expand their efforts.

Put it into practice: Create a 90-day integration plan that outlines specific actions and deadlines. Review progress at days 30 and 60 with the lateral and practice group leaders to maintain momentum.

The lateral launch toolkit

Key insight: A curated, practice-specific set of resources prepared before the lateral arrives sends a clear signal that the firm is invested in their success.

Building systematized support for laterals includes crafting a curated set of resources for their specific practice. The integration lead should walk them through the launch kit, which may include:

- A firm overview tailored to their client audiences.
- Practice-specific pitch materials and branded sample presentations.
- Email templates and outreach scripts for different types of relationships.
- A content development roadmap that suggests topics for articles, alerts, and speaking opportunities.
- An events calendar populated with practice-relevant opportunities in the next several months.
- Client opportunities matching firm clients to the lateral's practice.

Put it into practice: Develop a lateral launch toolkit template and customize it for each lateral. Assign a business development professional to manage each toolkit and ensure it is ready before the lateral's first day.

Avoiding common integration failures

Key insight: The cost of integration failure is not just the revenue that was never realized. It is the recruiting fees, signing bonus, compensation, morale impact, damaged client relationships, and reputational cost. Most of these failures are preventable.

Even the best integration plans can fail under the weight of mistakes, with the most common being:

- *Assuming they'll figure it out.* Talented, experienced lawyers are often reluctant to ask for help, especially when they are eager to demonstrate self-sufficiency. Proactive support and check-ins about what is missing or needed to help the lateral get comfortable and productive are essential and welcome.
- *Overwhelming them with firm history and politics.* Laterals need context, not comprehensive institutional history. Focus on what they need to know to be effective now.
- *No clear accountability for integration success.* Integration without ownership is hope without execution. When the 90-day plan is owned by a business development professional, the chance of success increases.
- *Treating marketing and business development teams as order-takers rather than strategic partners.* Proactively drive success by integrating these professionals into the lateral hiring ecosystem.

Put it into practice: At the 90-day mark, conduct an integration review with the lateral, practice group leaders, and the integration lead. Use this session to identify successes, areas for improvement, and future needs.

Beyond 90 days – sustaining success

Key insight: Integration does not end after 90 days. Long-term success requires ongoing support, data-driven measurement, and continuous improvement.

The momentum created in the first 90 days sets the tone for what happens later. The team should continue working with all attorneys to sustain their practices. The goal is to ensure that business development becomes habitual rather than episodic. Some suggestions include:

- *Regular client touchpoints.* A structured cadence of outreach, check-ins, and relationship-building activities supported by the firm's technology tools to sustain a long-term rhythm.
- *Thought leadership strategy.* A content plan keeps laterals visible. The team should facilitate opportunities for articles, alerts, speaking engagements, and webinars to demonstrate acumen and presence.
- *Cross-selling initiatives.* Internal opportunity spotting by the business development team further strengthens internal relationships and adds value to clients.
- *Event strategy.* Participating in relevant industry events, firm-hosted client events, and networking opportunities helps to keep relationships engaged.

Measuring what matters

Key insight: Firms that achieve the best returns on lateral-hiring investments are those that define and track honest metrics.

After the first 90 days, the integration team should conduct regular check-ins to keep the attorney on track with achieving business development goals. Quarterly connects during the first 18 months allow for adjustments before small problems become insurmountable. These conversations are data-driven, collaborative, problem-solving sessions that lead to better results. Some metrics worth tracking include:

- *Client retention rate.* What percentage of the lateral's clients transitioned with them?
- *New business generation.* Is the lateral generating new clients and matters?

- *Cross-selling success.* Are firm clients engaging the lateral's services? Is their network generating new referrals to other firm partners?
- *Market visibility.* Is the lateral building their profile through relevant subject matter speaking opportunities, published articles, and industry recognitions?
- *Profitability.* How much of the lateral's generated revenue and profitability?

Put it into practice: Create a performance dashboard to track metrics quarterly. Share it with the lateral before each check-in to ensure discussions are data-driven. If results are below expectations, use the check-in to identify issues and make adjustments.

Continuous improvement

Key insight: Every lateral integration, whether it is a success story or a cautionary tale, contains lessons to inform the next one.

After each integration cycle, conduct a retrospective about what worked, what needs tweaking, and where the system failed. Document these points and build them back into the process. Over time, this continuous improvement loop will transform the occasional lateral integration success into consistent, repeatable results.

Put it into practice: Conduct a formal integration retrospective with the lateral, practice group leaders, the integration lead, and the recruiter to support institutional learning and improvement.

Implementation framework – getting started

Firms with marketing and business development teams

Key insight: Successful lateral integration depends on involving marketing and business development teams from the beginning.

Folding the firm's marketing and business development professionals into the lateral hiring and integration process builds a robust infrastructure that increases the likelihood of successful lateral integration. To deploy this effort, here are a few practical starting points:

- *Involvement from the beginning.* As a firm policy, marketing and business development leadership should be included in lateral search conversations before candidates are identified.

- *Build a lateral integration playbook.* Create and document a clear, practical guide outlining team responsibilities at each stage. Design an uncomplicated, repeatable process.
- *Assign clear ownership.* Drawing upon natural strengths, choose marketing and business development professionals as the integration lead.
- *Pilot and learn.* Create a plan, document tactics, track results, and refine the process so that you may repeat your successes and course-correct any missteps.

Put it into practice: Before starting a lateral search, schedule a meeting with firm leadership, recruiting, marketing, and business development to define and agree on specific roles and responsibilities for program execution.

Firms without dedicated marketing and business development teams

Key insight: The absence of a dedicated marketing and business development team does not eliminate the need for strategic integration support. It just means the firm has to be more deliberate about where it focuses its resources.

Smaller firms and those without dedicated marketing and business development teams face constraints in this process, but the core principles still apply. Identifying who will coordinate strategic support throughout the lateral hiring lifecycle remains critical to success. Some practical adaptations for resource-constrained environments include:

- *Identify a partner champion.* Select a partner who understands the firm's culture, business development, and client relationships to be the integration lead. Importantly, this individual needs to be willing to play an active role.
- *Focus on the highest-impact activities.* The hiring team should focus on pre-arrival planning, 90-day launch support, and explicit expectation-setting to deliver the most value to a lateral hire.
- *Use external resources strategically.* Engaging marketing consultants, coaching professionals, and peer networks can supplement internal capacity for high-value integration and business development activities.
- *Start with process.* A checklist for each stage of onboarding is better

than no structure at all. Identify the typical to-dos and assign ownership for tactics and follow-through, and supplement with the list of needs specific to each lateral.

Put it into practice: If your firm lacks dedicated marketing and business development staff, appoint an individual to coordinate integration for each lateral hire. This could be a practice group leader or operations professional. Provide them with a clear mandate, a straightforward framework, and the authority to ensure accountability.

A self-assessment for your firm

Key insight: Evaluate your firm's lateral integration process to close gaps and ensure accountability.

Before lateral searches get underway, take an honest look at the firm's current approach to hiring. The goal is not perfection – it is continual progress. Start by answering these questions as candidly as possible:

- Is marketing and business development involved from the start, or only after a hire is made?
- Do we assess candidates on strategic fit and business development potential, or primarily on credentials and a self-reported book of business?
- Do we create a written launch plan before a lateral's first day?
- Do we provide structured, proactive business development support in the first 90 days, or are laterals tasked with asking for what they need?
- Do we measure success with explicit metrics and have honest conversations about results?

Designing for success

Lateral hiring always carries risk. Practice area landscapes shift, client relationships are more complex than they appear, and cultural fit can be hard to assess from the outside. These realities cannot be engineered away.

Most lateral failure is not the result of bad candidates. It is the result of predictable gaps – insufficient strategic vetting, missed recruiting opportunities, no pre-arrival planning, inadequate early support, and failure to measure outcomes. These are all solvable problems, especially when the right professionals are included.

The firms winning the lateral talent race are not doing so because they have bigger signing bonuses or stronger brands. They are winning because they design a better experience. They treat lateral integration as a strategic priority, not an administrative function. By deploying their marketing and business development teams accordingly, they get much deeper results.

The business case is straightforward. Lateral hiring is expensive, the stakes are high, and the failure rate is elevated for firms that manage reactively. A strategic, business development-centric approach demonstrates competitive advantage.

The closing thought that matters most is this – the best lateral integrations feel effortless to the lateral. They feel like the firm always knew exactly what they needed, anticipated their questions before they were asked, and built the conditions for their success before they walked in the door.

That experience does not happen by accident. It is designed. It is coordinated. And it is led, more often than not, by marketing and business development professionals who are given a seat at the table early enough to make a difference.

Start there. Invite them in earlier. Give them the mandate to lead. And then measure what happens. The results will speak for themselves.

Chapter 14:
How integrated client intelligence drives business development

By Nat Slavin, managing partner, Client Insight Ventures and CEO, ClientSignal

The real reason that business development struggles in law firms

For more than three decades I have been sitting across from general counsel, deputy GCs, chief operating officers, legal operations leaders, and procurement heads at the companies that law firms want to keep, and others want to steal. Across thousands of interviews and feedback survey data, the same patterns repeat. Clients want their lives made easier. They want to be made to look good internally. They want their firms to anticipate problems before they ask. And they want firms that know them, not just the law.

Yet in firm after firm, business development efforts struggle. Most of the diagnosis of why firms' efforts underachieve follows a similar pattern – partners do not pitch enough, associates need more BD training, the firm needs a better CRM, the most successful lawyers are too busy, and on and on. Underpinning this is one common reality: most firms project their own BD goals onto their clients. They assume what clients want, why those clients select firms, why those clients move work, and where the cross-sell opportunities are, in the absence of deep intelligence on what individual decision makers actually think. The reason business development struggles in most law firms is not effort. It is intelligence. Most partners are flying blind on their most important client relationships – not because they do not care, but because the intelligence they need to act on is fragmented across systems and people that do not connect.

Law firms are the rare businesses that expect to make more money every year, regardless of what happens to their clients. That orientation has produced a structural blind spot. The signals that should drive BD strategy – what clients want, where they would expand, why they would move work, what selection criteria they actually weight, and what unmet needs they have – all live somewhere inside the firm. They live in the heads of relationship partners. They sit in matter and billing data. They are buried in pitch logs, RFP responses, post-matter survey notes, eBilling platforms, alumni databases, and CRM entries written by people who have since left.

Few firms have any mechanism for assembling these fragments into a single, integrated picture of the relationship. This is a structural problem. The BD strategy of most firms is, in effect, the aggregated intuition of the relationship partners who have line of sight to their own clients but no visibility across the firm. That works in a market where the work flows reliably and the panel is stable. It does not work in a market where panels are consolidating, procurement is professionalizing, eBilling is depersonalizing, and AI is rewriting client expectations of what efficient legal service looks like. The firms that will lead BD over the next decade are those that integrate the intelligence they already have, surface the patterns it contains, and translate them into action.

This chapter is about what integration reveals. It draws on experience from nearly 20 years of client feedback interviews and the last decade of structured survey responses, verbatim comments, and panel-level analysis. The dataset is broad and covers all types of buyers of legal services – from paralegals to chief legal officers to business executives in the largest public companies and family businesses. All told, and for purposes of the research for this chapter, the data used is from the last decade and includes more than 17,000 individuals, providing feedback comments across more than a dozen topics; more simply it consists of more than 250,000 individual comments and ratings of firms from the last decade alone. The point is not the data. The point is that the data confirms, in scale and detail, what every firm already half-knows about its clients. Surfaced systematically, that knowledge becomes a BD strategy. Left disaggregated, it remains an unrealized asset. This work draws on ClientSignal's proprietary dataset where AI tooling was used to synthesize patterns across the data; all findings, framing and editorial judgment are the author's.

What integrated client intelligence reveals

When client intelligence is brought together across the silos that normally separate it, five things become visible that no single source can show. Each is a business development opportunity that almost every firm is leaving on the table.

1. What clients actually want from firms (and how it differs from what lawyers think they want)

Ask a partner what their best client wants from the firm and you will get a thoughtful, plausible answer. Ask the client and you will often get something different. In our research and data analysis, the most-wanted behavior in legal client relationships is not lower fees, not faster turnaround, and not better technology. It is, by a clear margin, this: understand our needs and align solutions to those needs. When clients are asked what they want their firm to do more of, proactive issue anticipation ranks first, ahead of better value, education about the firm's capabilities, more personal relationships, and technology investment. Technology ranks last. Yet most firms talk about technology more than they talk about anticipation.

The same data set reveals what actually keeps firms on the panel. Knowledge of the client's company and industry is the number one retention driver, beating expertise, rates, and quality of advice. Expertise, the thing firms market most aggressively, ranks third. Clients stay because the firm knows them, not just the law. That single distinction has direct implications for how firms invest non-billable time, which lawyers they put on which clients, and what they say about themselves in pitches.

In our analysis of 861 structured responses on how firms grow relationships from the last ten years, or more specifically the answer to the question, "How does this firm grow this relationship?", the data points in the same direction: 31 percent of clients ask for more relationship depth (more face time, more access, more knowing of the people behind the work). Twenty-three percent ask for billing innovation (alternative fee arrangements, predictability, creative structures). Twenty-one percent ask for proactive outreach (newsletters, CLE, relevant insight). Twenty percent ask for cross-practice introduction (show us what else you do). The first three of these together, 65 percent of all answers, are not legal work asks. They are relationship management asks. Most firm BD strategies are built around the legal work.

> *"It does not come up in those conversations, but I think it is a great selling point for any law firm. If we are made aware of something you are doing or investing in, that is an easy top-of-mind thing for us to have. So when things come up, we can say, oh, we talked to [a partner], and she mentioned they are doing that."*
>
> Chief legal officer, Fortune 500 company, 2025

2. How clients think about cross-selling (and why satisfaction is not the unlock)

If there is a single finding that should change how firms think about BD, it is this: on average, over the last decade, 71 percent of clients say they would consider using their primary firm for additional services beyond their current engagement. That number was 38 percent in 2015 and in 2025 grew to an astounding 92 percent. The trajectory is unambiguous. Clients are actively looking to deepen, not diversify, their firm relationships. The buyer is not the obstacle to cross-selling. The seller is.

The "why yes" breakdown confirms the desire to grow existing relationships. Fifty-six percent of responses cite relationship depth and loyalty as the primary reason to send more work. Thirteen percent cite the firm proactively surfacing capabilities the client did not know existed. The "why no" breakdown is even more useful for BD strategy. Twelve percent of all no responses are pure communication failures – the client is willing, the firm is capable, the conversation simply never happens. That is the single most converting target in any cross-sell program. It does not require new capabilities. It requires a phone call.

3. Why clients would move work (and what would make them stay)

The reasons clients leave firms are remarkably consistent, and almost all of them are predictable from data the firm already holds. Clients move work when the specific attorney they trust leaves and is not replaced with someone equally invested. They move work when too many new faces appear on their matters and institutional knowledge of their business is lost. They move work when billing surprises arrive without explanation. They move work when the firm goes quiet between matters and only reaches out at invoice time. They move work when the firm is reactive rather than proactive – only ever responding to what the client asks for, never bringing forward what the client did not yet know they needed.

In just a couple of scenarios that have been deeply researched, we see two patterns that deserve particular attention because they are silent and therefore invisible without diligence and attention. The first is the inherited relationship. When a new decision maker, like a general counsel, takes a role, the existing firm relationship defaults to continuation. However, the new GC carries no personal stake in the choices that put those firms on the panel, formal or otherwise. They evaluate with a fresh eye, and they are disproportionately likely to run an RFP, introduce a procurement tool, or reset outside counsel relationships. Our data from the last ten years (including 1,089 comments on how relationships are formed) validates this theory – 18 percent of relationship origin stories are inherited and these relationships have the highest churn risk in the data; that percentage has stayed in a narrow range over the time period. Critically, they almost never look risky from the firm's perspective. The relationship looks healthy because the work has continued. But loyalty was never personally considered and invested in.

The second silent pattern is what eBilling is doing to the firm–client relationship. Multiple platforms used for billing management have eliminated a quiet but important relationship touchpoint – the cover note that used to accompany an invoice, the phone call that explained an unusual entry, the brief summary that contextualized what was billed. In their place, invoices drop into a queue for anonymous processing. Multiple GCs have described this transition in our interviews as a depersonalization of the relationship. One was direct: *"When we moved to [a new billing platform], things became more impersonal, because instead of someone sending me a bill with a summary, it just goes into the system."* Firms that are surrendering relationship signal to a workflow they do not control.

4. How firms are actually selected (and why most BD assumptions are wrong about this)

Firms that invest heavily in pitch infrastructure often make the assumption that a competitive RFP is the dominant path to relationship formation. Again, the data says otherwise. In the same 1,089 comments mentioned above from the last decade regarding how relationships actually formed, only four percent began with a cold RFP. The rest were human. Here's more of what the data reveals:

- 14 percent of relationships began with a client following an attorney from a prior firm.
- 11 percent started with reputation – the client sought the firm out for a specific matter or practice.
- 18 percent were inherited.
- Three percent came from a peer or network referral.

The cold competitive process, despite consuming an outsized share of BD energy at most firms, accounts for a small minority of how relationships actually start.

Looking more deeply at RFPs, the data also tells a story that explains the law firm default habit around RFPs. RFP activity has tripled since 2019, but the function of an RFP in 2025 is not what most firms imagine. RFPs are now used predominantly to discipline incumbents on price, satisfy board or CFO mandates for competitive sourcing, give procurement institutional cover, and manage panel refresh cycles. Firms that engage with the client before the RFP launches have a massive competitive advantage. Firms that wait for the invitation to respond are already late.

The same dynamic applies to the procurement platforms companies use to manage RFPs. Clients using these platforms describe them slightly differently than the platform's stated purpose of "price-discovery". The individual attorney within the company controls who is invited to the auction. Expertise, institutional knowledge, and relationship consistently override price in final selection. One platform is, in the words of a client in late 2025, "a control mechanism with relationship loopholes". Winning the invite list, which is a relationship investment in the individual lawyer who controls it, is more strategically valuable than winning the auction itself.

On the question of what actually drives selection when the decision is made: across more than 6,000 structured responses to "why did you select this firm?" from the entire data set, the data reveals:

- Expertise, defined as not general expertise, but specific expertise related to the specific client need, leads at 46 percent.
- Personal relationship and trust sits at 21 percent.
- Existing relationship and incumbency is 19 percent.
- Price is only ten percent.

Digging deeper, the actual comments by buyers complicate how lawyers and firms, protect and win new business. Clients who cite specific expertise as the primary driver almost always pair it with a personal relationship that validates the expertise. Expertise gets you the call. Relationship gets you the work. Firms that pitch on expertise alone are answering only half the question.

> *"Cost being commensurate with experience is important from a business standpoint. The relationship piece is also highly influential. In [this relationship] we met at an event and started talking and found out they were from the same town and knew the same people. And now we are all on a texting basis. I feel like he is a friend that has our best interests in mind."*
> Chief legal officer, Am Law 100 client, 2026

5. Where unmet client needs reveal the next BD opportunity

Integrated intelligence does not just describe the present relationship. It identifies the gaps where unmet client needs are creating openings, both for the incumbent firm and for its competitors. Three of these openings stand out in current data.

The first is the technology expectations gap. Across our dataset, client ratings of their firms' technology have declined in six of the last seven years by nearly 20 percent. Whenever there is a decline in certain topics, like technology, it's not because it is less important – it's because the firms' use of, and deployment of, technological solutions is less of a distinguishing factor; firms that were lagging catch up; early mover status disappears.

Just look at the use of AI. Over the same period, client expectations about what AI should make possible have accelerated dramatically. Tech-related comments in client interviews increased 16-fold between 2022 and 2025. Being evaluated more expectantly on the use of technology solutions, particularly AI, is at an all-time high. The first firm in any given client relationship to bring a credible, concrete AI proposal to the table will gain a disproportionate advantage. Almost no firm is doing this consistently.

The second is the value–budget disconnect. In every year since 2008, clients have rated "value for fees" higher than "budget and billing". With AI now allowing firms to capture meaningful efficiencies, the gap is at risk of widening sharply if those efficiencies are kept by the firm and not shared with the client. Clients are watching this carefully. In 2025 alone, more than 35 percent of clients directly linked efficiency expectations to billing pressure. Firms that proactively address this conversation, before the client raises it, will earn loyalty and expansion. Firms that wait to be asked are at greater risk by comparison.

The third is the proactivity gap. Proactive issue anticipation is the number one client request from outside counsel in what more they can do beyond the legal work. The behavior clients most want is the behavior that least frequently shows up, even in the best relationships. That gap is the highest potential coaching advice because it is also the most direct connection between client intelligence and BD. A firm that systematically surfaces issues to clients has a natural, and massive, competitive advantage.

Market intelligence – objective and subjective

The solution for the challenges, and business development opportunities, described in this chapter relies on connecting and assessing two kinds of intelligence that most firms keep separate, and doing so in context.

Objective intelligence is the structured data the firm already holds – matter and billing data, realization rates by client and partner, panel rankings where available, win-loss records on competitive pitches, eBilling activity, OCG terms, and sentiment and data analysis of client feedback. This is the data that firm leadership regularly reviews and presents in a contextual story in the form of metrics, dashboards, and trend lines.

Subjective intelligence is the unstructured data the firm holds in less-organized forms – verbatim comments from client conversations, both formal and informal. The relationship language that clients use about other firms on their panels, extemporaneous comments about what they value, how their peers internally and externally talk about the firm and its lawyers. And even the things relationship partners hear at industry events that never make it into a system. This is the data the relationship partner and the marketing director must see, and then connect to the relationship (business development and client growth) goals. It produces context, sentiment, and direction.

Caveat emptor: either kind of intelligence alone is misleading. Objective data without context overweighs satisfaction signals such as NPS and underweighs the relational variables that actually drive cross-selling and retention. Subjective data without aggregation produces compelling anecdotes that are too often a reflection of past experience, not future opportunity or growth. It's the proverbial driving the car by looking only in the rear view mirror.

But together they reveal patterns that no single source can show. A client with a high loyalty score and a zero percent cross-sell rate means the firm simply has not asked for incremental work. Furthermore, clients are often transparent in where the work goes. A client who repeatedly refers to other firms by name is either announcing where the next competitive threat already exists, or where there is opportunity to capture work from those competitor firms. Too often, we see a relationship partner's confident assertion that the relationship is healthy, but that can be contradicted when the data shows the only client touchpoints beyond the delivery of work product is sending the monthly bill. Taking the time outside of the work to connect on client needs, and then listening for opportunities, is key to client growth.

But the landscape has changed. It is now possible to synthesize across the structured data a firm holds and the unstructured data it holds, at scale, in ways that were not previously feasible. The firms moving fastest are pairing that synthesis capability with the discipline to act on what it surfaces. Discipline supported by tools produces strategic clarity. Tools without discipline produce nothing useful.

What firms need to do: five moves

Translating integrated client intelligence into a business development strategy requires five disciplined moves at the leadership level. None of them is technically complex. All of them require a deliberate decision to operate the firm differently than the silos currently allow.

Move 1: Designate ownership for client intelligence at the firm level

The single biggest operational reason that integration does not happen at most firms is that no one owns it. Marketing owns feedback. Finance owns billing data. Pricing owns AFAs. Practice groups own the relationships. The CFO sees one slice; the CMO sees another; the partner sees a third. Until someone, typically a chief client officer, head of client value, or chief strategy officer, has explicit authority and access across all of these systems and the mandate to synthesize, integration will not occur. Designating ownership is the prerequisite. Everything else is downstream of it.

Move 2: Map the origin story of every key relationship

For each of the firm's top clients, document how the relationship actually began. Was it followed-from-a-prior-firm? Inherited from a predecessor GC? Won in a competitive pitch? Born of a referral? Built from a single matter? Different origins require different investment strategies, and inherited relationships in particular need a deliberate plan to convert default loyalty into chosen loyalty. The data is unambiguous – an inherited relationship gets fresh evaluation, and the firm that has not invested in that personal relationship will lose share when the panel is refreshed. Ultimately, when relationships are forged, the client will fight to keep the firm, even when there is change at the top of the organization and other firms are brought in for consideration.

Move 3: Build the cross-sell motion around capability communication

First, target decision makers, not influencers. These are clients who would say yes if they were asked, and they have never been asked. A proactive capability introduction strategy based on known client needs, and even gaps in where they are being served by other firms, organized around the clients' business needs is all opportunity and does not require change in the firm's capabilities. It's a simple process: ask the clients where they need help, offer a solution to that problem and then deliver against the promise and expectations.

Move 4: Treat the billing conversation as a relationship investment, not a negotiation

Twenty-three percent of clients even offer a simple recommendation when asked how a firm can grow the relationship: billing innovation. Clients who say they want more from the firm often say it in the language of fees – alternative fee arrangements, predictability, caps, success fees, value-based structures. Firms that approach billing as a place to defend rates lose the conversation before it begins. Firms that approach billing as a place to invest in the relationship, with creative structures the client did not have to ask for, earn disproportionate loyalty and the cross-sell expansion that follows.

The single most actionable risk-detection signal in the last decade of feedback data is value and budget scoring together. When both are weak, the relationship is in active attrition territory, whether or not the partner sees it.

Move 5: Replace what eBilling has stripped out

When invoices flow through billing platforms, the relationship signals that used to come with the bill disappears. Most firms have not noticed because the work has continued. The work continues until it does not. The fix is simple and within every firm's control – at invoice time, the relationship partner sends a brief, personal note summarizing the matter, the outcome, the rationale for what was billed, and the next thing the client should be thinking about. That note replaces what the platform stripped out. It also, not incidentally, creates a documented monthly relationship touchpoint that no procurement system can disintermediate.

Then, and most importantly, schedule regular meetings with the clients to discuss:

- What's next?
- What challenges do you see impacting you in the next quarter?
- Are there any areas where you need support where you aren't confident in who you are currently working with?
- How can we help solve your big, and small, internal challenges?
- And, most importantly, how can we make your life easier?

A self-assessment for leadership, and what to do first

Before any of these moves, leadership teams must answer six questions about their top clients. The questions are deliberately diagnostic. They reveal where the silos are.

1. For each of these clients, do we know whether the current decision maker personally chose us or inherited us?
2. Do we know which other firms each of these clients is using, on what kinds of work, and why?
3. Do we know what each of them weights most heavily in firm selection, and how that weighting has changed in the last two years?
4. When we last priced a major matter for any of these clients, whose voice from the client was actually in the room?
5. For each of these clients, what is the one piece of intelligence currently held in someone's head somewhere in the firm that would most change a strategic decision if it were known at the leadership table?
6. If we were to lose this relationship in the next 12 months, what would the loss most likely look like, and would we see it coming?

The answers, or the inability to produce them, will tell leadership exactly where to start. For most firms, the practical roadmap looks like this:

- Identify the top 25 strategic clients and assemble what is currently known about each across all internal sources.
- Designate a single firm-level owner for client intelligence with the authority to integrate across functions.
- Conduct rigorous feedback on the gaps the inventory reveals.
- Establish a monthly leadership review of integrated client intelligence on the strategic clients, tied to specific decisions on the table – pricing, staffing, panel position, expansion, and known client needs and service gaps.
- Train relationship partners on the small set of questions that yield the highest value intelligence in any client conversation, on or off the clock, and create a low-friction mechanism for what they hear to enter the firm's integrated view.
- Audit the firm's eBilling touchpoint coverage. For every client whose only firm contact in the last 60 days was a system-generated invoice notification, schedule a personal outreach within the week.
- Maybe most importantly, but also with the highest degree of difficulty, tie partner compensation, in some material way, to the discipline of capturing and sharing client intelligence rather than holding it.

A culture, not a project

Integrating client intelligence is not a project. It is not an initiative. It is not a quarterly survey or an annual feedback round. It is the way the firm operates. It is the discipline by which BD decisions get tested against what the firm has actually learned about the clients those decisions are meant to serve.

The firms that will lead business development in the coming years will not be the ones with the slickest slogans about client focus and service. They will be the ones whose leaders can describe their most important clients in detail. The ones who can speak credibly about what those clients want, where they would expand, why they might leave, and what they need that they have not yet asked for. The ones who have integrated the intelligence they already had, surfaced the patterns it contains, and used those patterns to decide where to invest.

The voice of the client is the client growth roadmap. Leadership's job is to use that as a GPS in following the growth roadmap. And every firm is different, just as every client is different. One size fits one. And the firms that operate that way, at scale, with discipline, every day, are the ones their clients will keep choosing. Just as law firms want to protect their best relationships, clients want the same. But how they define those best relationships needs to be uncovered, validated and then checked again over time.

Chapter 15:
Succession planning – ensuring client continuity when leaders retire

By Ida O. Abbott, founder, Ida Abbott Consulting

Partner retirements present valuable business opportunities. Losing lucrative clients and engagements when partners retire can be very costly, even catastrophic, for a law firm. Retiring partners are often rainmakers who control major client relationships and generate a disproportionate percentage of firm revenues. Keeping those clients is important to the continued health, stability, and economic vitality of the firm.

Preventing the loss of good clients when a partner retires requires careful planning, ample time, and concerted effort. Through well-planned and thoughtful client transitions, the firm can keep many of these clients. It can also enhance the leadership and rainmaking skills of successor partners and increase revenues and firm stability by strengthening and expanding the retiring partner's client relationships.

The challenge is how to manage client transitions properly. That's why it's so important for firms to have a client succession and transition process that is transparent, consistent, systematic, and fair. It's why retirement must be de-stigmatized and treated as a normal part of a lawyer's career, not the onset of obsolescence. All of that is easier in a culture where people trust each other, value collaboration, and honor legacy.

Case study: An effective and successful client transition

In this case study, a client of mine talks about their retirement process:

> *"I was deliberate about succession planning for years, long before anyone knew I was thinking of retiring. About a year before I retired, I told major colleagues on my team what I was thinking of doing so that they would know that they needed to step up to hold onto the business, and I fought for them to have the opportunities to prove themselves. Then I told the client of my plans.*
>
> *"To build trust, I shut up on client calls and made sure each of these team*

members was well-prepared to speak on their subject; I was transparent with the team about the client's preferences and concerns; and I made sure the key players had their own relationships with the client and had roles where the client could see them in action before they had to hire them on their own. It was also a team effort to hold onto the work. No one person likely could have done it, as they all played more specialized roles than I did.

"In the end, my client was happy for me, knew and trusted the team I trained and left behind, and hired them for a $20 million+ matter later the same year. These are significantly junior lawyers to me, but the client is comfortable because they've seen the team in action and know they provide excellent continuity. The client didn't hesitate to stay with them. It's wonderful for the client and for the team who have much more business – and credit – than they would have otherwise had at this stage in their careers."

Developing an effective client succession and transition process

Some partners thoughtfully plan and carry out client succession and transitions on their own initiative (see case study). Because many others do not, firms can prompt them to do it through a retirement policy that applies to all partners when they reach a designated age or career milestone. That policy should include a process describing what partners should do about client succession in the years before they retire. Firm partnership agreements often include terms relating to when or how partners may retire from the partnership (e.g., how much notice they must give), but they usually do not go into detail about the retirement process.

To increase the chances of client continuity, a retirement policy can provide a mechanism for transitioning clients to successors before the partner retires. The policy informs partners that, at a designated point, they will be expected to discuss with the firm the process to be followed, including how and to whom they will transfer their clients, when they do decide to retire. Knowing that all their colleagues will have similar conversations at the same point reduces partners' anxiety and facilitates frank discussions about the future.

To develop an effective client succession and transition process, firms first need to appreciate that the firm, clients, retiring lawyers, and successor lawyers all have their own interests and needs. The firm can then decide what it wants to achieve with a client transition policy and design a process that acknowledges diverse interests and needs, reconciles those that may conflict, and persuades partners that it is in their best interest to cooperate.

The firm's interests

It is in the firm's interests to have partners give as much advance notice as possible before they retire so that it can plan for and manage future staffing, financial, and leadership needs. If the firm wants to retain good clients, it needs strong leadership by other lawyers to replace the partners who retire. Effective succession practices ensure sufficient time to prepare for partner departures, carry out smooth client transitions, and advance the next generation of leaders and rainmakers.

Conversations asking partners about their retirement plans can be awkward. They require talking to partners who have devoted much of their lives to building and leading the firm about when and how they will leave it. Rather than risk upsetting or angering partners, firms delay discussions about retirement until they have no choice. But this avoidance poses problems.

Partners, too, may remain silent about their plans. They spend their last years at the firm focusing primarily on protecting themselves, especially their compensation. They hold tightly to their clients and leadership roles, frustrating the next generation of partners whose prospects for business growth, professional advancement, and leadership are blocked. They may coast along without exerting much effort, dragging down profits and further frustrating junior partners. When they do retire, it is often on short notice, making it difficult to plan smooth transitions of clients and leadership. As a result, junior partners may seek better career opportunities and clients may take their legal business elsewhere.

When the firm has a systematic retirement and succession process in place, it is more likely to retain both clients and junior partners. When successors are fully prepared and ready to take over, clients enjoy uninterrupted service and appreciate the smooth transfer of leadership. Junior lawyers can see a meaningful future in the firm because partners give them increasing responsibility, visibility, and credit; encourage them to develop their own relationships with the senior partners' clients; and share their contacts and opportunities to help successors build their own books of business.

By retaining and developing the firm's talent and leadership, the firm's reputation in the business and legal communities can be enhanced, not diminished, when a prominent partner leaves. Being known as a firm with a deep bench of talent, where lawyers can maintain continuous service when a key lawyer leaves, is attractive to potential clients, referral sources, and laterals looking for a firm where they can move up and ahead in their careers.

In some jurisdictions, an effective client succession policy is also a matter of professional responsibility. Some state bars have rules regarding the responsibility of lawyers to put in place succession plans to protect clients. Firms should be aware of the rules of the jurisdictions in which their lawyers practice.

The client's interests

Clients expect commitment, excellence, and reliability from their outside counsel. They expect high performance from lawyers they know and trust. When partners retire, clients expect all of that to continue seamlessly.

Clients value having a single contact who understands their needs and ensures they receive high quality service. But they also appreciate a team of outside counsel they can call upon if they can't reach their main contact or need help beyond that lawyer's expertise. If they have an assortment of legal needs, they value a team with experts in relevant areas.

Clients expect to be told well in advance about their lead counsel's retirement, and to be consulted and involved in the selection of a successor. The final decision is, after all, theirs. They expect timely succession discussions, thoughtful plans, and new relationship partners who are suitable, compatible, and fully prepared to take over. Ideally, the successor is someone they have worked with before who is familiar with the client's business and legal matters, and who they know to have the expertise and work ethic they value.

Clients do not want to be presented with a last-minute announcement that their lead partner is leaving. They don't want a successor chosen by the partner or firm without their input or prior agreement. When a partner moves to another firm, clients understand that the firm could not provide a lot of advance notice. When a partner retires, however, especially if it is planned (or could have been) well in advance, clients resent not being told in ample time to consider their options, whether in that firm or another.

The retiring lawyer's interests

Retirement is one of the hardest transitions in a lawyer's life. Lawyers often resist retiring, and they especially resist giving up client relationships. Some want to retire but fear negative repercussions if they announce too soon.

Understanding the reasons behind their resistance enables firms to create strategies and conditions that foster trust and engage senior partners in succession and client transitions.

All career changes are stressful, but retirement is different. Every partner going through a significant career change, like switching firms or becoming a managing partner, faces challenges but has a general idea of what lies ahead. Their training and experience have prepared them for the move, and their career progression continues in an upward or lateral direction. But when senior partners face retirement from the job that has been at the center of their life and identity for decades, the future is entirely uncharted territory, full of unknowns and uncertainties, and without guides or guideposts. Perhaps most important, they fear the loss of status and professional identity once they are no longer law firm partners and leaders.

Adding to this anxiety is the need to relinquish long-term client relationships that have been the source of their success. Partners may feel possessive of the relationships they built and nurtured over a lifetime of practice. They may believe no one can replace them or provide the same level of care and attention their client requires. They may simply feel a need to be in charge or to be needed.

Aging and ageism are also factors. Our society values youth – as do law firms. Retirement is associated with getting older. Retiring lawyers themselves may be perfectly healthy and capable, but view retiring as a sign of oncoming decline or a reminder of their own mortality. Older lawyers can be highly valuable, but retiring lawyers are often treated by others in the firm as no longer important or relevant. Their history of contributions may be appreciated but they represent the past – the firm is focused on the future.

Senior partners want to be treated with respect, dignity, and fairness when they retire – not as if they are being pushed aside. They want to know what the firm expects from them before they leave, what they can expect from the firm, and what will happen to them when they plan to depart. Few firms provide clear guidance or cultural environments that make partners feel secure and safe enough to discuss their retirement openly.

When they do exist, firm retirement policies often generate confusion. They rarely spell out clearly how to retire or what happens when you do. Sometimes firms make exceptions in "special cases" or treat retiring partners differently for subjective or unexplained reasons. Lack of transparency and consistency about what happens when they announce their intent to retire, and especially the fear of punitive financial consequences, creates suspicion and distrust.

Perhaps the biggest deterrent for senior partners is fear of losing compensation. The uncertainty of what will happen if they announce their retirement makes it especially hard to let go of the compensation and credits they've earned. It isn't necessarily that these partners need the money, it's what that money represents – wealth, importance, and power. They have reached the top compensation levels through years of hard work and don't want to lose what they have attained. A drop in compensation may be insignificant financially, but of major importance to their ego.

If policies or decision-making processes are ambiguous, it will be hard for the firm to overcome the partner's fear and distrust. But when firms have a clear policy that spells out criteria, processes, and calculations, and if it applies that policy consistently to all retiring partners, partners are more likely to believe they are being treated fairly and more willing to speak about their plans.

The successor partner's interests

The prospect of inheriting an established client should be appealing to a junior partner. However, potential successors want the security that comes from having their own clients. If they must choose between serving their own clients and working on another partner's clients, it makes sense for them to opt for the former. While inheriting an existing client may be easier, the possible successor wants some assurance that the client will actually be transferred to them, and that they will receive a fair share of credit and compensation during the transition. Without transparency and prior agreement, retiring partners may change their minds and decide not to retire, transfer the client, or share the credit, leaving the junior partner empty-handed and angry.

Successful client transitions show younger partners that upward mobility and future career success are real possibilities for them. When retiring partners carry out a plan for the eventual handover of their clients, successors can acquire increasing levels of responsibility, leadership, and client management skills. They are well positioned to earn the client's trust and deepen their own client relationships. They can build on the retiring partner's contacts and community leadership roles to gain prominence professionally. These are all important considerations for lawyers who want career advancement and for firms that want to attract and retain the best legal talent.

Preliminary steps

A client succession and transition process should be tailored to the specific culture and situation of each firm. Firms differ in countless ways. The descriptions above of the parties' varying interests apply generally but are not universal. To design an effective succession and transition process, you need to identify the needs, interests, and circumstances of your own firm, its lawyers, and clients. Designing a process that looks and sounds good is easy – designing one that is feasible and viable in your firm requires deeper analysis of the firm's culture.

Analyzing firm demographics

A demographic analysis of the firm is an initial step in undertaking the development of a client succession and transition process. Understanding the age range of the partnership generally and within specific practice groups or departments will help you estimate when partners will retire and anticipate what the firm will need to do to avoid disruption to its finances, personnel, and operations. Looking at the "average" ages and tenures at which partners have retired in the past (e.g., for the last five to ten years) may disclose pertinent trends, such as whether lawyers have been retiring at younger ages. This data should be straightforward and easy to obtain from firm records.

With a rough prediction of which and how many partners may retire in the next few years, you can assess how those departures may affect the firm, such as the financial impact if clients leave when the partner does; who the firm is counting on to meet future staffing and leadership needs; and the effort and cost of recruiting or developing successors for clients the firm wants to keep.

Understanding the firm's culture

Another important but more difficult preliminary step is to take a close look at the firm's culture. This includes partners' attitudes toward each other and the firm. Senior partners who feel well-treated and care about the firm's future are more likely to transfer clients to their successors. When lawyers share client management routinely, transitions are easier. On the other hand, in firms with a high level of distrust or self-centeredness, partners may focus more on protecting their own security with less regard for those they leave behind.

Some firms might want to use outside consultants to conduct a cultural assessment, but others may find that partners respond better to other partners. An internal committee should include a cross-section of the partnership in terms of seniority, gender, and practice areas. In multi-office firms, it would be useful to include partners in different locations.

Information can be obtained through confidential surveys, focus groups, or interviews. Outreach should include as many partners as possible, at every stage of practice.

In addition to collecting useful information, this process has other benefits. It serves to:

- Notify the partnership that a client succession and transition policy is being considered;
- Explain the reasons for it and the good intentions behind it;
- Educate partners that retirement is an integral part of lawyers' lifelong career development;
- Emphasize that retirement is a lengthy process, not a single or last-minute event;
- Remind partners of the importance of mentoring and developing lawyers;
- Discover objections, problematic attitudes, or unexpected issues;
- Find examples of partner retirements that were effective or not;
- Solicit ideas and suggestions from across the partnership; and
- Stimulate buy-in from the partnership.

What you learn should help you decide how to approach the subjects of retirement, succession planning, and client transitions, as well as what should be included or avoided, possible pitfalls, and how to overcome potential obstacles.

When surveying partners, here are examples of areas to inquire about:

- Does the firm currently have a retirement policy? If so, what do partners know about it? If they do not know much about it, why not?
- Are partners comfortable talking candidly with the firm about their retirement plans?
- How collaborative are partners? Are partners primarily looking out for themselves or do they care about helping colleagues? Will they be willing to sacrifice some short-term benefits (e.g., compensation during the transition period) for the future good of the firm?
- What will appeal to senior partners and make them willing to cooperate in the process?
- What assurance will possible successor partners need?

- What are partners' concerns about compensation and credit-sharing during the transition?
- How do lawyers perceive this initiative? What are their concerns? Are there any notable concerns or objections among lawyers at different career stages?

Designing the client succession and transition process

The specific components will be unique to your firm, but an effective process should contain a few key elements:

1. A clear statement of purpose and intent.
2. What will initiate the process.
3. Impact of the process on partner compensation.
4. What retiring partners are expected to do.
5. How the firm will support retiring partners.
6. Who will lead and oversee the process.

It is also helpful for firms to provide guidelines that explain the elements in greater detail, as well as templates, examples, and resources.

1. A clear statement of purpose and intent

A client succession and transition process is usually part of an overall retirement policy. The policy should state what it intends to achieve by establishing a succession and transition process, why it is important to the firm and to clients, and how it will benefit the firm's lawyers.

A retirement policy must also make very clear whether the policy requires partners to retire at a certain age or other specific point. If it does not, then it must reassure partners that the intent is not to force partners to retire, but to achieve the policy's stated purpose in a fair and orderly way when partners do decide to retire.

If the policy is mandatory and requires partners to retire at a certain point, then the reasons must be fully explained. The policy should also explain what happens to partners who reach the designated retirement time. Must they leave? Can they stay in a new non-equity status?

With any policy, the firm must be careful about making exceptions. If exceptions are made for "special cases", they must be pursuant to criteria plainly stated in the policy. Otherwise, some partners will remain in denial until the last moment, certain that they will receive special treatment.

2. What will initiate the process

The policy should state at what point partners will be expected to begin the succession and transition process.

Most policies initiate a retirement process by using partners' age, number of years in practice, or number of years in the firm. Others designate financial factors as process triggers, such as having a client, or portfolio of clients, that generate revenues of a certain amount. Individual partners can voluntarily start a transition process if they decide to retire before they reach the firm's designated starting point.

A retirement policy with a succession and transition process presents an easy way to open conversations with partners about retirement that might otherwise be awkward or difficult. Without a policy, when firms ask partners about their retirement plans on an ad hoc basis, partners may feel singled out, threatened, and defensive. But when every partner is asked about their future practice plans and needs as an ordinary, routine matter, it normalizes the subject and makes it easier to discuss openly. A good way to do that is to include those questions in annual practice surveys or compensation discussions.

Some firms' policies give the firm discretion to initiate the retirement process for reasons related to performance. This can be useful with a partner whose productivity drops significantly but who demands the same compensation they have been receiving. The transition process enables the firm to have serious conversations about how the partner's performance affects their compensation and continuation in the firm. The risk, however, is that people will perceive the policy as a disguised way to punish underperformers or push senior partners out.

3. Impact of the process on partner compensation

Every firm needs to decide how it can best calculate and allocate compensation during a retirement transition. Perhaps no factor has a greater effect on the success of a succession and transition process than how compensation is handled. To be viewed as fair, the firm must explain clearly how the partner's decision to retire and the transfer of their clients to successors will affect their compensation. It should also explain any situations where partners are entitled to continuing payments after they retire, such as contingency fees.

Each retiring partner is in a different situation and expects to be treated accordingly. But this personalized approach needs to take place within a framework that lays out the rules, formulas, or at least the factors and general approach that are used to determine compensation for everyone during their transition period. They should also address the impact on compensation as partners transfer client responsibilities and credit to the successor.

In determining how your firm will manage compensation during the transition period, factors to consider include:

- Expectations for partners' billable hours.
- Whether hours may be gradually reduced.
- Whether transitioning partners will be paid for non-billable and pro bono work.
- How to fairly allocate credit to successors.
- Time and expense required to prepare successors.

In deciding what approach it will take, the firm must balance the need for effective transitions with the costs it will incur during the process. For example, when successor preparation requires both retiring and successor partners to spend time on a matter, will the firm bill the client for that time or absorb the cost? If the firm intends to offer bonuses for successful client retention, how will those payments be funded?

4. What retiring partners are expected to do

An effective client transition must be carefully and thoughtfully planned. The firm should ask retiring partners to draft a written plan that lays out what the partner will do to select and groom successors, and how the partner will transition client work and control to the successor. Components of a client succession and transition plan include:

- Identification of clients.
- Identification of possible successors for each client.
- Actions the partner will take to prepare successors to take over.
- Expectations for ongoing workload and billable hour commitment.
- Arrangement for compensation andclient credit during the transition.
- Timetable for completing the transition.

Before partners can draft a proposed transition plan, the firm needs to give them some basic information about the planning process. This information should be set out in written guidelines, but the firm should also have designated individuals meet with the partner in advance to discuss firm expectations, policy provisions, and the planning approval process. They can explain any options or restrictions that the partner may not realize and address the partner's questions or concerns before the partner begins drafting a plan.

In addition, this firm representative can make sure the partner has other important information, such as:

- When and to whom they should submit their proposed plan.
- Who will be involved in negotiating the plan.
- Who will have authority to approve the plan.
- Role of the compensation committee.
- How frequently and with whom partners will meet to discuss their progress in effectuating the plan.
- Whether they will have to sign a formal agreement, memorializing the plan.

Identification of clients

Partners need to decide how they will transition each client. To help partners decide, the firm should give them as much relevant client data as possible, including a list of their current clients and for each client: a financial analysis, including revenues billed and collected; specific transactions, cases, and other legal matters billed to the client currently and in the past; and names of all lawyers who have billed hours to the client, the number of hours, and the kind of work they have done. Most of this data should be readily available from the accounting or financial services department.

It is also helpful for the partner to know if the firm wants to keep a client or not. Some clients are very profitable and from the firm's perspective, desirable, while others may not be. If the firm knows that there are types or categories of clients it can no longer support or is no longer interested in, they should let partners know in advance.

Partners should be asked to describe in their transition plans any possibilities for expanding a client relationship, or belief that a client's future legal needs may contract or change. This information can help the partner identify possible successors and help the partner and firm plan a strategy for client retention.

Identification of possible successors for each client

For each client, partners should identify lawyers with the potential to succeed them as lead partner. Partners should consider the qualifications necessary to lead client relationships generally and each client in particular.

Some successors are obvious. They already work closely with the client and are known and trusted by the client and the retiring partner. They demonstrate the expertise, work ethic, client relation skills, and leadership ability required for the role. If there is no apparent successor, the partner needs to look closely at other lawyers who have the potential to do the job. These are lawyers whose work and attitude show they strive to excel, are motivated to learn, and are eager to advance. Their talents might not be fully formed, but the transition period gives them time to learn from the retiring partner, and to develop and polish the skills needed to achieve their potential. For very large or important clients, it is wise to identify more than one potential successor for a client.

If there are no candidates within the firm, the firm can help the partner recruit and prepare a successor from elsewhere.

How the partner will prepare successors to take over

Partners should describe what they have done, and what they will do, to prepare the successors chosen for each client. A lawyer's capability, experience, motivation, and readiness to lead the client will determine the type and extent of preparation that will be needed, such as the work experiences, client interactions, mentoring, and introductions to provide. The retiring partner should also build in occasions to impart client insights, institutional knowledge, and professional wisdom.

Partners should be as specific as possible about what actions they will take. They might list any people who will need to be involved and resources that will need to be used. They should also give time estimates for how long the preparation will take. Table 1 shows the basic components of an action plan for successor preparation. Drop-down categories can be included in some of the columns to make it even easier to fill out.

Table 1. Successor preparation plan

Client	Successor(s)	Experience/ contact successor needs generally and with client	Actions I will take to prepare successor	People/ resources needed	Timetable	Notes

Expectations for ongoing workload and billable hour commitment
A partner's transition plan should state how much billable work the partner intends to do during the transition period. While some partners intend to work full-time until they retire, others prefer to retire gradually. Partners should be informed if they are expected to bill a minimum number of hours during their transition. If the policy permits a phased retirement (i.e. reducing their workload, billable hours, and firm responsibilities in stages), it should provide guidelines about how a phased retirement would work.

The plan should also address the amount of non-billable time the partner expects to spend in activities such as preparing successors, doing pro bono work, and fulfilling firm responsibilities (e.g., leadership roles, committee work).

Arrangement for compensation and client credit during the transition
The partner's transition plan should include a proposal for the compensation they want during the transition. If they elect to retire in phases, then they should propose how their work reductions will affect their compensation in each phase. They should also propose whether and how much billing and client relationship credit they will share with their successor during the transition. Doing this also acts as a reminder that they need to intentionally transfer client care and management responsibilities to the successor.

Timetable for completing the transition
The amount of time to create and complete a client succession and transition process depends on many factors, including complexity of the representation, depth of the retiring partner's relationship with the client, availability and readiness of successors, and the nature and breadth of the partner's entire practice. For some lawyers, the transition process may take a few weeks. For leaders and rainmakers with large books of business and clients with complex legal needs, it may take many years.

Transitions take longer than most people realize, so it's wise to set a broad timeframe, say three to five years or more, to complete the transition process. You can ask, encourage, and remind partners to start early and allow the longer time.

Setting timetables and interim milestones can help retiring partners focus and stay on track. Many things change or come up during a long transition period, so expected dates for events and milestones need to be flexible. But they provide a framework for accomplishing client transitions.

Notification of clients

Partners are expected to inform their clients of their plans to retire, but the decision about when and how to do it rests with the individual partner. Each partner–client relationship will necessarily determine how the partner will tell the client and how much advance notice they will give. Partners can be asked about this during their regular progress meetings.

5. How the firm will support retiring partners

Undertaking a client succession and transition process takes time, and most partners would rather spend that time doing other things. The firm should offer them guidance, support, and resources to make it as easy as possible for them at every step. That will make it more likely that partners will transition clients successfully.

There are many ways to help partners with their retirement and client transitions:

- Enlist firm personnel and departments to provide the information, direction, analyses, and advice partners need.
- Provide guidelines and planning templates. To make it even easier, firms can create drop-down questions that allow partners to check off boxes and minimize the need for written narratives (see Table 1).
- Utilize AI systems to facilitate the process. For example:
    - Conduct financial analyses of client engagements and create models of the long-term financial impact of retaining or losing clients.
    - Study lawyers' billed hours, experience, and professional development to analyze client relationships and successor readiness, and maybe even suggest possible successors.
    - Enhance successors' learning and preparation by capturing retiring partners' institutional and client knowledge.
- Use educational programs, social events, and marketing initiatives to intentionally connect junior and senior partners and encourage them to build relationships with each other and with clients.
- Offer training on client skills and succession planning or integrate the training into management and leadership programs.
- Track professional development and ensure associates and junior partners get increasing client responsibilities and contact.
- In firm programs that address lawyers' career development, include discussion of retirement as a natural career stage.

6. Who will lead and oversee the process

In many firms, the responsibility for managing the client succession and transition process rests with an individual like the managing partner, or a firm committee like the executive or management committee. Some firms establish a separate oversight committee for this purpose. These are the people in charge, expected to deal with any problems or questions that come up, such as resolving disputes or dealing with partners who fail to cooperate. They may also be responsible for assessing whether the process is achieving its stated purpose and which areas could be improved.

It is especially important to monitor the progress of partners as they carry out their individual transition plans. The firm may delegate that responsibility to designated individuals, people who hold specific positions (e.g., practice group leaders, management committee members), or members of the oversight committee. These people guide, assist, and monitor individual partners for the duration of the partners' retirement transition. They may help partners draft their plans, meet regularly with partners to follow their progress, and help them deal with any new needs or setbacks they encounter.

Conclusion

An effective client succession and transition process gives firms a competitive edge in retaining clients and future firm leaders. Clients are constantly courted by other firms seeking their business, and a lead partner's retirement is a natural time for them to explore other options. Firms that promise clients smooth transitions to fully prepared successors can protect client and leadership continuity.

Chapter 16:

How partner compensation models influence business development behaviors

By Tim Corcoran, principal, Corcoran Consulting Group

Every law firm strategic plan declares that growing the business is a top priority and every stakeholder – particularly partners – must play a role in furthering this mission. However, in most law firms, a relatively small number of partners are responsible for the majority of the firm's clients and matters. These partners are often among the highest paid. Firm managers are constantly exhorting all other partners to do more to grow their practices and the firm. Many firms employ marketing and business development professionals whose primary purpose is to promote the firm and support the lawyers' business development efforts. Yet, while many partners participate in training workshops, contribute thought leadership, and attend networking events, only a modest few make material progress each year in growing their practices. What can be done with those partners unable or unwilling to do more?

As it turns out, this is often a skewed or incomplete perception. This familiar pattern, repeated in so many law firms, may mean the battle isn't to convert apathetic partners into hard-charging rainmakers, but to overcome outdated partner compensation plans that impose significant and systemic barriers to generating more widespread business development success.

Finding the motivation

It's important to start by questioning the premise implied by this chapter's title. Is it safe to assume that law firm partner compensation plans do, in fact, influence partner behaviors? Those who have worked with or in close proximity to partners at private practice law firms know the answer is unassailably yes. Lawyers based in all the global jurisdictions in which we operate, working in law firms of varying sizes and practices, but particularly those who serve business clients with national or international needs, can and routinely do modify their behaviors to maximize available incentives. Partners who do this well can generate a very sizable income. So, does this imply that lawyers are greedy and motivated solely by money? Not at all! Lawyers are no more or no less greedy than other accomplished, driven, goal-oriented professionals. They have worked hard to achieve their expertise, and they expect to monetize that expertise. However, just because some lawyers are clearly motivated by incentives doesn't mean all are.

In fact, many law firms are successful primarily because some partners choose to knowingly act against their own economic self-interests. Or perhaps it's more accurate to say that partners in some law firms will do what needs to be done to ensure the firm's success, even if there is no cognizable recognition or reward for doing so. For some, the time commitment involved in doing what's right for the firm imposes an opportunity cost, meaning they forgo potential rewards they might have otherwise earned had they spent that time on pursuits deemed to have greater value, at least according to the compensation plan. For others, doing what's right for the firm may even incur a specific compensation penalty – partners who share origination credit or who transition client relationships in preparation for retirement are notable examples that I'll discuss in more detail later. A common root cause for the misalignment between *what's good for the partner* and *what's good for the partnership* is not partner naiveté, apathy, or greed, but poor incentive plan design.

Law firm compensation plans share some elements with other professional services firms, such as accounting or engineering firms. However, if the titans of industry leading law firm client businesses were to incorporate some of the common tenets of law firm partner compensation into their own senior executive or sales compensation plans, many would soon falter, and some would inevitably fail. Closely held family businesses and early-stage start-ups – entities that almost by definition require or foster an "all for one, one for all" mentality – might be able to withstand misaligned incentives, but many other businesses would struggle to recruit or retain top talent, particularly in executive or sales roles. If this sounds like a provocative statement, feel free to explain your plan to your most important client. The following anecdote is a true (if somewhat dramatized version of a) conversation shared with us:

> **Partner:** *Hi Monica, it's Arthur at Pearson Specter. We're reviewing our partner remuneration plan, and, given your business experience from your executive committee role and your other Board seats, I'd like to get your initial reaction to one of our most cherished remuneration elements.*

Client: *Hi Arthur, I'm delighted to help. Go ahead.*

Partner: *When one of our partners receives an inquiry from a potential client or attends a networking event with attendees who aren't currently firm clients, we "assign" these contacts to that partner, so he or she receives credit if one of these contacts becomes a client in the future.*

Client: *That sounds familiar. We do the same with our salespeople. But to avoid conflicts, salespeople are assigned a specific geographic territory where they have sole responsibility for all product sales. No one earns a commission for sales outside their territory. Some of our specialist product lines have their own dedicated salespeople with national territories. They will often collaborate with local salespeople, but only as needed, such as securing an introduction to a customer contact. As appropriate, both can earn a commission from subsequent sales.*

Partner: *Ah, our approach is much cleaner. Once assigned, each contact's company and all other companies or divisions in its corporate tree are permanently associated with that partner. If a contact ever takes a position with another company, the partner assignment to the original company remains intact, and the partner assignment will also transfer to the contact's new employer, if not already claimed. Partners coordinate with colleagues as needed, but they're under no obligation to share credit. Each partner may reassign credit at their discretion when they retire, of course.*

Client: *I'm not sure I understand. You make lifetime assignments between a single partner and entire corporations, irrespective of that partner's expertise, involvement, or understanding of what may very well be a quite diverse and geographically dispersed portfolio of businesses? Is this why you join every status conference I have with any other partners in your firm, even for matters far outside your specialty?*

Partner: *Exactly. The "responsible" partner may fully delegate both the delivery and supervision of matters outside their practice while retaining their credit, and many do, but I prefer to stay involved so I can be a better business advisor to you.*

Client: *You've just described a system seemingly intended to incentivize sales but that appears to actually incentivize claiming every company or contact possible in the hope that they become clients in the future, with no obligation to maintain contact, let alone nurture the relationship. If a different contact anywhere else in the far-flung client business at any time in the future assigns work to anyone else at your firm, the "responsible"* *partner exclusively receives fee credit or commissions from now until retirement. That's quite... generous. Do clients at least have some input into who takes over the client responsibility and credit at that time?*

Partner: *I admit, Monica, that some retiring partners in the past have assigned their credit to chums who are unfamiliar with the client, rather than assigning it to the lawyers closest to the client. We wish they'd do the right thing and select the client's preferred contact, but alas, we don't interfere in such decisions, and we've lost some good lawyers as a result. The good news is that some of our partners who have built up substantial credit over the decades are switching to part-time status instead of fully retiring, so we won't have to worry about their credit reassignments for another decade!*

Client: *Arthur, you're an excellent lawyer and I will always call on you when we need your subject matter expertise. But respectfully, I shall never seek business advice from you or any of your partners who agreed to this crazy plan.*

In days of yore, law firm partner compensation was predominantly "lockstep". This type of plan assumes a strong correlation between seniority and value, so as lawyers gain more tenure, their compensation rises. Lawyers with the same tenure earn the same compensation, irrespective of individual performance. This approach worked well when billing rates were more uniform, when there were far fewer lawyers to meet strong and unrelenting market demand, and when most law firms imposed a mandatory retirement age to ensure lawyers moved steadily through the compensation tiers until it was time to cede the stage to younger successors. Inevitably, however, some lawyers were not content to wait years, even decades, to reap the rewards commensurate with their significant contributions. Similarly, some lawyers at the peak of their professional capabilities (and, not coincidentally, at their peak earning capacity) approaching the mandatory retirement age felt they had much more to contribute and were not content to move on.

To retain younger partners who were growing impatient with longer timelines, and to recruit impatient partners departing other firms, compensation plans steadily began to incorporate performance-based incentives. Firm leaders quickly accepted the utility of a bonus pool to recognize exceptional individual contributions or to forestall threats of departures, and appreciated the flexibility to incorporate some new combination of subjective or objective performance criteria without discarding the entire compensation plan. Once in their grasp, they would not easily let go. Over time, the proportion of performance-based compensation grew. Fast forward to today, and lockstep compensation is practically extinct.

According to a 2025 study of the Am Law 200 law firms conducted by ALM's Pacesetter Research:

"The data results indicate how partner compensation models, to varying degrees, account for individual performance and contributions more than traditional lockstep models based solely on seniority, to no surprise, most bonus structures depend on individual performance for all attorneys."[1]

See Figure 1 below.

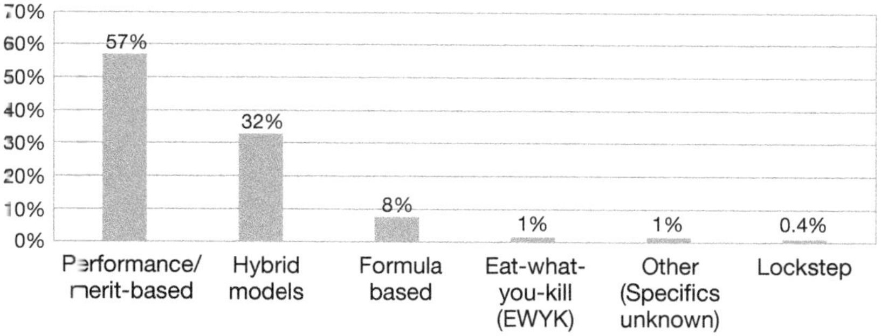

Figure 1: How equity partners are compensated. Source: ALM Compass Law.com Pacesetter Research© 2025

In the field of behavioral psychology, there are numerous theories of motivation. Of these, process theories refer to the emotional, cognitive, and decision-making processes that underlie human motivation. Expectancy Theory states that, *"To maximize motivation, organizations must make outcomes contingent on performance"*.[2] Most modern law firm partner compensation plans clearly embody this sentiment. Fundamental to this premise is that the highest value contributions should earn the highest value rewards. Yet, many law firm compensation plans reserve the highest rewards for partner contributions that, while fruitful, objectively do not deliver the greatest economic value. I'll explore that momentarily.

The Equity Theory of motivation states:

"Motivation is affected by the outcomes we receive for our inputs compared to the outcomes and inputs of other people. According to equity theory, our

reactions to the outcomes we receive from others (an employer) depend both on how we value those outcomes in an absolute sense and on the circumstances surrounding their receipt: Did I get as much out of this as I put into it? Did I get as much for my inputs as my coworkers got for theirs?"[3]

Equity Theory manifests in partner compensation in two prominent ways. Skeptical partners demand compensation metrics that are administered fairly, whilst busy partners demand compensation commensurate with the effort they put forth. I'll examine these structural limitations a little later.

The maths aren't mathing

Whether operating as a solo practitioner in a small town or as a senior partner in a global firm with thousands of lawyers, it's generally understood that when a lawyer bills more, compensation rises. Partner productivity, also known as working attorney or fee earner revenue, is measured in volume of billable hours multiplied by a high partner billing rate and is routinely characterized as a partner's greatest economic contribution to the firm, or "highest and best use". Accordingly, many partner compensation plans pay the most to high fee earners with high working attorney revenue. Not surprisingly, partners in high demand because of their specific skills or the brand strength of the firm see little value in engaging in long-term business development activities with an uncertain outcome, when it pays far more to sit at a desk and tackle client problems. The most creative chief marketing officer or practice group leader may find it quite challenging to dislodge top fee earners from their desks to jump on a plane to network at a conference, or sometimes to even write an article or contribute to a webinar. Seemingly endless demand for their billable expertise is hard to ignore.

Law firm performance financials have long favored production input metrics such as billable hours, billing rates, and collected cash, while minimizing metrics like quality or client satisfaction. However, law firms are steadily incorporating profitability measures, which is a key output metric. Put another way, a partner's billable hours and billing rate matter little if the net result generates no profits for the firm and its shareholders. Emphasizing profitability has the potential to unlock the value of technology innovation or process improvement or efficiency in the delivery of legal services. This is a welcome departure from the profession's dogged reliance on the billable hour – an extraordinarily inefficient approach for translating experience into income, and one that imposes a high mental health cost on the profession. Senior executives running multinational corporations undoubtedly work hard and put in a lot of hours, but not a single one would cite working an ever-increasing number of hours and raising prices far beyond what the market will bear as the best (let alone the only) method to earn high income. So, it's disappointing to see law firms embrace a methodology for calculating profitability that doubles down on productivity inputs and ignores all other partner contributions.

Writ large, profit is what remains after a firm's expenses are deducted from a firm's revenues. At the partner level, profit is what remains after a partner's compensation, direct costs, and overhead are deducted from the total value of a partner's economic contribution. In many law firm financial systems, working attorney or fee earner revenue is the sole consideration on the revenue side of the equation. No other partner contribution – originating new clients, originating new matters from existing clients, mentoring young lawyers, chairing a committee, serving in a firm- or practice-management role, being a good citizen within the firm or the community, or even delivering quality legal work – has any economic value whatsoever when measuring partner profitability.

Consequently, many partner compensation plans require partners "to work hard", which is measured solely through billable hours and fee collections. A partner who's rewarded with higher compensation after generating exhausting but lucrative productivity metrics must bill even more hours or charge high rates in subsequent years, because the higher compensation inevitably reduces the partner's profitability. Reduced profitability, in turn, will negatively impact future compensation. The reward for success is to bill even more just to maintain current compensation.

Despite the relative scarcity of accomplished rainmakers in most law firms, compensation plans like this quickly eliminate the motivation for young lawyers to learn business development skills. This also means that seasoned rainmakers who wish to justify high compensation must, at some point during the year, stop selling new work for themselves and others, and get back to the office to bill time. In our work advising law firms on partner compensation, without exception, each of our clients has one or more rainmakers with large books of business who are confident in their ability to generate even more business for the firm, but the compensation plan punishes them if they don't also bill time to client files. It's certainly within the purview of law firm partners to establish a requirement that all partners must bill a target number of hours, but it's often based on the false premise that "busy" partners generate the most favorable economic outcome for the firm. This is far from true.

"Increase leverage and partner profits increase, if all else remains the same"[4]

Law firms and other professional services firms tend to have pyramid-shaped organizational structures, with relatively few shareholders/partners at the top of the organization and a much larger number of non-shareholder timekeepers below them. Professor Bill Henderson states that:

> *"In the context of law firms, the term 'leverage' refers to a very specific concept: the extent to which partners, who own the firm, maximize the firm's revenues (and presumably profits) by billing out the time of lawyers who work for the firm as employees. Leverage is often measured as the ratio of associates to partners."*[5]

A firm with many associates and few partners has high leverage. A top-heavy firm with more partners than non-partner timekeepers has low leverage. Leverage can be a significant profit engine for professional services firms. While junior lawyers bill at lower rates than senior partners, junior lawyers are also paid far less than senior partners. The excess profit purposely generated from this differential flows upward, directly into partner pockets.

In this context, a partner who's incentivized to work at full capacity or utilization before delegating work to others – maximizing fee earner or working attorney revenue – contributes demonstrably less economic value to the firm than partners who balance their personal workload by regularly delegating work to junior lawyers. I routinely encounter law firms where partners earn the highest compensation by generating just enough work to keep themselves busy. This *"win the work, do the work"* approach may pay individuals well, but it leaves very little profit on the table for other partners to share. A compensation plan that allows a partner to not only place their individual financial self-interests above the firm's, but rewards them handsomely for doing so, is better suited for a group of solo lawyers sharing little more than a logo on a business card and some overhead costs than it is for partners who want to collectively build and sustain a thriving law firm. Compensation plans that reward self-interest also tend to starve associates of work, leading to retention and recruiting issues today, and a thin bench for success planning in the future. A firm can offer competitive salaries that keep pace with deep-pocketed competitors and yet still struggle to find and keep capable junior lawyers when senior partners are paid more to hoard work than to keep junior lawyers busy. Of course, partners are free to choose the kind of business they'd like to own and operate, but they should do so with eyes wide open.

It's important to note that, in today's fast-evolving legal marketplace, clients are increasingly reluctant to pay for services that once were routinely delegated to junior lawyers. Consultant Jim Cotterman explains this succinctly:

> *"Clients are less willing to pay for process and more willing to pay for judgment, experience, and expertise. The watchwords for leverage today should be flexibility and adaptability. Firms must respond to changing and differing client buying preferences while at the same time investigating, implementing and 'leveraging' technology – all in an environment of rapid technological change."*[6]

The client's perception of value always matters. In some cases, a client may be pleased to see partners delegate work to junior lawyers, thereby reducing the client's legal budget. However, there's a growing need to deliver legal work using technology, artificial intelligence, or process improvements to lower the cost even more to the client without compromising quality. Partners incentivized to bill high rates and high hours may soon find themselves priced out of work that once kept them busy. Partners who have long ignored business development while billing more hours may find themselves at a significant disadvantage in a changing marketplace.

Penny wise, partner foolish

In addition to over-rewarding some partner contributions while under-rewarding others, the structures of some partner compensation plans are specifically designed to limit incentives for contributions that might boost revenue and profits. In a classic example of game theory, The Prisoner's Dilemma, two captured criminals must decide whether to confess or stay silent. The punishment is minimal if both stay silent. If one confesses and the other stays silent, the criminal who confesses goes free and the silent criminal receives a harsh punishment. If both confess, each earns a modest punishment. Since the two criminals can't compare notes, and neither trusts the other to act in their collective best interest, each is likely to consider their own self-interest and conclude that the optimal course is to confess. It may be sensible for two criminals to not trust each other. But surely law firm partners who have made the conscious choice to own and operate a business together, and who will earn greater rewards if all partners act in their collective best interests, can trust their colleagues to place their collective best interests over their own? Alas, the answer is often no.

"Consider a team performance-driven firm. Everyone benefits if anyone's performance improves. Partners help one another."
According to Nanda and Prusiner:

> *"Consider individual performance-driven firm. Its partners focus only on their own performance. If helping their partners takes time away from their own production, they will avoid helping. Everyone sinks or swims on the basis of their individual performance."*[7]

Dr Larry Richards and others have long noted that lawyers have a much higher risk aversion and skepticism than the average population.[8] These personality traits, well-suited for helping clients to manage risk, are less desirable as foundational principles for running a business. In the game theory of compensation, partners are wary of incentives that may provide significant benefits to others while offering *de minimis* benefits to themselves. Even when incentivizing certain partner contributions demonstrably increases the size of the proverbial pie of profits that all partners share, some partners still prefer to limit these incentives. Profits may be lower, but... at least they all learn less together? Two recurring elements in partner compensation limit business development effectiveness – rewarding only results, not effort, and rewarding only "tangible" contributions.

Success is effortless

I have observed many clever and well-designed business development campaigns intended to encourage lawyers to get up from their desks and meet with clients or prospective clients, with the highest achievers receiving special recognition and even a modest bonus, only to see these campaigns fall flat. If a law firm's marketing and business development team proposes a three-month contest that offers, say, £100 for every documented lunch with a prospective client, what the marketers may not know is that some partners won't support such a campaign because of the risk it might be gamed by nefarious colleagues repeatedly buying lunches for law school chums who will never become firm clients. Law school training and years of advising clients on all the ways that something can go wrong have cynically led some partners to demand compensation plans that have zero risk of being gamed. An unaudited claim of multiple lunches with "potential clients" is risky. What's not risky is rewarding results that have already happened – such as fee earner or working attorney revenue that has already been worked, documented, invoiced, and collected.

Results matter, but so do the efforts that lead to the result. Consider a client business that manufactures widgets. Salespeople travel to prospective customer sites to meet with potential users and discuss the merits of utilizing these widgets compared to the customer's current approach. Product managers, marketers, and executives travel to industry conferences and trade shows, demonstrating the company's widgets in exhibit halls or educating potential users from the podium through use cases incorporating the widgets. Account managers are tasked with managing existing customer relationships by responding to questions, taking the point on service-related issues, or discussing ways the customer can improve workflow through better use of the company's widgets. That's a lot of activity taking place long before anyone secures a signature on a new purchase contract, but selling widgets isn't possible without these efforts.

Were the company to reward employees only when a new sale is made and pay out the rewards only after the widget has been shipped, deployed, invoices paid, and payments cleared, there would be a lot fewer employees and very few sales. Companies selling big ticket items like airplanes or enterprise software require multi-year sales cycles. Salespeople are expected to engage in actions that are known to lead to sales, and their performance is measured both by sales made this year and the efforts that will generate sales next year. No company would minimize the importance of these efforts by paying only for completed sales.

Business development in a law firm is also a process. It starts by promoting the firm's brand and service offerings and promoting individual partner expertise. Partners demonstrate expertise through thought leadership, engaging in fact-finding with potential clients, positioning the firm's unique combination of expertise, bench strength, and service quality as a critical differentiator, preparing customized proposals and fee arrangements, and finally securing an engagement letter. Few partners do all this well, so in law firms that have embraced a business development culture, everyone plays a role based on their particular skill, and this generates better results than individual partners working alone. Nearly all this effort is invisible or de-emphasized in partner compensation plans.

David Maister, who developed over a long career a comprehensive understanding of law firm structures and practices, weighs in to reinforce the need to recognize and reward business development efforts that precede results:

> *"In many firms, rewards for marketing success are based upon exactly that: success. There is no credit within the systems or, perhaps more important, the culture of the firm to reward marketing contributions that cannot be linked to a specific piece of business. There is no 'origination credit' for writing a good article or putting on a good seminar. There is no bonus for contributing a new tax idea that everyone else in the firm got to tell their clients about. Unless you were the one to tell your client and you were the one who got the 'here's a deal' call from the client, you don't get acknowledged."*[9]

Raw effort itself isn't sufficient to earn rewards, but efforts that are planned and budgeted in an annual business planning process linked to the firm's strategic priorities and approved by management, that are documented in the firm's client relationship management or document management systems, and that are monitored by management during the year, are excellent candidates for incentives. The way to reduce gaming or over-rewarding inefficient effort is to develop a strong understanding of the difference between efforts that improve the probability of securing a client engagement and random acts of lunch.

In money matters, only money matters

Because there's no universal agreement on the relative value of so-called "intangible" or non-financial contributions, or even if such contributions can be accurately measured, most partner compensation plans focus on long-standing metrics like billable hours, fee revenue, or collected revenue. This perspective is and always has been myopic. Executive compensation plans in many business segments incorporate non-financial contributions, some of which are easily measured and given equal footing with financial performance. In law firms, however, contributions that can't be tidily measured in hours or collected euros or dollars may be deemed to have little economic value, and contributions that appear susceptible to gaming are either eliminated from partner compensation plans, or allocated only modest and subjective rewards, e.g., *"There's no added bonus for being a great mentor or chairing the recruiting committee, but exceptional performance in these areas might justify keeping your compensation flat if you have a particularly bad year."*

Some law firm partnership agreements obligate partners to devote a certain amount of time to necessary non-financial contributions, noting that these are baseline expectations for becoming and remaining a partner, so they will not earn incremental rewards. Not surprisingly, when there are no such baseline expectations, and there are minimal or no rewards allocated to non-financial contributions, some partners will devote no time or energy to them. These tasks then fall to those relatively few partners willing to incur the opportunity cost for doing so. As noted above, every law firm has multiple partners willing to set aside their self-interest to further the firm's collective interests. Still, someone at our client firms sooner or later shares some version of, *"I'm not claiming that chairing the pro bono committee or doing on-campus recruiting is worth as much as billing time, but surely, it's worth something. At the very least, it'd be nice if the compensation committee acknowledged the time I've invested in these firm activities instead of treating me as if I work part-time because I missed my hours target."*

It's a misnomer to refer to contributions outside of billable hours and fee revenue as "intangible" or "non-financial". I routinely encounter the question of whether to incentivize practice group leaders or executive committee members. The argument for is the same in any successful business: A leader skilled at clarifying strategic priorities and removing organizational roadblocks, with the charisma to motivate the team to peak performance, is hard to find, so pay them well and get out of their way. The argument against is usually, *"Our best people should be doing billable work, not managing"*, or *"If we pay managers, then unproductive partners will move into management rather than improve their performance"*. Simply put, the accretive impact of an effective manager will always generate more economic value for the firm than that partner could ever generate through individual billings. There's nothing non-financial about it.

Space doesn't allow an explanation for every intangible contribution, but I'll offer one example. Figure 2 below is an anonymized but real scorecard for rating the effectiveness of a partner as a mentor to junior lawyers. During a lively discussion in one firm, I learned that nobody monitors whether partners even meet with their assigned mentees. Before engaging in esoteric debates about KPIs and rating scales, I suggest starting with the fundamentals.

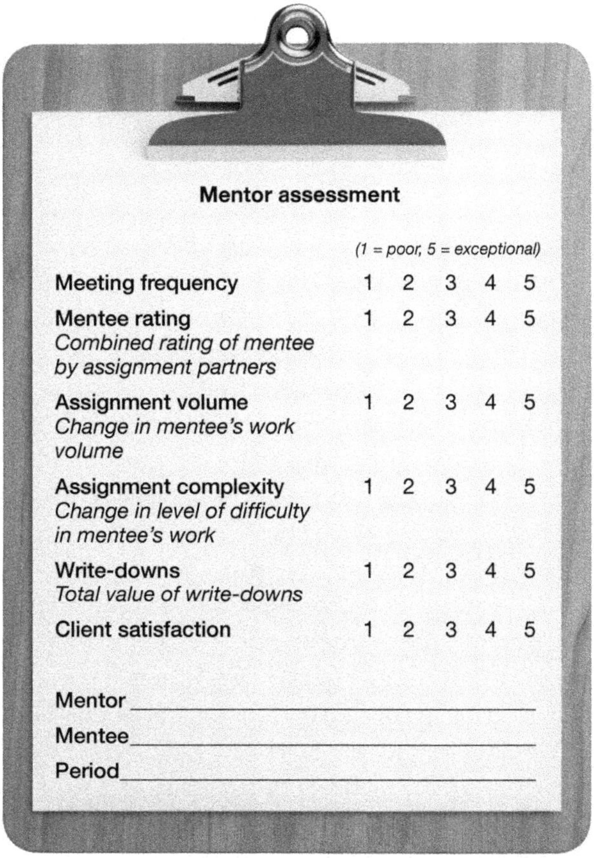

Figure 2: Scorecard to rate the effectiveness of a partner as a mentor. Source: Corcoran Consulting Group archive

As it turns out, monitoring changes in a mentee's quality (assignment redos), quantity (assignments), and financial impact (amount of write-downs not driven by rate negotiations or client billing guidelines) can provide a lot of insight into a mentor's effectiveness. Similarly, I've observed enough variations of such scorecards to confidently assert that there are plenty of criteria available to fairly assess a partner's performance in all other "intangible" partner contributions.

When risk aversion and skepticism lead to compensation plans that impede business development activity, it's almost certain to limit revenue growth and distributable profit. To be clear, some skepticism is warranted. I acknowledge that gaming the system does occur, but I tend to see more opportunistic and possibly conveniently naïve lawyers working a compensation plan to their advantage than bad actors pursuing unjust enrichment at the expense of their colleagues. The appropriate response to this concern is not to eliminate all incentives for good faith efforts or for non-financial contributions, but to reward only efforts correlated with business development success and to implement performance metrics for all important contributions.

The origin of origination

This brings us to origination – an incentive element that is implemented with good intentions but can be quite divisive. When I'm called in to referee and reconcile competing and strongly held views about origination by warring factions, I hear the same laments:

- Is origination supposed to reward past contributions, present contributions, or future contributions?
- Is origination intended to foster collaboration or hoarding?
- What's the value of origination relative to fee revenue or other partner contributions?
- What's the relationship between origination and business development?

I routinely encounter law firms that don't track or reward origination but have fostered a culture of collaboration, so they don't need it or want it. I also routinely encounter law firms with such deep-seated trauma related to origination that the partners won't even use the term, yet they acknowledge it as a meaningful driver of new business generation and cross-selling. Most often, I encounter law firms that reward origination in some fashion because they believe it drives desirable behaviors, but they know they're not managing it effectively because there are pockets of dissatisfied partners. Let's unwind when and why origination credit is awarded.

- Origination is sales commission. It's an incentive paid to reward one or more lawyers ("hunting in packs") for landing a new client for the firm. The amount of the incentive varies according to the magnitude of the workload generated by the new client. In this context, origination is intended to reward present contributions (new client billings), even though the business development efforts to land the client concluded before billings started.
- Some partner compensation plans maintain origination assignments

for a new client in perpetuity, so over time the originating partner can earn a tidy sum whether he or she remains involved in some or all of the client's work. In this context, origination is intended to reward past contributions.

- More recently, compensation plans have begun to differentiate matter origination from client origination. Landing a new client takes one set of skills, but ensuring the client is satisfied and continues to assign more work to the firm takes another. Those receiving matter origination may include lawyers billing time to the client, lawyers supervising the work but billing minimal time to the client, and the originating lawyer(s) who landed the client initially. In this context, origination is intended to reward present contributions. Some firms create a new matter origination category; others simply split a single origination category differently.
- Matter origination may also apply to landing new assignments from the client in new areas ("cross-selling"). Navigating a client organization to identify and capture new lines of work often requires the same skills as client origination, so in this context it's intended to reward present contributions.

Origination starts to provoke controversy when the lines are blurred and it's no longer clear which contributions are being rewarded. A lawyer whose contribution is material to landing a new client is upset when a more powerful colleague unilaterally decides not to share any credit. When a new client generates significant work, it can lead to unrest as the monetary value of the origination becomes wildly disproportionate to the initial or ongoing contribution. When a client has been generating work for quite some time, often across multiple practices, there's a question of the suitability of offering the same level of rewards for landing new clients as for servicing established or "institutional" clients.

There's unrest when originating partners with the option to share credit choose not to share, and when those who do share credit do so inconsistently. Originating partners may be offended if an in-demand lawyer declines an assignment unless it comes with shared credit, since it's not intended to reward doing the work. But originating partners may share credit to position a junior lawyer for promotion to partner, to boost a partner into a higher tier, or to reward and retain lawyers working on their client files. Some originating partners negotiate credit splits up front, while others choose to wait until year-end to ensure they've first retained enough credit to maximize their own compensation.

Senior lawyers approaching retirement are often reluctant to share credit (and lower their income) with successors too early in the process. Partners taking over these client relationships believe credit should transfer when taking on the responsibilities. If they lack enough influence to make this happen, they want certainty on the amount and date that credit will be transferred. This is typically a reaction to originating partners who have, upon retirement, gifted significant credit to friends uninvolved with clients being transitioned, sometimes completely bypassing the lawyer(s) who now have full client responsibility.

Occasionally a partner will land a new client, only to have another partner swoop in and claim the credit even though the client has been dormant for a decade. When an unhappy partner asks firm management to resolve this or other disputes about shared credit, everyone's unhappy when firm management claims to have no jurisdiction and "encourages the partners to work it out themselves".

These are just the headlines. Every scenario involving origination credit has multiple nuances and variations. I've written and commented quite a lot on this topic previously, including this:

> *"Too many plans treat origination of a single matter as a perpetual annuity, crowding out any incentive to cross-sell, or for older partners to transition key client relationships to up-and-coming younger partners. Other plans allow partners to stake a claim on all future business from clients they initially generate, whether or not that partner is ever again involved in winning another engagement."*[10]

Consultant David Freeman goes on to observe:

> *"A protectionist attitude towards origination credit often creates an internal barrier to cross-selling. In most firms, there's a lot of internal deal-making going on, with lawyers realizing it's better to get 50 per cent of something than 100 per cent of nothing."*[11]

There is movement afoot to create and enforce standard credit-sharing guidelines. Allowing individual partners to have full discretion to choose if and how much credit to share is a nice sentiment, but whether through self-interest or merely the usual differences in scale between practices in a multi-practice firm, the inevitable outcome is unnecessary variability. Partners in smaller practices have less credit to share even when they're team oriented. Partners in larger practices can share a much smaller proportion of credit but it can still be more impactful due to volume. No set of sharing guidelines will cover every scenario, but the "legislative intent" underlying the guidelines should be made clear. It's even better when management proactively monitors compliance, so it's not left to a junior lawyer to take on the career risk of challenging a corner office partner.

Aside from impairing business development, poorly managed credit sharing increases the risk that partners who amass significant credit become shadow leaders with unfettered power to influence decisions related to lawyer hiring or promotions, becoming or remaining a partner, and compensation allocations – often gaining more influence than management, whose actions are usually constrained by the firm's partnership or operating agreement. To be clear, rainmakers with responsibility for critical client relationships have always had influence and will always have influence. Putting guard rails such as credit sharing guidelines in place helps to limit the firm's exposure to an influential partner who goes rogue.

Says Matthew Winings:

> *"Dominant rainmakers have been able to reallocate firm income in their favor and dictate firm governance. Indeed, the partners who control the most important clients are well positioned to continue to wield a colossal amount of influence on virtually all aspects of the firm."*[12]

When origination takes on a negative connotation, some firms will change terms and refer to Billing credit or Responsible credit, which are standard labels in most financial systems, but most law firms use only one, sometimes two. Changing nomenclature provides air cover when leaders claim the firm does not track origination and is therefore not a cut-throat "eat what you kill" firm. As a practical matter, "eat what you kill" refers as much to culture as it does compensation structure. I've seen partners put their firm's needs above their own even when the compensation plan is wired to reward selfishness. I've also seen how self-interested partners will always find a way to work even the most benign compensation plan to their advantage.

The casual interchangeability of origination, responsible, and billing labels, and sharing credit for "off label" purposes have another unintended outcome

– the critical contributions of managing a client relationship and leveraging that relationship for the mutual benefit of the client and the firm are often overlooked because there is no standard label for the role. Every business of a certain scale understands the distinction between selling and account management. Many partner compensation plans have a blind spot for the law firm version of an account manager. Lawyers who bill time to the client's file receive fee revenue credit. Originating partners can earn origination credit, sometimes with no ongoing involvement. A more effective use of the Responsible Partner label is to recognize the contributions of lawyers who neither originate nor bill substantial time to the client. They may supervise junior lawyers working on client matters, they may serve as the firm's liaison for billing questions or for an entire matter. They may also have responsibility for a significant slice of the client relationship or oversee the entire relationship. However, partners filling this role are often invisible when reviewing standard productivity metrics.

I see this play out regularly with partners who receive work assignments from a client and then delegate and oversee the work of others. Leveraging the work can boost matter profitability and please price-conscious clients, but with minimal billings or origination credit to demonstrate the partner's value, compensation committees regularly penalize client responsible partners for doing what's right for the client and the firm.

As I have written previously, *"It takes a combination of skills including technical lawyering expertise, project management, people management, budget management, and client relationship management to successfully manage matters and clients."*[13]

Harvard professor Heidi Gardner has written extensively on this topic, calling out the significant financial advantages for law firms operating more as an integrated business than as a hotel for lawyers:

> *"When firms can get their partners to collaborate across practices, offices, jurisdictions or other internal boundaries, the financial gains to the firm are unambiguous. One of the clearest measures of this finding is the link between cross-practice collaboration and revenues. The more practices that are involved in servicing a client, the greater the annual average revenue that client generates. Client projects involving offices in several countries are significantly more lucrative than single-office engagements."*[14]

An effective but underutilized opportunity is to define the obligations and expectations for a Responsible Partner so only those doing the role can earn this credit, then track the effort involved, possibly by using non-billable task codes. Then, offer incentives for improving client retention (repeat business) and client penetration (cross-selling). If your firm is ready to incorporate profitability metrics, incentivize growth in client profitability – keeping in mind that alternative or fixed fees coupled with technology or practice innovations can be far more profitable than increasing rates and hours.

Don't hate the player, hate the game

A central thesis of this chapter is that many partner compensation plans are outdated, or poorly designed, or poorly managed, so they not only can fall short in driving desirable behaviors and lucrative financial outcomes (like business development), but they might even offer substantial incentives for behaviors and contributions that actively hinder the firm's growth. I very infrequently encounter bad actors who appear to be nefariously gaming their firm's compensation plan in a mad dash for cash. More often, I see good people trying to strike the right balance between furthering their own financial interests with the firm's long-term financial health. I also see earnest, dedicated firm managers and compensation committee members put forth significant effort to wrangle a complex, time-consuming, and critical task, knowing that no decision will result in universal happiness.

There is a clear connection between partner compensation and the zeal with which partners pursue business development, or not, in some cases. It's helpful for firm leaders to periodically assess the partner compensation plan to ensure it remains fit for purpose. A compensation plan developed during a time of plenty likely under-values contributions to generate new clients. A plan devised by founders may rely substantially on the shared belief that partners will always place the firm's financial interests above their own, but the partners' shared beliefs tend to change when founders and first-generation partners have exited the stage.

Law firms are not homogenous organizations that look and act the same, irrespective of size and location. Despite similarities in market position or size, firms can have widely varying cultures that value and reward very different contributions. What works to boost business development in one law firm may be wholly unnecessary in another law firm where the commitment to firm growth is a baseline expectation of partners. This dichotomy reflects that what each law firm needs, and what motivates its partners, is constantly evolving based on market conditions.

Maister acknowledges that compensation plans may compel partners to adjust their behavior to maximize their rewards, but such plans may also serve to decelerate behaviors and contributions that aren't explicitly rewarded:

> *"Alfie Kohn published an important book,* Punished by Rewards *(Mariner Books), in which he pointed out that all incentive schemes are doomed to failure because they divert people's attention away from inherent meaning, purpose, fulfillment or fun in the activity. Rather than these things, all motivation is shifted to getting the reward... Say 'Do it and I'll pay you' and they will immediately translate it into 'I'm not going to do anything you don't pay me for!'"*[15]

By contrast, Cotterman believes that many partners engage in certain behaviors, particularly business development, because they can, not because they're motivated by compensation:

> *"Lawyers who generate business do so because they have the innate ability to do so and they understand its importance. Lawyers who don't generate business don't generate it because they can't. Of the group that can't, there are probably two subgroups: those who could if properly trained, coached and supported, and those who just do not have the temperament to do so. It is not the compensation system that creates either the ability or the drive to engage in marketing."*[16]

There is no one "right" approach to partner compensation when it comes to recognizing and rewarding business development. Multiple approaches may be equally effective. However, I suggest that there is one clear "wrong" approach: doing nothing. I encourage firm leaders to periodically assess the suitability of their partner incentives to support the firm's strategy and to motivate the behaviors and contributions that the owners have deemed most valuable for the firm's success.

I've shared a lot of insights into what can go wrong with partner compensation. I'll close with a checklist of best practices to consider, and blind spots to avoid, to boost business development:

- Determine the current importance of rainmaking and business development relative to other shared partner values. If the relative importance is not aligned with compensation, adjust the allocation of compensation accordingly or restate the values to align with the what the firm rewards.

- If the firm tracks and rewards origination (or billing or responsible) credit, check that it motivates the desired behaviors, paying particular attention to:
  - Which pays better: winning new clients and matters or amassing origination credit?
  - Which pays better: hoarding origination credit or sharing origination credit to foster regular collaborations with colleagues to win new clients and cross-sell?
  - Which pays better: winning a new client ten years ago that's now a top client due to the efforts of others or regularly generating new clients and new matter revenue and maintaining active involvement?
  - How sufficient are credit sharing policies and safeguards to ensure consistent and equitable credit sharing, including prohibiting the sharing of credit for off label purposes?
- How well does management balance the allocation of marketing and business development budgets and resources between established and highly visible practices and less visible or smaller practices with significant growth potential? (This isn't usually driven directly by partner compensation, but some firms hold partners accountable for repeatedly wasting firm resources on low-ROI tactics by dinging compensation or requiring partners to front future investments from their own draw.)
- Clarify the baseline contributions expected of partners that aren't incentivized, and implement policies or adjust compensation to improve compliance (some firms use this to ensure partners attend practice group meetings, participate in client feedback or key client programs, or engage in annual planning).
- Clarify the "intangible" or "non-financial" partner contributions critical to business development success and implement quantitative and qualitative performance metrics to better inform compensation committees.
- Ensure that partners actively serving in client responsible roles are recognized for the appropriate use of leverage, for ensuring client satisfaction and growth, particularly those who collaborate rather than hoarding work or credit.
- Ensure the annual business planning process incorporates tasks correlated with business development success, particularly when these

efforts are not expected to immediately bear fruit, and allocate some rewards for successful completion of these tasks.

- Ensure that the path to partnership adjusts targets to allow sufficient time for high potential lawyers on the rise to develop business development skills.

References

1 Sierra, R., *Innovation in Law Firm Partner Compensation Models*, p.17, New York: ALM Law.com Compass Pacesetter Research, 2025

2 Bright, D. and Cortes, A., *Principles of Management*, §14.3, Houston: OpenStax, 2019

3 *Ibid.*

4 Cotterman, J., Evolving Leverage, Cotterman on Compensation blog, Newtown Square: Altman Weil, 2016

5 Henderson, W., *An Empirical Study of Single-Tier Versus Two-Tier Partnerships in the Am Law 200*, p.1722, Chapel Hill: North Carolina Law Review, Vol 84, 2006

6 Cotterman, *Ibid.*

7 Nanda A. and Prusiner, L., *Compensation in Professional Service Firms*, p.3, Harvard Business School, 9-905-039, Boston: President and Fellows of Harvard College, 2004

8 Richard, L., *Herding Cats: The Lawyer Personality Revealed*, Hildebrandt Baker Robbins, 2002

9 Maister, D., "Doing It for the Money", London: *International Financial Law Review*, 2005

10 Corcoran, T., "Linking Business Development to Partner Compensation", Philadelphia: *Legal Intelligencer*, ALM Media Properties, 2014

11 Freeman, D., *Secrets of the Masters: The Business Development Guide for Lawyers*, p.53, London: Ark Group, 2013

12 Winings, M., "The Power of Law Firm Partnership: Why Dominant Rainmakers Will Impede the Immediate, Widespread Implementation of an Autocratic Management Structure", p.175, Des Moines: *Drake Law Review*, Vol 55, 2015

13 Corcoran, T., *Human Capital in the New Legal Ecosystem*, p.8, London: Ark Group, 2020

14 Gardner H., "Collaboration in Law Firms: The New Wave of Client Service", p.2, *The Practice*, Boston: Harvard Law School Center on the Legal Profession, Vol 1, Issue 6, 2015

15 Maister, *Ibid.*

16 Cotterman, J., *Compensating Business Origination*, p.5, Newtown Square: Altman Weil Report to Legal Management, 2005

Chapter 17: Digital presence and online reputation

By Jaron Rubenstein, tech strategist, Rubenstein Ventures

A strong digital presence and online reputation are non-negotiable strategic assets for successful business development, impacting lawyers at the individual, practice, and firm levels. Developing a clear, disciplined strategy and enforcing it throughout your firm's culture are key leadership responsibilities that accelerate future growth. This chapter covers the critical topics that firm leadership must govern and leverage, including how to maximize the effectiveness of AI-driven tools and services:

- How to define your target audience and personas for market amplification.
- The strategic imperative of a user-focused website that provides a modern User Experience (UX) and surfaces key information to validate expertise.
- Ensuring dominant visibility in search engines, leveraging traditional Search Engine Optimization (SEO) and anticipating future Answer Engine Optimization (AEO) and Generative Engine Optimization (GEO) techniques to surface the firm's expertise in today's AI-driven world.
- Developing firm-wide social media strategies to elevate practice groups and establish thought leaders for your target audience, including fostering a culture of high-quality publication and self-promotion.

The chapter concludes with a brief self-assessment tool for leaders to assess the maturity of their firm's digital presence and a methodology to prioritize an implementation roadmap based on that assessment.

For most law firms, the majority of their business originates from relationships and referrals. The practice of law is fundamentally a relationship -based service. While relationships are formed through in-person interaction, long-term cultivation, and referral networks, a prospective client's journey no longer ends with a name.

Buyers of legal services are on a due diligence journey. Even when referred, most buyers – especially sophisticated, digitally-savvy in-house counsel and executives – will use the firm's and the lawyer's digital presence as a critical factor in their decision. They will seek to validate the referral, assess the brand, and determine its compatibility with their own organizational requirements. For example, a client who values efficiency and ease of transaction will interpret a firm's clunky or outdated website as a proxy for the administrative friction they can expect when working with the firm.

A firm's digital presence serves as an authentic projection of its brand and service delivery model. Therefore, the website must be clean, strategically clear, easy to navigate, and include readily searchable information and recent thought leadership. The digital platform's goal is to reinforce the reasons a specific lawyer or firm is the superior professional choice for the buyer's complex legal needs.

In a management context, ensuring a universally strong digital presence across the firm must be driven from the top. The managing partner, executive committee, and other leaders must not only participate but enforce sophisticated, active approaches that embody the firm's brand. This leadership-led effort is effective in keeping clients and prospects engaged, ensuring that the target personas receive the necessary thought leadership, and, most importantly, modeling the required behavior for all lawyers.

Defining your target audience and personas for amplification

By this point in your firm's business development journey, your Ideal Client Profile (ICP) should be clearly defined. The next strategic step is to define your target audience with maximum specificity, then develop tangible personas for the key decision makers within those audience segments.

This rigor is necessary because strategy definition and execution must always be centered on the actual audience and how your content and outreach mechanisms will serve them most effectively. Granular persona definition directly enables more targeted, resource-efficient business development and marketing content. Personas help leadership strategically hone in on the best methods to reach the audience and identify strategic shifts in market approach.

Consider a corporate law firm focusing on commercial real estate law. The target ICP might be:

- *Primary industries:* REITs, private equity firms, commercial developers, mid-to-large retail chains, and tech companies with significant physical footprints (data centers).

- *Company size:* $50m – $2bn in annual revenue (mid-market to enterprise).
- *Geographic focus:* Multi-state or international operations (where legal complexity increases).
- *Transaction volume:* Organizations closing three or more major acquisitions, dispositions, or complex leases annually.

With this ICP, leadership must identify the primary decision-maker personas. For example:

- *The chief executive officer:* Leader of the business, may be heavily involved in legal negotiations or completely hands-off, typically focused on end results, risk, and revenue.
- *The general counsel (GC):* They care about fiduciary risk mitigation and specialized expertise that their in-house team lacks.
- *VP of real estate / head of portfolio:* They care about operational velocity and *deal-making* legal advice rather than *deal-breaking* hurdles.

Let's craft a more detailed persona of the general counsel for a deeper strategic profile.

Persona: Strategic Sarah
Title: General counsel (GC) / chief legal officer
Typical age: 45-55
Reports to: CEO or CFO

Strategic profile: Sarah oversees a small in-house legal team (two to five people). She is a generalist by necessity but a strategist by trade. She lacks the bandwidth to micro-manage every transaction, but she is professionally responsible if a deal fails or a regulatory error incurs significant cost.

Sarah's primary goals (the firm's focus):

- *Risk allocation:* Ensuring maximum company protection in complex agreements (e.g., Sale-Leaseback or Triple Net Lease (NNN)).
- *Operational velocity:* Preventing legal from becoming the *bottleneck* that slows down the real estate acquisition team.
- *Cost management:* Balancing the legal budget and demanding

predictable, high-value billing, not *sticker shock* from firms that bill for every six-minute phone call.
- *Standardization:* Developing an efficient *playbook* for real estate transactions to ensure consistency across different states/regions.

Sarah's key pain points (opportunities for the firm):
- "I'm paying Big Law rates for a first-year associate to learn on my dime."
- "Our local counsel is slow, and it's making our VP of real estate look bad to the board."
- "My internal team is buried – I need someone I can trust to run point on a closing without me micro-managing."
- "Is our current portfolio compliant with the new environmental ESG regulations?"

Communication style and preferences (firm's mandate):
- *Format:* Concise, bulleted emails. Sarah requires a three-sentence summary of the risk and a clear recommendation, not a ten-page memo.
- *Value signal:* Proactive updates are essential. If Sarah has to call the firm for an update on a closing, trust has been fundamentally broken.
- *Social proof:* Sarah relies heavily on her trusted peer network (e.g., Association of Corporate Counsel) and LinkedIn for firm recommendations.

Firm leadership should mandate creating at least three to four unique personas. Once developed, these personas become the ultimate filters for strategic decision making:
- *Targeted events:* Given the personas' details, which industry-specific conferences or private events are they most likely to attend? How can partners be positioned as speakers at these events to gain trust?
- *Strategic positioning:* What is the most effective firm-wide positioning?
    - *Example:* To win more business, position the firm at the intersection of *high expertise and low management overhead*, since GCs at our ICP are clearly overwhelmed.
- *Competitive differentiation:* What factors matter most to our personas that the competition is overlooking?

- *Example:* If clients are deeply concerned about new regulatory changes affecting building efficiency and the bottom line, position the firm as the undisputed leader in understanding these regulations. The digital presence is then built around this – a dedicated section of the website, regular LinkedIn posts by partners, and firmwide thought leadership on the topic.

In addition to targeting individual personas, leadership should identify the *common denominators* across all personas. If all personas are geographically dispersed, a regional event may be ineffective, suggesting resources should be allocated to digital delivery, such as a high-production webinar series on complex regulatory changes. Specificity in audience definition is the engine that allows the firm to tailor its business development and marketing activities, successfully differentiating from the competition as prospects progress along their buying journey.

Your firm website – a strategic asset

A firm's website is the foundation of its digital presence and a primary vehicle for demonstrating value to both clients and prospects. The era of the simple brochureware site – with outdated photos, minimal lawyer biographies, and no relevant information – is over. Such a site signals to sophisticated buyers that the firm has failed to keep pace with modern business practices. The most critical consideration for the firm's website is its *usability*, or User Experience (UX).

The interaction a visitor has with your website is a powerful, often first, representation of your organization. A firm with an archaic website – dated fonts, antiquated photography, or poor navigation – is conveying a negative, frustrating experience. At a bare minimum, leadership must ensure the website is modern, fresh, implements best practices in navigation, and is fully responsive on mobile devices and tablets, which are frequently used by executives.

The design should feature modern, easy-to-read fonts and high-quality photography that ideally shows your professionals interacting with clients and each other, signaling a superior client experience. Furthermore, governance must ensure content is meaningful, modern, and up to date, including the use of current social media icons (e.g., the X social media network logo instead of the old Twitter logo).

Your firm's brand is conveyed by your website via clear content, key headlines and phrases, visual design and layouts, and carefully curated images. Brand is an important attribute that conveys who your firm is and how one will work with you. Are you a Compassionate Advisor, a Fearless Challenger, or an Elite Specialist firm? Are you primarily a local firm, one with regional focus, or national/global? These details are powerful signals to buyers of legal services that indicate a potential fit, or lack thereof.

For any firm beyond the smallest size, a fast, fully functional website search is mandatory. Visitors, often executives, seek specific information – a lawyer's biography, thought leadership on a niche topic, or an office location. The search functionality must surface this information instantly and efficiently. A non-functional or inaccurate search creates a frustrating experience that reflects poorly on the firm's brand and suggests a similar lack of efficiency in service delivery. This is an opportunity for leadership to mandate a client-centric experience that mirrors the quality of the firm's legal representation.

Beyond UX, leadership must prioritize *website accessibility* for visitors with impairments. Adherence to established website accessibility standards, such as the Web Content Accessibility Guidelines (WCAG), is not merely a legal or ethical obligation, but a strategic one. Ensuring content is accessible also directly supports Search Engine Optimization (SEO) as well as the emerging Answer Engine Optimization (AEO) and Generative Engine Optimization (GEO) disciplines. SEO, AEO, and GEO are paramount for ensuring the firm's name, brand, and expertise are surfaced by traditional search engines and the new wave of generative AI models (e.g., ChatGPT, Claude, Gemini, Perplexity).

Finally, a firm-wide mandate must be placed on the quality of lawyer biographies. They must be robust, accurate, and up to date. The most important component of a biography is the list of successfully completed deals or representative matters, which should be updated quarterly. A buyer's major factor in selection is seeing relevant expertise validated by results. A bio that lists "most recent matters" from five years ago raises immediate, critical questions about the lawyer's current practice activity and expertise. Leadership must ensure that lawyers regularly provide updated matter information to the marketing/business development team for immediate publication, often utilizing matter management databases as a core data source. Clear, concise, and well-written descriptions of these matters offer immense value, allowing prospective clients to see the breadth and depth of expertise and, ideally, similarity to their own complex legal needs.

Lawyer visibility via SEO and GEO

Few firm-wide business development efforts are more important than ensuring lawyer biographies, thought leadership, and key expertise are robust, up-to-date, and *easily found* by clients and prospects.

This is executed via disciplined SEO, AEO, and GEO techniques. These techniques ensure the firm's content is properly indexed and positioned within search engines and generative AI systems. Modern search engine features, such as Google's AI overviews, use generative AI to provide instant, summarized answers at the top of search results, helping users quickly understand complex topics. For a given lawyer's name or a niche legal query, the firm's website and corresponding content should dominate the results.

While the technical details of SEO/AEO/GEO are constantly in flux, the high-level guidance for firm leaders remains clear and unchanging – *you must create relevant, accurate, and comprehensive thought leadership for your target audience and personas.* This is an executive-level mandate that often requires the strategic allocation of resources to specialized outside agencies or internal writers.

A successful Am Law 100 firm, for instance, took the decisive step of realigning a seasoned, practicing partner as the firm-wide head of content development. This strategic move led to prolific publishing and positioned the firm ahead of its peers in a highly competitive practice area. This success was a direct result of content that was not only timely and relevant but backed by the deep, firsthand insights and knowledge only a practicing lawyer could provide.

True thought leadership is *leading the sector with your thinking.* This strategic approach establishes an undeniable position of expertise and grants the firm a consistent audience and following, ultimately translating into a more predictable pipeline of business.

Social media strategies for practice and firm elevation

A social media strategy, driven by leadership, must center on the regular publication of true thought leadership to a carefully cultivated network. The goal is to constantly expand that network, thereby building a larger, more engaged audience for the firm's expertise.

A frequently overlooked strategic aspect is cross-promoting thought leadership between partners and professionals. Leadership must foster a culture where lawyers actively engage with, like, comment on, and repost each other's content. This simple internal discipline significantly expands the audience and increases the firm's thought leadership reach without additional external spend. Beyond marketing, social media is a crucial platform for business development. Real conversation happens here – it is not a one-way broadcast. Firm leaders must mandate that lawyers carve out time not just to create and post content, but also to actively interact with others on the appropriate platforms for the target audience. It is a strategic imperative to reach out and engage with prospective clients who are connections, as this interaction is the first step toward generating more legal work for the firm. There are numerous tools and services available to assist lawyers and law firm marketing teams with this mandate.

Measuring digital performance – the mandate for data analytics

For law firm leaders, business development can often feel driven by intuition or past relationships. However, a modern, high-performing digital presence must be governed by evidence. Relying solely on anecdotal feedback or vanity metrics (like total website visits) is insufficient. The imperative is to shift to a data-driven marketing discipline, which uses objective metrics to connect digital activity directly to business outcomes. This ensures marketing spend is a strategic investment, not a cost center.

Your leadership team must demand answers to the fundamental question: *Which digital activities are reliably creating new client conversations and revenue?*

Two key strategies for building this data-driven capability are:

1. *Conversion rate optimization (CRO) by persona.* Move beyond simply tracking traffic to tracking *action*. For each of your key personas (e.g., Strategic Sarah, the GC), define the exact "conversion" they should take on your website – whether it's downloading a gated whitepaper, signing up for a specific alert, or using a lawyer contact form. Measure the percentage of targeted visitors who complete this action. This directly links your website's performance to your most valuable prospects' needs and highlights areas where the User Experience (UX) requires immediate attention.
2. *Closed-loop lead-to-revenue tracking.* Mandate the integration of your website analytics with your CRM (client relationship management) system. The marketing team must be able to trace a prospect's entire journey – from the initial search engine query (SEO/AEO/GEO) or social media post that first brought them to your site, through to a

signed engagement letter. This "closed-loop" view identifies the most profitable digital channels and content topics, enabling leadership to confidently shift resources toward activities proven to drive new business.

Creating a culture of publication and self-promotion

The foundation for a strong, firm-wide digital presence must originate and be consistently modeled by leadership – the managing partner, executive committee, and other high-level partners. They must be active, sophisticated users who embody the firm's brand, keeping clients and prospects engaged and ensuring that target personas consistently learn from the firm's thought leaders.

A content calendar is a powerful management tool for institutionalizing content generation. This defines a periodic schedule for publishing content on predetermined topics, allowing the rotation of content development responsibilities among partners or lawyers, and giving them adequate advance notice of their writing assignments. Many firms successfully employ external marketers or ghostwriters, and increasingly, AI-driven tools, to assist or even generate content.

However, a critical leadership distinction must be made – true thought leadership involves *leading* topics and market sectors. Simply regurgitating information already readily available online is insufficient to establish oneself as an authority or gain significant traction.

Finally, encouraging a culture of self-promotion is equally important. Leaders must constantly remind their audience and potential clients of their value. This involves simple, systematic actions – including a link to an upcoming webinar in their email footer, linking to recent articles in their LinkedIn profile, and ensuring their most critical, recent accomplishments are easily accessible through all digital channels. Making this information visible and accessible is vital for building a following and strengthening the firm's thought leadership presence.

Assessing your firm's maturity

As your firm works to enhance its digital presence and online reputation, a critical first step is a frank assessment of its current standing relative to its strategic goals. While a few firms may achieve rapid, transformational change, sustainable growth and maturity are more common. The pace and focus of your development should be strategically guided by the highest priorities for the firm, its clients, and its prospects. This initial assessment will clearly identify areas for immediate focus and prioritized investment.

Law firm digital maturity and reputation assessment tool

Look at the below questions and rate your firm on a scale of 0 to 5 for each question:

0: Not doing this at all / no awareness.

5: Exceptional investment / industry-leading execution.

	0	1	2	3	4	5
1. *Website UX and conversion.* Is your website mobile-responsive, fast-loading, and designed with clear "call to actions" (CTAs) for desired personas?						
2. *Content authority (thought leadership).* Do you consistently publish high-value insights (white papers, legal alerts, or case studies) that solve specific problems for your ICP?						
3. *Search Engine Optimization (SEO).* Does your firm rank on the first page of Google for "intent-based" keywords (e.g., "Corporate real estate attorney [Your City]")?						
4. *Google business profile and local presence.* Is your Google business profile fully optimized, featuring accurate data, recent photos, and a high volume of 4.5+ star reviews?						
5. *Proactive review acquisition.* Do you have a formalized, automated system for requesting and managing client reviews and testimonials after a successful closing?						
6. *LinkedIn presence and executive branding.* Are your firm's partners active on LinkedIn, sharing insights and engaging with the target audience (e.g., tagging GCs or reacting to industry news) on a regular basis?						

	0	1	2	3	4	5
7. *Social proof and case results.* Is your website prominently displaying client logos (where permitted), success metrics, or "representative matters" to build immediate trust?						
8. *Online reputation monitoring.* Do you use tools (like Google Alerts or Clay) to monitor when your firm or your key partners are mentioned online to respond to or leverage that press?						
9. *Lead capture and nurture architecture.* Do you have a mechanism (like a gated PDF or newsletter signup) to capture visitor data and nurture those leads through an automated email sequence?						
10. *Data and analytics oversight.* Do you review monthly reports on website traffic, lead sources, and engagement metrics to make data-driven marketing decisions?						

How to interpret your score:

0-15: The invisible firm. You are likely losing business to competitors because prospects can't find or verify your expertise online.

16-30: The reactive firm. You have the basics, but you aren't using the web to generate new business – only to validate referrals.

31-45: The emerging leader. You have a strong presence and are likely winning business away from larger, less-agile firms.

46-50: The digital authority. Your digital presence is a competitive moat. GCs likely find you and trust you before they even speak to a partner.

Prioritizing for maximum impact

Few firms can – or should – attempt to address all ten areas of the digital maturity assessment simultaneously. Prioritization is a core strategic responsibility of firm leadership. Your mandate is to review the assessment results and strategically identify the two or three areas that promise the highest return on investment for your firm's specific market, client base, and growth goals.

The correct path depends on your firm's current state. For example:

- A regional firm will find more immediate value in dedicating resources to Google business profile and local presence (assessment area 4) than in a costly national intent-based SEO campaign.
- A firm with a robust website but a passive culture should focus its energy on LinkedIn presence and executive branding (area 6) and proactive review acquisition (area 5).

Regardless of the approach you select, a foundational commitment to measurement and content is non-negotiable.

- *Content is king*. Remember that without well-written, clear, and helpful content (content authority, area 2), efforts across all other categories – from website UX (area 1) to social proof (area 7) – are meaningless. True thought leadership is the fuel for your SEO and GEO visibility (area 3).
- *Focus on the audience*. Every priority you choose must be filtered through the lens of your defined ideal client profile (ICP) and personas. Prioritize the activities that most directly address the pain points and communication preferences of your "Strategic Sarah" GC.
- *Mandate measurement*. Define and track baselines for metrics like website traffic, lead sources, and engagement (data and analytics oversight, area 10). Monitor these metrics to establish a clear connection to business outcomes – opportunities generated or case revenue. As your revenue grows, leadership must mandate that a portion is strategically reinvested to fuel this marketing flywheel.

By focusing on a disciplined, prioritized roadmap, your digital presence will transform from a passive brochure into a powerful, competitive asset, helping you achieve the digital authority status you seek.

About Globe Law and Business

Globe Law and Business was established in 2005. From the very beginning, we set out to create legal books that are sufficiently high level to be of real use to the experienced professional, yet still accessible and easy to navigate. Most of our authors are drawn from Magic Circle and other top commercial firms, both in the United Kingdom and internationally. Our titles are carefully produced, with the utmost attention paid to editorial, design and production processes. We hope this results in high-quality publications that are easy to read and a pleasure to own.

In 2021, we were very pleased to announce the start of a new chapter for Globe Law and Business following the acquisition of law books under the imprint Ark Publishing. Our law firm management list is now significantly expanded with many well-known and loved Ark Publishing titles.

We are also pleased to announce the launch of our online content platform, Globe Law Online, which allows for easy access across firms. Details of all titles included can be found at www.globelawonline.com. Email glo@globelawandbusiness.com for further details and to arrange a free trial for you or your firm.

We'd very much like to hear from you with your thoughts and ideas for improving what we offer. Please do feel free to email me on sian@globelawandbusiness.com. Happy reading and thank you for your time.

Sian O'Neill
Managing director
Globe Law and Business
www.globelawandbusiness.com